THE ESSENTIAL TORAH

Norbert Weinberg

THE

ESSENTIAL TORAH

Bloch Publishing Company

New York

The author gratefully acknowledges the permission
of The Soncino Press to quote from the Pentateuch and
Haftorahs by J. H. Hertz

Printed in the United States of America

Library of Congress Catalog Card Number 73-77282

ISBN: 0-8197-0282-X

Dedicated to the Sacred Memory
of my
Beloved Father
DR. SELIGMANN WEINBERG

"And all thy children shall be taught of the Lord,
And great shall be the peace of thy children."

ISAIAH—54, 13.

Table of Contents

The Essential Torah / Contents

Contents

ix

Preface

𝒯HE STORY IS told of the Baal Shem Tov—the founder of Hasidism—that he was asked a difficult question regarding Jewish law. As he pondered the ramifications of the problem, he opened at random a book of Torah, looked into it for awhile, and then gave a clear and lucid answer to the question.

When asked how it was possible for him to receive such inspiration by simply immersing himself in the first book of the Torah that came to his hand, he gave the following answer:

"We know that God created light at the very dawn of the existence of the universe. On the fourth day, He created the sun to provide light during the day. What was the nature of the original light and what happened to it after the sun was created?

"Our tradition teaches that this light was of a very special spiritual nature. So strong was its mysterious power, that God deemed it to be too potent for man. He therefore hid it for future righteous generations, replacing it with the illumination of the sun.

"Now where," continued the Baal Shem Tov, "did God hide this light? . . . It was hidden in the Torah. Anyone who wants a spark of its splendor simply has to delve into its pages and he will be blessed with a vision of the majesty and eternity of the universe. Many of his problems will thus be solved."

As I saw the many problems confronting my congregants and religious school students, I was utterly dismayed at the lack of knowledge regarding the very foundations of the Jewish faith, the words of the Torah. The basic facts, the chronology of the lives of even the most famous biblical personalities, were seldom known by the average person.

My wonder increased as I set about looking for a text, in simple and popular language, which could be used by the layman to gain an appreciation of the facts and profound truths which are contained in the Torah. While I found a number of books on the subject, I saw none which treat the texts in a systematic and comprehensive manner.

This need and search, with its unsatisfactory ending, led me to write THE ESSENTIAL TORAH. By no means does it seek to serve as a substitute for the original Hebrew text or the classic commentaries which accompany the Written Word. It does, however, attempt to introduce the reader to a basic and systematic understanding of each weekly Torah section as it is read in the synagogue. It is my fervent hope that everyone who takes this book in hand will master the essential teachings, and then go on to a more intensive study.

To demonstrate the importance of the commentaries for a deeper understanding of the biblical text, a selected number of excerpts from their teachings appear in each chapter.

To complete the study session of each Sabbath morning service, a synopsis of the Haftorah, the weekly reading from the Prophets, appears at the conclusion of every Torah reading.

A number of years have gone into the research and preparation of the manuscript. During this period, I have enjoyed the encouragement of many friends and pedagogues who share with me the conviction that such a text was vitally needed.

While I am grateful for everyone's help, there are a few individuals whose support was so valuable that this book would not have seen the light of day without them.

Mr. Charles Bloch, president of Bloch Publishing Company, saw the educational value of this work from the very beginning. His professional ingenuity and personal friendship were constant stimuli for me to forge ahead.

The textual matter, both its style and content, owes a great debt to Mr. Samuel Gross, former editor of Bloch Publishing Company. His scholarship, coupled with keen insight into the problems of exposition, prodded me into many rewritings and revisions. I came to deeply appreciate his meticulousness and I am certain the reader will benefit from it as I have.

In the spirit of "the last is most dear", I convey my sincerest gratitude to my wife, Shoshana, who not only patiently permitted me to pore over my manuscript for many hours, but constantly encouraged me to finish the work despite the many pressures of rabbinical duties. She added a great deal of literary and technical assistance during the progress of the book.

I trust that THE ESSENTIAL TORAH will be utilized by schools, adult education seminars and Jews in all walks of life, to become another step toward the prophetic vision . . .

". . . for the earth shall be full of the knowledge of the Lord, as the waters cover the sea."—(Isaiah—11, 9).

Fall River Massachusetts   NORBERT WEINBERG
Elul, 5733
September, 1973

THE BOOK OF
GENESIS

סֵפֶר בְּרֵאשִׁית

The first book of the Torah reviews the Dawn of Creation and the earliest origins of mankind. It describes the beginnings of the Jewish People through the lives of the forefathers; Abraham, Isaac and Jacob.

The evolvement of history continues with the birth of the sons of Jacob who became the founders of the Twelve Tribes of Israel. Driven by his brothers' hatred, Joseph found himself in Egypt, where the stage was set for the entry of Jacob and his entire family.

More than just a book of laws, the Torah embodies universal concepts of God and justice, commandments to the Jewish People, ethics and history.

The entire Torah demonstrates God's involvement with Man and Man's involvement with God.

בראשית

Bereshit

CHAPTERS I–IV, 8

In the beginning God created the heaven and the earth.

*W*ITH THESE WORDS, the Torah opens the account of the dawn of creation.[1] The entire universe was called into being by the will and command of God during a period of six days.

First, heaven and earth were called into being. A sky divided the waters upon the earth and those of the mists and vapors which lingered in the atmosphere. As the waters drained into oceans and seas, dry land began to appear. Soon the land turned green with grass and other forms of vegetation. Fruit-giving trees appeared and all the plants contained seeds so they could reproduce their own species.

The sun, moon and planets next appeared, followed by the lower forms of life. Soon the waters swarmed with fish and other sea life. Birds soared through the skies and animals roamed the earth. All this new life was blessed by God and given the means by which to reproduce, each according to their species.

Finally, on the eve of the sixth day of creation, God said:

Let us make man in our image after our likeness.

On the one hand, Adam was created from the "dust of the earth" like the animals. On the other hand, he bordered on the

---

[1]Rabbi Judah asked: Why did the Almighty record the creation of heaven and earth first, when in fact the angels, the Throne of Glory, and many of the supernatural aspects of creation came first? So that man should not meditate on things which are hidden from the eye and which are impossible to comprehend.

—MIDRASH HANE'ELAM, BERESHIT, ZOHAR HADASH 6

divine since he was created in the spiritual likeness of God. While man shared the bodily functions and physical traits of the animal world, he was given a higher degree of intelligence; the capacity to differentiate between right and wrong; and freedom of choice to determine his actions. These divine capacities were to be an eternal challenge to Man.[2]

Adam was placed in the Garden of Eden where he lived in peace with himself and the animal world.[3] The earth gave willingly of its produce with no labor on his part. Loneliness was his only affliction: he had no mate like the other living creatures. God caused a deep sleep to fall over Adam, during which He created Eve from one of his ribs.

All the good things of the Garden of Eden were accessible to Adam and Eve, with the exception of the Tree of Life and the Tree of Knowledge from which they were forbidden to eat. However, the serpent spoke to Eve and convinced her to eat from the Tree of Knowledge. When she had done so, she gave some of the forbidden fruit to Adam, who ate it. When God asked them about their transgression, they refused to admit their sin and were punished. Henceforth, the serpent had to crawl on its belly; Eve was to have pain in childbirth; and Adam had to till the ground which had been cursed and yielded its produce only with great difficulty. Adam and Eve were banished from the Garden of Eden.[4]

---

[2]Man alone among all living creatures is endowed, like his Creator, with moral freedom and will. He is capable of knowing and loving God and of experiencing spiritual communion with Him. Man alone can guide his actions in accordance with Reason. On this account he is said to have been made in the form and image of the Almighty.

—MAIMONIDES

[3]God created man only after providing for all his needs. The Torah thereby demonstrates proper behavior: a man should not invite another to a feast before making all the necessary preparations for his proper requirements.

—MIDRASH TANHUMA YASHAN

[4]Beware of the unhappy results of sin! Adam committed one sin and his stature was diminished, his glory dwindled, his food supply

4

Adam and Eve had many sons and daughters. Since there were no laws of marriage as we know them today, it was from these sons and daughters that the human race developed.

There were two sons of whom the Torah speaks in detail because of a tragedy which occurred through them. Cain, the eldest, was a farmer and one day he brought a sacrifice to God. At about the same time, his shepherd brother, Abel, also offered a sacrifice from the very best of his flock. Abel's sacrifice must have been more sincere, since God accepted it, while rejecting Cain's. Instead of trying to achieve sincerity in his worship, Cain went into a jealous rage, turned on his brother, and murdered him.

When God inquired of Cain where his brother was, Cain impudently replied:

Am I my brother's keeper?[5]

In punishment for this great crime, he was made to wander the earth.[6] Cain pleaded with God for some token of mercy,

---

diminished and he became a fugitive and wandered over the face of the earth.

—MIDRASH HAGADOL BERESHIT

[5]This is comparable to the man who entered a garden, gathered mulberries, and ate them. The owner of the garden ran after him, demanding, "What are you holding?" "Nothing," he replied. "But your hands are stained with juice!" When Cain defiantly answered, "Am I my brother's keeper?", God hurled at him the accusation, "Wretch! The voice of your brother's blood cries unto Me from the ground."

—GENESIS RABBAH

[6]The Mishna states: How do we impress witnesses in cases involving life and death with the grave consequences of their testimony? We tell them: Know well that capital cases are quite different from monetary questions where a false witness is guilty of shedding the blood of his victim and that of his children and children's children till the end of time.

—MISHNA SANHEDRIN 37A

5

since he feared that anyone who heard about the murder would kill him in revenge. In answer to his plea, God placed the "mark of Cain" upon him. This mark was a sign to prevent people from harming him as he trudged from land to land. Although the sign was meant to protect him, it was also a mark of shame. Throughout history, the expression "mark of Cain" was applied to a person or nation that had committed such crimes.

Just as Adam, Eve, and Cain, sinned at the very birth of civilization, so people continued to act wickedly as new generations were born, so much so that God began to regret that He had created Man. Civilization was on the verge of destruction and was saved by the appearance of one man, Noah.

Haftorah Bereshit

Isaiah XLII, 5– XLIII, 10

The Haftorah, which means *conclusion,* is read in the synagogue after the Torah reading on Sabbath mornings, as well as on festivals and fast days. Talmudic sources trace the origin of the reading of the Haftorah back to Moses and Ezra.

A Spanish teacher of the fourteenth century, Abudraham, notes that the reading of the Haftorah began during the persecutions of Antiochus IV (168–165 B.C.E.) when Jews were forbidden to read from the Torah. Ingeniously, they selected portions from the Prophets— whose readings had not been banned—which closely paralleled the Torah reading. This practice, which began as a necessity, became an established custom even after the decree had been withdrawn.

The first Haftorah introduces us to the words of Isaiah. He declares God to be the Creator of heaven and earth, an obvious link to the Sidrah.

The prophet is addressing himself to the Jews of Babylonia who had been exiled to this land after the destruction of the Holy Temple (586 B.C.E.). They yearned to return to their homeland to rebuild the

Temple and their fallen nation. Throughout this period of despair, Isaiah's words keep their spirit aloft by assuring the people that they will be remembered by God.

Isaiah continues to explain that the punishment of God which brought about the exile was not the result of divine hatred, but a necessary lesson which the people had to endure. They had gone contrary to the ways of God's teachings, and their punishment was a divine act of love to cause them to return. Isaiah assures the people that God will certainly gather His people together again for the Return.

As Israel passes through this exile, and those to come, they will be witnesses to the Presence and Will of God. They will show the way of salvation to all the nations of the earth.

Ye are My witnesses, saith the Lord,
And My servants whom I have chosen;
That ye may know and believe Me, and understand that I
*   am He;*
Before Me there was no God formed,
Neither shall any be after Me.

נֹחַ

Noach

CHAPTERS VI, 9–XI, 32

Noah was in his generation a man righteous and whole-hearted. Noah walked with God.[1]

*A*LTHOUGH GOD FOUND Noah to be a good man, the rest of his generation was steeped in violence and evil. Mankind had not improved since the sins of Adam, Eve, and Cain: Violence and evil had increased.

God came to regret having created Mankind and was ready to destroy them. It was only because Noah stood out among all the others as a righteous person that future generations were spared.

One day the voice of God spoke to Noah:

The end of all flesh is come before Me for the earth is filled with violence. . . . Make an ark of gopher wood with rooms.

This vessel was to provide space for himself and his family, and for all the species of animals and birds. The construction of this huge vessel was to take many years so the people could see it take shape. It was hoped they would take warning and change their way of life for a better one.

As they questioned Noah about his strange behavior, he

---

[1]"Noah was righteous and whole-hearted in his generation." Rabbi Yochanan said: 'Noah was righteous in *his* generation, but would not have been so considered in other generations.' Reish Lakish said: 'If he was righteous in that [evil] generation, he would certainly have been more so in other generations.'

—SANHEDRIN 108 (a)

explained to them that this Ark was to be a shelter for him and representatives of the animal kingdom from a flood which God was to bring on all the earth. Unfortunately, the people just laughed and thought him a fool.[2]

Finally, after many years had passed and the Ark was completed, Noah brought seven pairs of clean animals and one pair of the unclean species into the huge ship. He also sent his wife and their three sons, Shem, Ham and Japheth, together with their wives into the Ark and the doors and windows were sealed.

On that day all the fountains of the great Deep were broken open and the windows of heaven were opened and the rain was upon the earth for forty days and forty nights.

As the rains stormed down and the rivers spilled over their banks, the Great Flood began. The waters rose over the entire earth and all life perished. The Ark bobbed over the stormy waters and rose with the rising tide far over the peaks of the highest mountains.

The Ark floated for one hundred and fifty days. Finally, the winds began to drive the waters away and the flood waters began to recede.

During these many long days, Noah often tested the height of the waters. First he sent a raven through an open window, but it flitted back to the Ark, having found no place to rest. Soon after, he sent out a dove which was also forced to return when it could not find dry land. Noah waited seven more days and

---

[2]Rabbi Huna said in the name of Rabbi Yose: 'The Almighty admonished that generation for one hundred and twenty years in the hope they would repent. He said to Noah, 'Build an Ark!'. Noah thereupon planted cedar trees. When the people asked what he was doing, Noah told them of the flood which was coming. But the people mocked and laughed at him. Noah watered the trees and they grew. Again the people asked and again they scorned him. Finally, Noah cut down the trees and nailed them together. When they saw the Ark and still refused to repent, God brought the Flood upon them.'

—BERESHIT RABBAH 31

again sent out the dove. This time it returned holding an olive branch in its beak, showing that the waters were receding and the tops of the trees had appeared.[3] After waiting another seven days, the dove was sent out again: this time it did not return. Shortly after, the Ark came to rest on Mount Ararat.[4]

Noah opened the roof of the huge ship and walked out upon dry land. His wife, his family and all the animals aboard also left the Ark to begin a new life. God vowed that never again would He curse the ground or destroy Mankind. He blessed Noah and his family so that they would replenish the world again.

A covenant was entered into between God and Mankind:

And God said to Noah: I have set My rainbow in the cloud and it shall be a sign of a covenant between Me and the earth.

Noah also received the seven commandments, which were to serve as the basis of future civilization. These laws binding on all people, regardless of their religion, deal with respect for God, for man and for beast.[5]

---

[3]The dove said to the Almighty: 'Creator of the Universe! I would rather that my very sustenance be as bitter as this olive branch and given to me by Your bounty, than sweet as honey but doled out from the hands of man.'

—SANHEDRIN 108 (a)

[4]*And God said to Noah: Go forth from the Ark.* Rabbi Yudan said: 'Had I been on the Ark, I would have broken the door down [as soon as it landed on the mountain] and gone out. Noah reasoned, however, that just as he entered the Ark on God's command, so would he wait for God's command to leave.'

—BERESHIT RABBAH 34

[5]The seven "Noachide Commandments"—the basis for all civilized behavior—are:

1 the command to establish courts of justice
2 the prohibition of blasphemy
3 the prohibition of idol-worship

As the earth began to be repopulated, an event occurred which greatly displeased God. In the Valley of Shinar, the people began to build a huge tower.

The people said:

Come, let us build a city and a tower with its top in Heaven, and let us make a name for ourselves, lest we be scattered abroad upon the face of the whole earth.

They actually wanted to wage war against God in the manner of that age by casting spears and arrows over the clouds. They also had no regard for human life. When a brick fell and was smashed, they were grief-stricken, but when a person fell to the ground dead they weren't bothered in the least.

At that time people still spoke only one language. God decided that if speaking one language could bring people to such degradation, He would frustrate the project by causing them to speak in different tongues. When this happened, they were no longer able to understand each other and all the work on the tower ceased.[6] "Babel," means confusion, and this project was always remembered as the "Tower of Babel".

A young man, destined to become the father of a great nation and a new faith, sadly watched the people working on this tower and then wandering off in separate groups. This man was Abram.

---

4   the prohibition of incest
5   the prohibition of murder
6   the prohibition of robbery
7   the prohibition of eating flesh cut from a living animal. (The flesh of animals, previously forbidden, was now permitted.)

[6]Their languages were confused: "When one worker said to the other, 'Bring me water!', he brought him earth, causing the first to strike and wound him. If one said, 'Bring me a shovel!', the other handed him a rake. And he would strike and wound him."

—YALKUT SHIMONI 28

Haftorah Noach

ISAIAH LIV–LV, 5

The Prophet continues the theme of the previous Haftorah, assuring Israel of its return to their Homeland. Isaiah promises his listeners that a new nation will rise from the Babylonian destruction. As terrible as the downfall of Jerusalem was, it had to occur to bring about a better future.

A similar catastrophe befell the world as described in the Torah reading. A terrible flood engulfed all mankind. Its tragic effects were almost total. Had it not come, mankind would have destroyed itself through its utter corruption. But the future was assured through the survival of the righteous Noah.

Isaiah promises the Jewish exiles in Babylonia that their punishment is only temporary. God will soon relent and forgive them.

"In a little wrath I hid My face from thee for a moment;
But with everlasting kindness will I have compassion on
thee, Saith the Lord thy Redeemer."

The Prophet then draws a direct parallel between the Flood and the exile which the Jewish people were enduring.

For this is as the waters of Noah unto Me;
For as I have sworn that the waters of Noah
Should no more go over the earth,
So have I sworn that I would not be wroth with thee,
Nor rebuke thee.

The Jewish people shall live in righteousness and security and the knowledge of God which shall be taught will bring everlasting peace.

And all thy children shall be taught of the Lord;
And great shall be the peace of thy children.

לֶךְ–לְךָ

Lech Lecha

CHAPTERS XII, 1–XXV, 18

*I*N THIS TORAH reading, we are introduced to the beginnings of the Jewish people.[1] Abram, who lived in the city of Ur, in Chaldea, could not bring himself to believe in the idol-worship of his day.[2] Terach, his father, was a merchant who dealt in idols, but his son rebelled against this pagan worship. Abram struggled to find the source of life and existence and he finally rediscovered the God who had addressed Adam, Eve, Cain, Abel and Noah.[3]

And the Lord said unto Abram: Get thee out of thy country, and from thy kindred, and from thy father's house, unto the land that I will show thee. And I will make of thee a

---

[1]There were ten generations from Noah to Abraham and the Almighty spoke with none of them until Abraham.

—BERESHIT RABBAH 39

[2]Abram, the Ivri (from the Hebrew meaning 'side'). Rabbi Judah said: "The whole world was on one side and Abraham was on the other side."

—BERESHIT RABBAH 42

[3]When Abraham was three years old, he began to wonder. "Who created heaven, earth, and myself?" He prayed all day to the sun. In the evening the sun descended in the west and the moon shone forth from the east. When he saw the moon shining surrounded by the stars, he said, "The moon created heaven and earth and me, and the stars surrounding it are its officers and servants. Thereupon he stayed up all night and prayed to the moon. The next morning, the moon went down in the west and the sun rose again in the east. He then said: "These creations have no power. There is a Master over them and to Him will I bow in prayer."

—MIDRASH

great nation, and I will bless thee and make thy name great; and be thou a blessing.

This command of God sent Abram from his homeland, together with his wife, Sarai and his nephew, Lot. The land of his destination was Canaan, later to be known as the Land of Israel.[4]

God continued:

And I will bless them that bless thee, and him that curseth thee will I curse; and in thee shall all the nations of the world be blessed.

Throughout Jewish history, this promise has always come true.

Abram and Sarai had many encounters in the lands through which they passed and with the people whom they met. In all these encounters, Abram was always a man of peace and always tried to avoid hostility and strife. Once, he nearly had a conflict with his nephew, Lot, when the shepherds of the two men began to fight over grazing lands for their flocks. To avoid warfare, Abram offered his nephew the first choice of land. Although it was known to be a place of wickedness, Lot chose the green and fertile plains of Sodom and Abram remained in Canaan.

God was so pleased with Abram's choice that He chose this moment to promise the Land of Canaan to him and all his descendants.[5]

And the Lord said unto Abram:

---

[4]Wherever Abraham travelled, he brought people into his home, fed them, showed them love and kindness and brought them to the worship of God.

—SIFRE: VA-ETCHANAN

[5]Until Abraham appeared in the world, God was the recognized King only of the heavens. Once Abraham began to teach the presence of God and His Torah, the Almighty became King of the heavens and the earth.

—SIFRE 313

Lift up thine eyes and see the place where thou art, north-
ward and southward and eastward and westward; for the
land which thou seest, to thee will I give it and to thy seed
forever . . . Arise, walk through the land in the length of
it and in the breadth of it, for unto thee will I give it.

It was on the strength of this divine promise that the Jewish
people have laid claim to the Land of Israel ever since.

There was one matter in Abram's life which caused him
great concern. His wife, Sarai, had not been blessed with a child
and he desperately wanted a son to carry on the tradition he had
begun. When Sarai realized that she could not have children,
she suggested to Abram that he take Hagar, a maidservant, as
a second wife, which was permitted in those days. Abram followed her advice and a son was born to Hagar whom they named
Ishmael.

In later years, Sarai was very unhappy with Hagar and Ishmael, since she felt that they did not follow the ways of the
household and they were sent away. Ishmael, however, survived
all dangers and became the father of the Arab peoples.

Soon after Ishmael's birth, God again appeared to Abram
and gave him a commandment which he and his family were to
observe, as well as all Jewish males after him. He was to circumcise himself and Ishmael as a covenant between God and the
Jewish people for all future generations. This act, known as
"Brit Milah", was to be done on the eighth day of the life of a
male child. It was symbolic of man's need to constantly strive for
completion and perfection, and for a pure and good heart.

During this period, God changed the name of Abram to
Abraham which means "the father of a great multitude" and
Sarai's name was changed to Sarah, indicating that she was a
princess among her people.

Because Ishmael did not follow the life-pattern set for him
by his father, Abraham was again saddened. What good was it,
he asked himself, to have a son, if the child rejects the traditions
of his parents? Although Sarah was now an old woman, God
promised that she would yet be blessed with a son. Abraham
laughed when he received this news since he thought Sarah too

old to bear a child. But God fulfilled His promise that the covenant He had established with Abraham would continue through Sarah's son.

Haftorah Lech Lecha

ISAIAH XL, 27–XLI, 16

The Sidrah describes the birth of our People through God's selection of Abraham as the first Jew. It was Abraham who, through his gentle teachings and saintliness brought about the beginnings of the Jewish faith and its way of life.

One of the highlights of Abraham's life was God's promise to him that his descendants would inherit the Promised Land. Even if they are driven from the Land, they will invariably return.

The Prophet, speaking to the downtrodden exiles in Babylonia, reminds them of this divine assurance and keeps the hope and faith of the people alive.

A direct connection with the Sidrah occurs in Isaiah's proclamation:

> *But thou, Israel, My servant,*
> *Jacob whom I have chosen,*
> *The seed of Abraham, My friend;*
> *Thou whom I have taken hold of from the ends of the*
> *earth,*
> *And called thee from the uttermost parts thereof,*
> *And said unto thee: 'Thou art My servant',*
> *I have chosen thee and not cast thee away.*

וירא

Va-Yera

CHAPTERS XVIII–XXII

IT WAS THE custom of Abraham to sit at the door of his tent looking for stray wanderers he might invite into his home. In this Torah reading, we learn how the response of three such guests to Abraham's hospitality and his response to them, had a deep effect on Abraham's life, and on the future of the Jewish people.

One day, as Abraham sat in the noon heat, God appeared to him just as he noticed three strangers trudging through the desert.[1] Taking leave of God, and rushing after the strangers, he invited them to pause from their journey and come to his tent to refresh themselves. After serving them food and drink, Abraham came to realize that these were no ordinary travelers.[2] They asked Abraham where his wife, Sarah, was. Being told that she was in the tent, one of the three spoke:

I will certainly return unto thee when the season cometh round; and lo, Sarah thy wife shall have a son.

This time it was Sarah who could not refrain from laughing —as Abraham had done before. She felt she was much too old to bear a child. Nevertheless, Abraham was assured that God would certainly make this promise come true and that it would happen the following year.

---

[1]These three guests were messengers of God. Rashi explains that God visited Abraham because he was sick. As Rabbi Hanna, the son of Hanina puts it: "It was the third day following his circumcision and the Holy One, Blessed be He, came to inquire about his health."

[2]One, to bring the tidings that Sarah would give birth to a son, the second to overthrow Sodom, and the third to heal Abraham; the last also went on from there to save Lot. This division took place because one angel cannot perform more than one type of errand.

—BERESHIT RABBAH

More and more Abraham realized that these strangers were messengers—or angels—of God. A second one informed him that the cities of Sodom and Amorah were to be destroyed because of the wickedness of their inhabitants. Abraham, who deeply loved all his fellow-men, was horrified to learn of this impending tragedy and pleaded with God to save the cities. He drew near to God and asked:

Wilt Thou indeed sweep away the righteous with the wicked? If there are fifty righteous within the city, wilt Thou indeed sweep away and not forgive the place for the fifty righteous that are therein?

God informed Abraham that he would spare the cities if fifty good people could be found in them. When Abraham realized there weren't fifty righteous people there, he lowered the amount of people through whose merits the cities should be spared. In each case, God agreed to save the cities for that number of people. Finally, Abraham pleaded with God not to destroy Sodom and Amorah even if only ten just people could be found there. When God agreed and Abraham could not count even ten righteous people, he realized that the fate of the cities was sealed. The only people worthy of survival were Lot and his family who had gone there to live when he and Abraham had separated their flocks.

That evening, two of the angels who had visited Abraham, came to the city of Sodom and accepted the hospitality of Lot. One of the grave sins of the people of this city was their refusal to permit strangers to lodge within their gates.[5] As a result, Lot's house was soon surrounded by an angry mob which demanded

---

[5]They hated all strangers and punished those who helped their fellow-man. The following legend will demonstrate their attitude. A girl of Sodom gave food to a poor stranger. When this was discovered, she was stripped, tied and covered with honey. Then she was placed on a roof under the hot sun to be eaten by the bees. This was the "cry of Sodom" which reached God.

—Sanhedrin 109 (b)

that the two strangers be brought out. Lot pleaded with them, but to no avail. As they continued to press against the house, the strangers extended their hands and the people were struck with blindness. Lot was told to flee the city with his family as quickly as possible, since the destruction was about to take place. He was to escape to the city of Zoar and neither he, nor any member of his family, was to stop or turn around. Lot asked the husbands of his two daughters to flee with the family, but they thought he was a madman.

The destruction quickly overtook the cities:

Then the Lord caused to rain upon Sodom and upon Amorah brimstone and fire from the Lord out of heaven, and He overthrew those cities, and all the Plain, and all the inhabitants of the cities, and that which grew upon the ground. But his wife looked back from behind him, and she became a pillar of salt.[6] *And Abraham got up early in the morning to the place where he had stood before the Lord. And he looked out toward Sodom and Amorah, and toward all the land of the Plain, and behold, and lo, the smoke of the land went up as the smoke of a furnace.*

A year passed and God's promise to Abraham was fulfilled: his wife, Sarah, gave birth to a son. Remembering how they laughed when they first received the good news, they named the child "Isaac", from the Hebrew for "laughter". True to his covenant with God, Abraham circumcised Isaac when he was eight days old.

---

[6]Rabbi Isaac said: Because she had sinned regarding salt. On the night that the angels came to Lot, he said to his wife, 'Give these guests some salt'. She replied to him, 'Do you want to teach this bad custom of hospitality here in Sodom?' What did she do? She went to all her neighbors and said to them, 'Give me salt for we have guests'. By so doing, she hoped that the men of the city would realize that strangers were present in Lot's home.

—BERESHIT RABBAH

But Hagar and her son, Ishmael, did not fare too well in Abraham's household. Ishmael grew up to be a hunter with a violent personality unlike his half-brother, Isaac. Sarah insisted that both Hagar and her son leave Abraham's home. It was with great unhappiness that Abraham sent them away, but God told him to do what Sarah had asked.

Hagar and Ishmael wandered off to the wilderness of Beersheba. When their supply of water was gone, Hagar feared for the life of her child and began to cry. A heavenly voice reassured her:

Fear not, Hagar, for God has heard the voice of the lad where he is. Arise, lift up the lad; for I will make him a great nation.

Hagar then saw a well of water which saved their lives. They settled in the desert of Paran where God told Hagar that her son would be the father of a large nation, which was to become the Arab people.

Abraham now faced one of the greatest trials of his life. The voice of God came to him:

Take now thy son, thine only son, whom thou lovest— Isaac—and get thee into the land of Moriah,[7] and offer him there for a burnt—offering upon one of the mountains which I will tell thee of.

Because of his deep faith in the justice of God, Abraham offered no objections and went up to the mountain. There, he tied up his son, who also offered no complaint or resistance. As Abraham raised his arm and was ready to strike with the knife,

---

[7]Moriah is Jerusalem. The Rabbis explained that this area was called Moriah because it is related to the Hebrew word for "teaching" (*hora'ah*), which went forth from there to the world. (The Holy Temple was later built on this mountain).

—RASHI

the voice of God stopped him from bringing it down. God told him that He wanted only to test his faith—that He did not require human sacrifice. Abraham saw a ram caught in the bushes and he sacrificed the ram instead. From that day on the ram's horn was used as the "shofar", symbolizing dedication to God.

This episode in Abraham's life was concluded with a sublime blessing by God:

By Myself have I sworn, saith the Lord: because thou hast done this thing, and has not withheld thy son, thine only son, that in blessing I will bless thee, and in multiplying I will multiply thy seed as the stars of the heaven, and as the sand which is upon the seashore; and thy seed shall possess the gate of his enemies; and in thy seed shall all the nations of the earth be blessed; because thou hast hearkened to My voice.[8]

Haftorah Va-Yera

II KINGS, IV, 1–37

The loving and compassionate personality of Abraham is apparent throughout the Torah reading. He attempts to save the people of Sodom and Amorah; form an alliance with his neighbors; and demonstrates the deep love he feels for Isaac, his son. It was only his unquestioning loyalty to God which enabled him to carry out the near-sacrifice of his beloved son.

---

[8]The promise of the Land of Israel had already been made by God (Genesis Chapter 15 Verse 18). The present oath was that never would Abraham's descendants forfeit the Land for all time; nor be so completely destroyed or fall into the hands of their enemies, so they could not rise again. This was in essence a promise of ultimate redemption.

—NACHMANIDES

The section of the Book of Kings which gives us this Haftorah describes a similar personality. Elisha was the disciple of the great prophet Elijah. Like Abraham, he wanted to help people wherever and whenever he could.

A number of miracles are recounted in this narrative. A woman who was destitute had asked Elisha to help pay her debts. The prophet tells her to collect as many vessels as possible and pour the last bit of oil which she had into them. The oil multiplied until all the vessels were filled.

Elisha then tells the woman:

Go, sell the oil, and pay thy debt, and live thou and thy sons of the rest.

A striking parallel with the Sidrah occurs when Elisha attempts to repay the kindness of a woman. She explains that like Sarah she could not have a child and her husband had reached old age. Elisha promises that she will have a son the following year. Despite her doubts, she gave birth to a child exactly as the Prophet had foretold.

When the son became a young man, he was struck by an illness which brought him to the brink of death. His mother rushed to Mount Carmel to inform Elisha. They returned to the stricken lad and Elisha placed his body to that of the boy and breathed into his mouth until he was revived.

Both the Sidrah and the Haftorah demonstrate the love and compassion which people can have for each other, and the never-ceasing involvement of God in the affairs of man.

Cha-Ye Sarah

CHAPTERS XXIII–XXV, 18

*A*BRAHAM HAD LIVED a long and fruitful life. He had traveled great distances and shared many experiences with his wife, Sarah. In this Torah reading, Abraham sustains a great personal loss: the death of his beloved wife.[1]

> *And the life of Sarah was one hundred and seven and twenty years; these were the days of the life of Sarah. And Sarah died in Kiriath-arba—which is Hebron—in the land of Canaan; and Abraham came to mourn for Sarah, and to weep for her.*[2]

It was now Abraham's task to find a proper burial place for Sarah. He went to the inhabitants of Heth and spoke to Ephron, who was the owner of a large cave which was to become the burial ground of the forebears of the Jewish people. Although Ephron first offered the Cave of Machpela as a gift, Abraham insisted on paying the full price, so that there would never be a question as to its ownership, and the cave would always remain as a testimony that the very first Jews lived and died in the land of Canaan which God had promised to their descendants.

After having buried his wife, Abraham realized that there

---

[1]The death of Sarah was recorded following the "binding of Isaac" (see previous chapter), since when she heard that her son had been prepared for sacrifice and almost been slaughtered, her soul left her body and she died.

—RASHI

[2]Sarah died after Rebeccah—who was fit to replace her—was born, since one righteous person does not die before another is born.

—SFORNO

was one more task which must be done to complete his life's work. He happily observed that his son Isaac was growing up in a manner which truly made him a fine representative of his faith, but it was essential to find a proper wife for him—especially since his mother Sarah had died.

> *And Abraham was old, well advanced in age; and the Lord had blessed Abraham in all things. And Abraham said unto his servant, the elder of his house, who ruled over all that he had: Put, I pray thee, thy hand under my thigh, and I will make thee swear by the Lord, the God of heaven and the God of the earth, that thou shalt not take a wife for my son of the daughters of the Canaanites, among whom I dwell. But thou shalt go unto my country, and to my kindred, and take a wife for my son, for Isaac.*

The people of Canaan were not of the type that would understand or be willing to live by Isaac's new faith. Abraham told his trusted servant Eliezer to travel to Chaldea, to find a wife for Isaac. It was there that Abraham grew up, and his relatives still lived there. Eliezer was uncertain: he had no notion of how to go about finding the right bride, and even if he did find her, he feared she might not want to follow him back to the land of Canaan. To make matters more difficult, Abraham would not permit his servant to take Isaac along. He did not want him exposed to the same place which God had told Abraham, many years earlier, to leave.

Eliezer, however, had great faith in God, no doubt developed by observing his master. He prayed to God for assistance in finding the young woman who would have the same virtues of love and hospitality which he had seen in Sarah and in his master's home. He prayed that a woman would come to the well where he and his camels rested after the journey and offer water not only to himself, but for the camels as well.

No sooner had Eliezer completed his prayer, than Rebeccah came to the well with her pitcher. Eliezer asked her for water and she immediately dipped her bucket into the well. As soon as he had finished drinking, she began to give water to all the camels, whose capacity was enormous.[3] Eliezer understood that God had answered his prayers: Rebeccah was the woman who would make a fitting wife for Isaac.

They returned to Rebeccah's home, where Eliezer told of the course of events and the mission which had brought him there. Both Bethuel, Rebeccah's father, and Laban, her brother gave Rebeccah their blessings[4] when she asked[5] to journey to Abraham's household and become the wife of Isaac.

And Rebeccah lifted up her eyes, and when she saw Isaac, she alighted from the camel. And she said unto the servant: 'What man is this that walketh in the field to meet us?'[6] And the servant said: 'It is my master.' And she took her veil and covered herself. And the servant told Isaac all the things that he had done. And Isaac brought her into his mother Sarah's tent, and took Rebeccah, and she became his wife; and he loved her. And Isaac was comforted for his mother.[7]

[3]Then Eliezer understood that God had brought him what he sought.

—RASHBAM

[4]The blessing was: "You and your seed shall receive that blessing which was stated to Abraham on Mount Moriah, 'And I shall surely multiply thy seed' ".

—RASHI

[5]From here we learn that a woman can be given in marriage only with her consent.

—RASHI

[6]She saw his distinguished appearance and she was very impressed with him.

—BERESHIT RABBAH

[7]Isaac brought her into the tent, and behold: she was Sarah his mother—that is, she became like Sarah his mother. As long as Sarah lived, there was a light burning from one Sabbath eve to the other, the dough was blessed, and a divine cloud hung over her tent. When she died, these ceased. When Rebeccah entered the tent, they returned.

—BERESHIT RABBAH

Having accomplished his many tasks, Abraham's life now drew to a close.

And Abraham expired, and died in a good old age, an old man and full of years;[8] *and he was gathered to his people.*[9]

He was buried in the Cave of Machpela by his sons Isaac and Ishmael. The Torah tells us that God now blessed Isaac, who was destined to continue the tradition of Judaism which his father had begun.[10]

Haftorah Cha-Ye Sarah

I KINGS I, 1–31

The Sidrah depicts the last days of Abraham and the care which he exercises to assure the future of the Jewish faith through his son, Isaac. Throughout this period Isaac is a faithful son who is prepared to carry on his father's tradition.

In the Haftorah, David, the second king of Israel is an old man who is about to die. Unlike Abraham's loyal son Isaac, one of David's sons prepares to lead a revolt and become king immediately after his father's death.

---

[8]He saw all the desires of his heart fulfilled and was satisfied with all that he wished to see and do.

—NACHMANIDES

[9]He was gathered into the bond of eternal life together with the righteous of all generations who, being like him in that respect, were "his people".

—SFORNO

[10]Rabbi Chanan, the son of Rabbah said in the name of Rav: "On the day that Abraham our father died, all the great men of the world exclaimed: 'Woe to the world that has lost its leader! Woe to the ship that has lost its helmsman!' "

—BABA BATRA 16 (b)

In a dramatic scene, Bath-Sheba, the king's wife, approaches him at his death-bed. She asks if he did not designate her son Solomon to be the next king. At that very moment, the prophet Nathan enters the king's chamber with the same question.

After learning of Adonijah's planned revolt, the king gave his firm decision that Solomon shall rule after him. He thus established and continued the dynasty of the House of David which ruled Israel for many years.

The long reign of Solomon was marked by peace and prosperity and the first Holy Temple in Jerusalem was built during his reign.

תולדות

Toledot

CHAPTERS XXV, 19–XXIII, 9

*T*HE THIRD GENERATION of the Jewish people begins in this Torah reading. Rebeccah had married Isaac and, after quite a long time, was about to give birth. Strangely, she felt more pain during the period of her expectancy than other women. She prayed to God for an explanation of this unusual situation. The voice of God came to her:[1]

> *Two nations are in thy womb,*
> *And two people shall be separated from thee;*
> *And the one people shall be stronger than the*
> *other people;*
> *And the elder shall serve the younger.*

Since these two peoples were destined to be so different, even as unborn children they were already struggling within her.

When the time for the birth came, Rebeccah became the mother of twins. The child born first was named Esau and he had a ruddy and hairy complexion. The second boy, Jacob,[2] was fair skinned and had a smooth complexion. Because he was born after Esau, he could not be considered the first-born and this was to have serious consequences for the family.

As the boys grew up, it became apparent that Esau the

---

[1]The voice spoke through a prophet, or through Abraham, who was still alive and did not die until [Rebeccah's] sons were fifteen years old.

—IBN EZRA

[2]Jacob was so named because at birth, he held Essau's heel, trying to prevent him from being born first (the Hebrew "eikev" meaning heel).

—RASHI

outdoors type liked to hunt. Jacob, on the other hand, enjoyed sitting in the tents and devoting his time to meditation and study. Their father, Isaac, who was almost blind, favored Esau, since the older brother took good care of him and regularly brought him food. But Rebeccah loved Jacob more; she knew that he was destined to carry on the faith of Abraham and Isaac.[3]

One day, Esau came home very tired from the hunt. He brusquely asked Jacob for food, seeing that Jacob was cooking a pot of lentils.[4] He offered to give his brother the lentils in exchange for his birthright. This right belonged to the firstborn giving the eldest son the right to become the head of his family and tribe. Esau thought he was starving to death and quickly told Jacob that he could have the birthright in exchange for a bowl of lentils.

Isaac was becoming an old man and his eyesight had become dim.[5] Like his father Abraham, he was very grateful for the life he had led. God had blessed him in the same manner as his

---

[3]Each parent had a favorite child, which was to lead to the breakup of the household. "Love thy children with an impartial love" is the wise admonition of a medieval teacher.

—HERTZ

[4]This was the day on which Abraham had died, so that he would be spared seeing his grandson (Esau) begin a life of wickedness. Had he lived to see it, he would not have enjoyed the "good old age" promised to him by God. As a result, God took him away from the world five years before his time, for he lived five years less than his son, Isaac. Jacob had prepared this meal of lentils for the mourners' meal. And why lentils?—because just as lentils are round and roll, so does mourning roll from one person to another, i.e.-sooner or later it comes to everyone. Another reason: as lentils have no opening, so must a mourner not open his mouth to speak of any matters except those related to his mourning.

—RASHI

[5]Rabbi Elazar ben Azariah said: "His vision was dimmed to prevent him from seeing a wicked son (Esau). The Holy One, blessed be He said: "Isaac will go out to the marketplace and people will say: 'That is the father of that wicked person.' Therefore, I will strike his vision and he will remain in his home."

—BERESHIT RABBAH

father and promised he would be the father of a great nation, and that this nation would possess the Land of Israel.

When Isaac saw that his death was rapidly approaching,[6] he called Esau and asked him to go out to the fields to hunt some food. He wanted to strengthen himself so he could give his last blessing to Esau. When Rebeccah overheard this conversation, she called Jacob and told him that it was very important for him to receive this blessing instead of his brother. Jacob was very hesitant about tricking his blind father by posing as Esau. Even if Isaac could not see him, he might recognize him in other ways. Rebeccah solved this problem by placing furs on his arms so that they would resemble Esau's complexion. She then prepared the type of food which Isaac loved and sent Jacob to bring the meal to his father.

The respectful voice and mannerisms of Jacob confused his father, who was used to a much gruffer approach from Esau. He asked Jacob to come forward and felt his arms. When they resembled those of Esau, he exclaimed—still perplexed:

The voice is the voice of Jacob, but the hands are the hands of Esau.

Nevertheless, Isaac gave the full blessing to Jacob which he had intended for the first-born:

See, the smell of my son is as the smell of a field which the Lord has blessed.
So God give thee of the dew of heaven and of the fat places of the earth
And plenty of corn and wine.
Let peoples serve thee and nations bow down to thee.

---

[6]Rabbi Joshua ben Korcha said: "When a man approaches the life span of his fathers, he should concern himself [with his own death] five years prior to and five years after that time."

—QUOTED BY RASHI

*Be lord over thy brethren and let thy mother's sons bow
down to thee.
Cursed be everyone that curseth thee and blessed be
everyone that blesseth thee.*

When Isaac completed this blessing and Jacob had just left
the room, Esau entered with the food for his father. With great
trembling, Isaac told his son that he had already bestowed his
major blessing upon Jacob. Esau was furious, and weeping, he
asked that he also be blessed. Although Isaac blessed Esau in the
best possible manner, he did not revoke his blessing given to
Jacob.

*Behold, of the fat places of the earth shall be thy dwelling,
And of the dew of heaven from above;
And by thy sword shalt thou live and thou shalt serve thy
brother;
And it shall come to pass when thou shalt break loose,
That thou shalt shake his yoke from off thy neck.*

Esau now hated Jacob and resolved to kill him as soon as
his father died.[7] When Rebeccah learned of his intent, she and
Isaac decided to send him to Padan-Aram, the home of Rebeccah's brother, Laban. This was the home from which Rebeccah
traveled to Canaan to marry Isaac after Abraham's servant,
Eliezer, met her at a well. It was hoped that Jacob would also find
a wife there.

Isaac bade his son farewell with a fond blessing which firmly
established Jacob as the inheritor of the tradition of the Jewish
people.

*Thou shalt not take a wife of the daughters of Canaan.
Arise, go to Padan-Aram, to the house of Bethuel thy*

---

[7]Esau did not wish to grieve his father by taking revenge while he
was alive.

—RASHI

mother's father; and take thee a wife from thence of the daughters of Laban thy mother's brother.

And God Almighty bless thee, and make thee fruitful, and multiply thee, that thou mayest be a congregation of peoples; and give thee the blessings of Abraham, to thee, and to thy seed with thee;

That thou mayest inherit the land of thy sojournings, which God gave unto Abraham.[8]

Haftorah Toledot

MALACHI I–II, 7

Malachi, the last of the prophets, spoke to the returned exiles from Babylonia who had rebuilt the Second Holy Temple. Although their dream of returning to their beloved homeland had come true, their faith in God was nevertheless weak. While other nations claimed belief in God, both the priests and the people of Israel were very passive about their religion and actually doubted God's Presence.

The Prophet speaks out fiercely against this disbelief. He proclaims God as King even though He cannot be seen. He denounces the evil and corruption stemming from the people's lack of faith. The priests are called upon to offer sacrifices in a spirit of dignity and faith. Only then, Malachi insists, will they be accepted by God.

Finally, he affirms God's choice of Israel to be His people and to teach the divine way of life to mankind.

---

[8]God's blessing to Abraham was that he should teach man the knowledge of the true God which would become a blessing to him. Isaac now blessed Jacob that his seed might be worthy to continue such teaching, through the merit of which they would possess the Promised Land.

—SFORNO

Toledot

The Prophet describes the evil ways of Esau, who was the father of the Edomites. Although he was Jacob's brother, his corruption caused God to reject him. These are the parallels which the Prophet draws with the Sidrah.

Malachi then declares the virtues of Jacob, who continued the Jewish tradition. As Jacob was loved by God, the Prophet concludes, so too can the Jewish People come close to Him if they faithfully follow His commandments.

וַיֵּצֵא

Va-Ye-Tse

CHAPTERS XXIII, 10–XXXII, 3

And Jacob went out from Beer-Sheba and went toward Haran.[1]

JACOB HAD TAKEN both the birthright and the blessing from his older brother, Esau. When it became apparent that Esau, in his wrath, was going to kill Jacob following their father's death, Jacob was sent to stay with Rebeccah's family in Haran.

During the trip to his uncle Laban's home, he stopped along the way to rest through the night. Finding no inn where he might stay, he placed his head upon a rock and fell asleep. In a dream he saw a ladder reaching from the earth to heaven with angels of God going up and coming down the ladder. Then he heard the voice of God:

I am the Lord, the God of Abraham thy father, and the God of Isaac. The land whereon thou liest, to thee will I give it, and to thy seed. And thy seed shall be as the dust of the earth,[2] *and thou shalt spread abroad to the west, and to the east, and to the north, and to the south. And in thee and in thy seed shall all the families of the earth*

---

[1]The Torah had only to state that Jacob went toward Haran, but his departure from Beer-sheba is also mentioned to inform us that the departure of a righteous man from a place makes an impact. While he is in the city, he is its glory, its splendor, its crown; when he leaves, the city's glory, its splendor, its crown leave with him.

—RASHI

[2]Only after your seed has reached the lowest depth of misery and degradation and is treated like the very dust of the earth, will they achieve salvation ("and thou shalt spread abroad").

—SFORNO

be blessed.[3] *And, behold, I am with thee, and will keep thee withersoever thou goest, and will bring thee back into this land; for I will not leave thee,*[4] *until I have done that which I have spoken to thee of.*

The next morning, Jacob approached a well where he met a group of shepherds from Haran, and he knew that his journey was just about over. His uncle Laban's daughter, Rachel, came to the well. Jacob immediately fell in love with her, and they returned together to Laban's house. When Jacob told his uncle that he would like to remain with his family for a period of time, Laban readily welcomed him. Jacob began to work for the family and Laban offered him wages for his labors.[5] Instead of asking for money, Jacob told Laban that he was willing to work for seven years if at the end of this time he could marry Rachel. Jacob's love for Rachel was so great that he knew the seven years would seem a short time for him. Laban agreed to this arrangement.

So well did Jacob do his work during this time, that Laban sought to trick him in order to extend his stay. When the time came to marry Rachel, Laban told his older daughter, Leah, to put on the bridal veil instead. At the wedding feast, Jacob was greatly shocked when he realized that he had not married his beloved Rachel, but her sister, Leah.[6]

---

[3]All the families of the earth shall join you.

—RASHBAM

[4]I will not abandon you when you are travelling on the road, since then a man needs more than the usual protection.

—RASHBAM

[5]From the outset, Jacob seems to have decided not to be indebted to his uncle, but to earn his maintenance.

—HERTZ

[6]Jacob—not trusting Laban—had arranged a sign before the wedding whereby he would know that it was Rachel who was under the veil. But when Rachel saw that she was being replaced by Leah, she gave the sign to Leah, so that her sister would not be put to shame.

—RASHI

When Jacob complained about this trickery to Laban,[7] he was told that the local custom was to have the older daughter marry before the younger. Since Leah was the older of the two sisters, she had to be his first bride.[8] However, if Jacob would consent to work another seven years, Rachel could certainly become his wife. Because of his deep love for Rachel, Jacob agreed to this new task and Rachel also became his wife.

In those days, it was still proper for a man to have more than one wife. Besides the two sisters, Jacob also married two of their maids. Children were born to all of them, and Jacob became the father of twelve sons and one daughter. These sons were to become the fathers of the Twelve Tribes of Israel. The two sons born to Rachel, whom Jacob loved even more than his other children were Joseph and Benjamin.

After these many years, Jacob yearned to return to his father's home:

And it came to pass when Rachel had borne Joseph, that Jacob said unto Laban: 'Send me away, that I may return unto mine own place, and to my country. Give me my wives and my children for whom I have served thee, and let me go; for thou knowest my service wherewith I have served thee'.

Despite the fact that Jacob had greatly enriched his uncle through many years of diligent work, he had to go through great struggles with Laban to determine his final wages. Only after

---

[7]Rabbi Chanin said in the name of Samuel, the son of Rabbi Isaac: "When Jacob, our father saw the deceit of Leah against her sister, he wanted to divorce her. When God then granted Leah children, Jacob changed his mind and said, 'Can I divorce the mother of these children?' "

BERESHIT RABBAH 71

[8]Laban defended himself by his claim that the people would not have permitted him to keep his original promise to Jacob.

—SFORNO

Laban actually pursued him on the road was the matter finally settled.

Of course, it was difficult for Leah and Rachel to leave their father's home even though he had not dealt kindly with their husband. Jacob explained to them before their departure that it was his wish to return to his family and the Promised Land. They consented to go along with him, and finally, Laban blessed his daughters and wished them well.[9]

Jacob, the man who came as a lonely traveler to flee from his brother, Esau, now left with a large family and many flocks of sheep and herds of cattle.

Jacob left Laban's home with great fears. He was glad to leave the strife and discontent of his uncle and return to his family. He did not know, however, if his brother still harbored hatred towards him for taking his birthright and blessing. Esau had vowed to kill his brother after their father's death. Would Jacob be able to defend himself and his family if attacked by his brother along the way?

It was both with fear and a great faith in the protection of God that Jacob and the entire caravan journeyed toward the Mountains of Gilead and began to wend their way to Canaan, the Holy Land.

Haftorah Va-Ye-Tse

HOSEA XII, 13–XIV, 10

The link between the Sidrah and Haftorah is provided at the very beginning of the reading, as the Prophet takes his listeners back to the early days of their history.

---

[9]Even the blessing of an insignificant man should not be taken lightly. When a parent offers a blessing to a child, it will probably take hold, for it is the image of God which gives the blessing.

—SFORNO

Hosea reminds the people how Jacob, despite difficulties, was constantly saved by God. He reviews the miraculous Exodus of the Jewish people from Egyptian bondage.

The Prophet was speaking to a difficult generation. He preached in the northern kingdom of Israel shortly before it was destroyed by the Assyrian Empire. The entire population of that country was dispersed as the result of this calamity.

Instead of returning to the ways of God and their tradition, thereby averting their downfall, the people wallowed in luxury and idolatry. They were not satisfied with their very special Torah way of life. Instead, they aped the politics and morals of other nations.

In beautiful and moving phrases, Hosea pleads with the people to return to their God who, in the end, will be their only salvation.

Return, O Israel, unto the Lord thy God;
For thou hast stumbled in thine iniquity. . . .
Whoso is wise, let him understand these things,
Whoso is prudent, let him know them.
For the ways of the Lord are right,
And the just do walk in them;
But transgressors do stumble therein.

וישׁלח

Va-Yishlach

*A*s JACOB BEGAN his journey back to Canaan, he knew that he would soon meet his brother, Esau, from whom he had been separated for many years. After Jacob had deprived his older brother of his birthright and his father's blessing, Esau had determined to kill Jacob in revenge. To guard against sudden attack, Jacob sent scouts ahead of his caravan. These scouts were also to act as messengers of peace and good-will.

As Jacob's entire procession neared Canaan, these messengers reported that they had seen Esau approaching with an army of four hundred men.[1] Jacob, a man of peace, was extremely frightened. It seemed to him that Esau had not forgotten his vow for vengeance. In order to protect as many in his camp as possible, Jacob divided the entire group into two sections, so that if Esau attacked one, the other could escape.[2]

Then, he fervently prayed to God for divine protection:

And Jacob said: 'O God of my father Abraham, and God
of my father Isaac, O Lord, who saidst unto me: Return

---

[1] This episode is recorded to show how God saved his servant from an enemy stronger than himself. It further teaches that Jacob did not rely on his own merits, but took all possible precautions to protect himself and his camp. Another lesson: whatever happened to the patriarchs was also to happen to their descendants. Therefore, we too should make a three-fold response to our enemies (Esau's descendants) through prayer, gifts of friendship, and battle.

—NACHMANIDES

[2] This symbolizes the destiny of the Jewish people in exile. They will never be destroyed. Should one king decree their destruction, another one will take pity and offer them shelter.

—NACHMANIDES

unto thy country, and to thy kindred, and I will do thee good; I am not worthy of all the mercies, and of all the truth, which Thou hast shown unto Thy servant; for with my staff I passed over this Jordan; and now I am become two camps. Deliver me, I pray Thee, from the hand of my brother, from the hand of Esau for I fear him, lest he come and smite me, the mother with the children.[3] And Thou saidst: I will surely do thee good, and make thy seed as the sand of the sea, which cannot be numbered for multitude.'

In a final effort to avert war with his brother, Jacob sent many flocks and cattle as presents to Esau. He hoped that this gesture of friendship would bring peace to the two camps.

That night a strange thing happened to Jacob as he stood by himself. An unknown being attacked him and wrestled with him through the night.[4] Although Jacob was struck in the thigh by his assailant and badly wounded, he would not withdraw. When dawn began to break, the being asked to be released. Jacob, sensing some divine significance, said he would relax his grip only if the stranger blessed him. It was then that the angel blessed him:

Thy name shall no more be called Jacob,[5] but Israel; for thou hast striven with God and with men, and hast prevailed.

---

[3]Jacob was afraid that he might be killed or he might have to kill his brother.

—RASHI

[4]To prevent Jacob from fleeing, so that he may witness how God kept His promise that he would not be harmed.

—RASHBAM

[5]It will no longer be claimed that you gained the blessings by "supplanting" (Hebrew—"akab"), but through "superiority" (Hebrew—"sar").

—RASHI

The next morning, Esau and the four hundred men were seen approaching Jacob's camp. As was the custom in those days, Jacob bowed deeply seven times as he walked toward his brother. Whatever Esau's original intentions were, Jacob's efforts for peace succeeded. Esau ran to greet his brother and embraced him in peaceful welcome. Jacob declined his brother's offers for the two camps to move together and, after some time, Esau went back to his home in Seir. Jacob and his camp arrived safely in the city of Shechem which is in the land of Canaan.

An incident then occurred in Jacob's life which was contrary to his usual pursuit of peace and grieved him greatly. His daughter, Dinah, was kidnapped and nearly forced into marriage by Shechem, one of the princes residing in the area. Simeon and Levi, two of Dinah's brothers were outraged. They tricked the men of the city into agreeing to be circumcised, and while they were still weak, the brothers attacked the city and completely destroyed it. Although they did it to avenge their sister's honor, Jacob was disturbed by their behavior to the very end of his life.

Jacob continued his travels through the land of Canaan, journeying to Beth-El. Once more, God blessed him:

And God said unto him: 'Thy name is Jacob: thy name shall not be called any more Jacob, but Israel shall be thy name'; and He called his name Israel. And God said unto him: 'I am God Almighty. Be fruitful and multiply; a nation and a company of nations shall be of thee, and kings shall come out of thy loins; and the land which I gave unto Abraham and Isaac, to thee will I give it, and to thy seed after thee will I give the land.'[6]

On the road between Beth-el and Ephrath, toward which Jacob now travelled, one of the saddest events in his life occurred. Rachel gave birth to another child and died in childbirth.

---

[6]God explained that His promise to Jacob should be looked upon as an oath, as He extended it to Abraham and Isaac.

—NACHMANIDES

41

The baby was named Benjamin, meaning "Son of my affliction." Jacob buried his beloved Rachel by the road to Bethlehem, and her grave is a holy place of pilgrimage for the Jewish people to this day.[7]

Isaac, the second of the patriarchs of the Jewish people, was now an old man, and he died. Although the ways of Jacob and Esau were very different and they seldom shared each other's company, they joined in burying their father Isaac with great respect and honor.

The twelve sons of Jacob, the forebears of the Twelve Tribes of Israel, were born. Leah gave birth to Reuben, Simeon, Levi, Judah, Issachar, and Zebulun. Rachel bore Joseph and Benjamin. Jacob had two other wives, Bilhah and Zilpah, and Bilhah gave birth to Dan and Naphtali, and Zilpah bore Gad and Asher.

It was a large and wonderful family, but they were to be torn by brotherly strife.

Haftorah Va-Yishlach

THE BOOK OF OVADIAH

In the Sidrah, we read how Jacob continues in the traditions of Abraham and Isaac. Through him, the Jewish faith moves forward and is transmitted to his sons, the fathers of the Twelve Tribes of Israel.

Esau, Jacob's twin brother, broke away into different ways of life. He became a hunter and a man of violence. Esau was the father of Edom, a nation which often oppressed the Jewish people.

---

[7]What compelled Jacob, our father to bury Rachel on the road to Ephrath? The reason was that Jacob foresaw that future exiles (from Jerusalem) were going to pass on that road to their captivity. Being buried there, Rachel would be able to plead for them,-as it is written: "A voice is heard in Ramah, Rachel weeping for her children." (Jeremiah xxxi. 15)

—BERESHIT RABBAH

Ovadiah was aware of the hatred which the nations felt against his people. He warns all those bent on Israel's destruction that such a course will invariably end in their own destruction.

At the end of his message, the Prophet predicts that the forces of righteousness which the Jewish people embody by living in the ways prescribed by God, will continue to triumph until the end of days.

> *And saviors shall come up on Mount Zion*
> *To judge the mount of Esau*
> *And the kingdom shall be the Lord's.*

וישב

Va-Ye-Shev

*A*FTER HE RETURNED to Canaan from the home of his uncle Laban, Jacob continued to live in the Promised Land.[1] He and his family suffered a great deal. His beloved wife, Rachel, had died on the way to Bethlehem and Jacob was left with twelve sons and one daughter, Dinah. Having loved Rachel so deeply, Jacob had a special fondness for Joseph,[2] Rachel's son. This greatly angered Joseph's brothers and because of their jealousy they began to hate him.

One day, they saw that their father had made a beautiful coat of many colors for Joseph.[3] When this coat was presented to Joseph, they hated him even more.

To make matters worse, Joseph, then a youth of seventeen years,[4] had a number of dreams which he related to his family.

> *And he said unto them: 'Hear, I pray you, this dream which I have dreamed: for, behold, we were binding sheaves in the field, and, lo, my sheaf arose, and also stood upright; and, behold, your sheaves came round about, and*

---

[1]Esau had gone to a different country, but Jacob remained in the land of his father, because the birthright was his and he was to inherit the land.

—RASHBAM

[2]Jacob erred in differentiating between his sons.

—SFORNO

[3]The coat was a sign that Jacob had marked him for leadership.

—SFORNO

[4]From this we learn that he was separated from his father for twenty-two years, since he was thirty-nine years old when they were reunited.

—RASHBAM

bowed down to my sheaf.' And his brethren said to him: 'Shalt thou indeed reign over us? Or shalt thou indeed have dominion over us?' And they hated him yet the more for his dreams, and for his words.

He then told them of a dream in which he saw the sun, the moon, and eleven stars bowing down to him. His brothers were furious. Even Jacob was shocked, but he did not take the dream lightly.

The hatred of his brothers was climaxed when Jacob asked his son, Joseph, to go to the fields and see how his brothers were faring while they were out tending the sheep. When his brothers saw him approaching them, their fury reached a peak, and they decided to do away with him. It was only through the intervention of Reuben, the oldest brother, that Joseph's life was spared. Instead of being killed, he was thrown into a pit. Reuben hoped the desire for violence in the brothers would be calmed, and that he could then safely return Joseph to his father. But while Reuben was away, the others saw a caravan of Ishmaelite merchants and sold Joseph into slavery. When Reuben returned to the group, he was shocked and frightened at what had happened. Being the eldest, he felt he would be held responsible.

The brothers took Joseph's hated coat, dipped it into the blood of a slain animal, and presented it to Jacob as evidence that Joseph had been attacked and killed by a wild animal. The grief this caused their father knew no bounds, and he refused to be comforted.[5]

The many adventures that Joseph was to encounter in Egypt now began to unfold. He was bought as a slave by Potiphar, one of the very important men of Egypt. Joseph worked hard in this household. So well did he do his work that Potiphar began to notice him and finally placed him in charge of all the affairs of his home.

Trouble swiftly returned to Joseph when Potiphar's wife

---

[5]No person can be comforted for a living child whom he thinks dead. It is a divine decree that the dead be forgotten, but not the living.
—RASHI

began to make advances toward him.[6] Joseph told her that he feared God and that her actions were wrong and unfair to her husband. She became so angry that she snatched one of his garments and ran out into the street with it, claiming that Joseph had tried to attack her. Luckily, Joseph escaped with his life, though he was thrown into an Egyptian prison.[7]

Even in prison, he performed his appointed tasks with such diligence and success that he became the chief trustee. It was at this time that the fortunes of Joseph began to change. The chief butler and the head baker of Pharaoh, the ruler of Egypt, were thrown into prison. Joseph was charged with attending to their needs. One day, both these men were troubled by dreams which they could not explain.

Joseph asked them to relate their dreams. The chief butler spoke first:

> *In my dream, behold, a vine was before me; and in the vine were three branches; and as it was budding, its blossoms shot forth, and the clusters thereof brought forth ripe grapes; and Pharaoh's cup was in my hand; and I took the grapes, and pressed them into Pharaoh's cup, and I gave the cup into Pharaoh's hand.*

Joseph interpreted the dream to mean that within three days Pharaoh would pardon him and return him to his former rank. Joseph asked the butler to remember him when he again

---

[6]When Joseph received this important position, he began to eat and drink well, and to curl his hair. He said to himself: "Blessed be the Lord who has helped me forget my father's home." God then said: "Your father mourns for you in sackcloth and ashes and you eat, drink, and curl your hair!? By your life, I shall incite the bear (Potiphar's wife) against you!"

—BERESHIT RABBA

[7]Potiphar spared Joseph because he loved him. It is also possible that he doubted the truth of his wife's accusation.

—NACHMANIDES

stood before Pharaoh. He wanted him to tell the ruler that he was innocent and to seek a pardon for him.

The head baker then related his dream to Joseph:

I also saw in my dream, and, behold, three baskets of white bread were on my head; and in the uppermost basket there was all manner of baked food for Pharaoh; and the birds did eat them out of the basket upon my head.

Joseph informed the baker that Pharaoh would order him to be executed within the next three days.

On Pharaoh's birthday, three days later, everything happened exactly as Joseph had predicted: the baker was hanged and the chief butler was returned to his former position. But the butler did not mention Joseph to Pharaoh, and for the time being forgot about him.[8]

Haftorah Va-Ye-Shev

AMOS II, 6–III, 8

Amos was a fiery prophet whose life was spent as a simple herdsman in the hills of Judea. He strongly condemned all nations which acted contrary to human decency and righteousness.

Israel was not exempt from the Prophet's warnings and condemnation. Because God chose the Jewish People to teach His prescribed way of life, they were especially vulnerable to punishment if they betrayed this trust.

At the beginning of the Haftorah, Amos declares that God will

---

[8]The chief butler's forgetfulness in the enjoyment of his own good fortune, is sadly natural. Nothing, alas, is more common than ingratitude. Man forgets; but God does not forget his own. And when the night is darkest, the dawn is near.

—HERTZ

punish those who "sell the righteous for silver". In those days, poor people could be sold into slavery for a debt which they were unable to pay. This statement by Amos is an allusion to the Sidrah in which Joseph was sold by his brothers for twenty pieces of silver.

The Prophet constantly expresses the hope that his listeners will respond to his teachings and repent from their evil ways.

> *For the Lord will do nothing,*
> *But He revealeth His counsel unto His servants the*
>   *prophets.*
> *The lion hath roared,*
> *Who will not fear?*
> *The Lord God hath spoken,*
> *Who can but prophecy?*

מִקֵּץ

Mi-Ketz

CHAPTERS XLI–XLIV, 17

JOSEPH REMAINED IN the Egyptian prison for two years after he had correctly interpreted the dreams of the chief butler and baker. Then dreams again played a major role in his life. This time Pharaoh the ruler of Egypt had two dreams which greatly troubled him and none of his advisors could give an acceptable explanation. Now that it was to his advantage, the chief butler told Pharaoh of his experiences in prison, where Joseph had interpreted his dream.

Pharaoh was impressed and Joseph was quickly summoned and brought before the monarch. True to his faith, Joseph first told the king that he could explain only that which God had made clear to him, and then he asked Pharaoh to relate his dreams.

And Pharaoh spoke unto Joseph: 'In my dream, behold, I stood upon the brink of the river.[1] And, behold, there came up out of the river seven kine, fat-fleshed and well-favoured; and they fed in the reed-grass. And behold, seven other kine came up after them, poor and very ill-favoured and lean-fleshed, such as I never saw in all the land of Egypt for badness. And the lean and ill-favoured kine did eat up the first seven fat kine.[2] And when they had eaten them up, it could not be known that they had eaten them; but they were ill-favoured as at the beginning.

---

[1]Because famine and plenty in Egypt depended upon the Nile, Pharaoh saw the cows coming up out of the river.

—NACHMANIDES

[2]This symbolized that all the joy of the years of plenty would be forgotten during the famine.

—RASHI

*So I awoke. And I saw in my dream and, behold, seven ears
came up upon one stalk, full and good. And, behold, seven
ears, withered, thin, and blasted with the east wind,
sprung up after them. And the thin ears swallowed up the
seven good ears. And I told it unto the magicians; but there
was none that could declare it to me.'*

Although the two dreams were quite similar, Joseph told
Pharaoh that they were necessary to emphasize what they foretold would happen very soon. The seven fat cows and the seven
healthy ears of corn represented seven years of plenty which
were about to come to Egypt. The seven lean and sickly cows,
as well as the seven shabby ears of corn, represented seven years
of famine which would follow the seven good years. Joseph
advised Pharaoh to immediately appoint someone to store up
the food from the seven years of plenty to provide for the famine
which would follow.

Pharaoh and his advisors were so impressed with this explanation that Joseph was appointed to rule over Egypt second only
to Pharaoh. He acquired great fame and honor throughout the
land. During the seven years of plenty, all the surplus food was
carefully stored according to Joseph's instructions.

When the famine struck in Egypt, as well as in the neighbor-
ing countries, Joseph was ready to sell food to the population.
When the hunger in Canaan also became severe, Jacob sent ten
of his sons to Egypt to purchase food.[3] He kept Benjamin home,
fearing that harm might come to him. Having lost Joseph, this
son was the only remaining child of his beloved Rachel.

When the brothers were brought before Joseph, they did
not recognize him[4] because he had been quite young when they

---

[3]Jacob said to them: "My sons, you are all strong men; you are all
handsome. Do not enter Egypt together through one gate, and do not
congregate together in one place, lest the Evil Eye (trouble) shall have
sway over you.

—MIDRASH TANHUMA

[4]Joseph acted as though he were a stranger and spoke harshly with
them.

—RASHI

sold him.[5] But Joseph immediately recognized them. Remembering all that had happened, he accused them of being spies. The brothers strongly denied this charge and told him:

We thy servants are twelve brethren,[6] the sons of one man in the land of Canaan; and, behold, the youngest is this day with our father, and one is not.

But Joseph insisted they were spies and had them jailed for three days. After releasing them, Joseph took Simeon as a hostage and informed the brothers that they must bring Benjamin with them when they returned if they wanted their brother Simeon to be freed. Joseph told them he wanted to see Benjamin to determine if they were telling the truth about who they actually were.

With great sadness the brothers returned to Canaan. They sensed that their inhumanity to Joseph had somehow brought on their present trouble. When they told their father of Joseph's demand to see Benjamin, Jacob refused to permit his son to go, fearing he would lose him too. But when the famine grew worse and the hunger became more severe, Jacob had no choice but to consent.[7]

Judah took responsibility for Benjamin's safety:

And Judah said unto Israel his father: 'Send the lad with me, and we will arise and go, that we may live, and not die, both we, and also our little ones. I will be surety for him; of my hand shalt thou require him; if I bring him not

---

[5]Joseph now had a beard. When the brothers were in his power, he recognized them as brothers and was merciful to them; but when Joseph was in their power they "knew him not."

—RASHI

[6]The Divine Spirit entered into them and so they unwittingly included Joseph in the "we."

—RASHI

[7]Jacob did not believe what they had said and thought that they were looking for an opportunity to kill Benjamin [Rachel's other son].

—RASHI

*unto thee, and set him before thee, then let me bear the
blame for ever. . . .'*

When the brothers again stood before Joseph, Benjamin
stood alongside them. Joseph now began to act more kindly. He
had Simeon released and sat down with them to a feast.[8] So
happy was he to again see his young and beloved brother, Benjamin,
that he left the room and wept.

When the time came for the brothers to return to Canaan,
Joseph had their sacks filled with food. As he did the first time,
Joseph returned their payment for the food by placing their
money into their sacks. This time, however, he ordered his servant
to hide his own silver cup in Benjamin's sack.

As the caravan was leaving Egypt, Joseph had the brothers
overtaken and they were accused of stealing the cup. Naturally
they firmly denied this charge and they hastily agreed to have
the one in whose sack the cup was found slain in punishment.
But it was agreed that if the cup was found on any of them, he
would have to remain in Egypt as a servant.

The cup was found in Benjamin's sack.[9] The brothers were
horrified and returned to Joseph together. They pleaded with
Joseph and offered to remain themselves as servants. Joseph

---

[8]This feast was intended as a test for his brothers. Joseph wanted
to see how they would behave toward Benjamin and if they would show
envy toward him when he would give Benjamin larger portions than
the rest.

—SFORNO

[9]When the cup was found in Benjamin's sack, the shocked brothers
beat him on the shoulders, saying to him: "Thief, the son of a
woman thief; you have shamed us! You are a true son of your mother
[Rachel] who shamed our father [when she permitted Leah to take her
place as his bride!]"

Because of these blows which Benjamin endured, he merited to
have the Divine Presence rest upon his shoulders as we read in Jacob's
blessing to him (Deuteronomy 33:12) "Of Benjamin he said, 'The
beloved of the Lord shall dwell in safety by Him; He covereth Him all
the day; and He dwelleth between his shoulders' ".

—MIDRASH TANHUMA

declined this proposal and told them to return to their father—
only Benjamin was to remain.

The dramatic revelation of Joseph to his brothers was now
at hand.

Haftorah Mi-Ketz

I KINGS III, 15–IV, 1

Dreams play an important role both in the Sidrah and Haftorah. The
dreams of Pharaoh change the fate of Egypt and elevate Joseph from
prison to the exalted position of viceroy of Egypt. The Haftorah begins
with the last verses of a dream of King Solomon. He heard the voice
of God asking him what he most desired. According to Rabbinic tradition, Solomon assumed the throne when he was only twelve years old.
(Some historians claim that he was somewhat older).

Being so young, and aware of his awesome responsibilities as king,
he asked God to bestow on him "an understanding heart to judge Thy
people, that I may discern between good and evil; for who is able to
judge this Thy great people?"

God was very pleased with this request since Solomon asked nothing for himself—only the wisdom to better serve his people. His wish
was granted and he received a "wise and understanding heart; so that
there hath been none like thee before thee, neither after thee, neither
after thee shall arise any like unto thee."

The Haftorah describes a brilliant judgment which King Solomon
rendered. He was confronted by two women, each claiming that a
recently born baby belonged to her. The King asked for a sword and
ordered the child to be divided between the two women. While one
of the women readily agreed, the other immediately offered to give up
the child so long as no harm shall befall it. King Solomon declared
that woman to be the true mother.

And all Israel heard of the judgment which the King had
judged; and they feared the King for they saw that the
wisdom of God was in him, to do justice.

ויגש

Va-Yigash

CHAPTERS XLIV, 18–XLVII, 27

JOSEPH'S BROTHERS STOOD before him in Egypt. They realized
that their brother Benjamin was in serious danger of having to
remain as a servant in that country. After Joseph's cup was found
in Benjamin's sack, they had no arguments for his release. At
this critical moment, Judah stepped forward with a stirring plea
to Joseph:

> Oh my lord, let thy servant, I pray thee, speak a word in
> my lord's ears, and let not thine anger burn against thy
> servant;[1] for thou art even as Pharaoh. . . . thy servant
> my father said unto us: Ye know that my wife bore me two
> sons, and the one went out from me, and I said: Surely he
> is torn in pieces; And I have not seen him since, and if ye
> take this one also from me, and harm befall him, ye
> will bring down my gray hairs with sorrow to the
> grave. . . . Now, therefore, let thy servant, I pray thee,
> abide instead of the lad a bondman to my lord; and let the
> lad go up with his brethren. For how shall I go up to my
> father, if the lad be not with me? lest I look upon the evil
> that shall come to my father.

Hearing these words, it was impossible for Joseph to continue to conceal his identity. He was now convinced of his brothers genuine love for their father and each other. He sensed their
sorrow for the crime they had committed against him. He was
ready to forgive them completely.

---

[1] This fear on Judah's part indicates that he spoke to Joseph in a
harsh manner.

—RASHI

Sending the Egyptians out of the room,[2] Joseph told his brothers that he was their long-lost brother. Their reaction was shock and fright. They realized that Joseph's dreams about their bowing down to him had come true. What would happen to them now? Joseph quickly reassured them and put them at ease. He reasoned with them: God surely must have desired this chain of events, since he was now able to supply them with food during these years of famine.

The report of the reunion of Joseph with his brothers reached Pharaoh's ears and he was very pleased.[3] He told Joseph to prepare wagons for the entire family. Supplied with food and their other needs, the brothers were to return with the caravan to Canaan. They were to invite Jacob to come to Egypt, where the most desirable part of the country would be available to them.

At first Jacob could not believe the report that his beloved Joseph was still alive, and that he was the viceroy of Egypt. But

---

[2] Joseph could not bear that the onlookers should see his brothers put to shame when he revealed his true identity to them.

—RASHI

Also, it would not have been wise to let the Egyptians know all that happened between Joseph and his brothers. Being aware of all these troubles, they might have refused to let the Jews settle in their country. If the brothers could act so against their own flesh and blood, how much worse might they act against Egyptians. The knowledge of this background might also cause the Egyptians to lose faith in Joseph.

—NACHMANIDES

[3] It had been humiliating for Egypt to be governed by a slave released from prison. Joseph had told them that his family was honored in Canaan, but only now did they have proof of it.

—NACHMANIDES

The Egyptians were also pleased that with the coming of Joseph's family to Egypt, he would no longer consider himself a stranger, but a citizen with all his interests in that country.

—SFORNO

when he heard all the tales of his sons and saw the long caravan with which they returned, he realized that it was true, and he prepared to journey to Egypt.

And Israel took his journey with all that he had, and came to Beer-sheba, and offered sacrifices unto the God of his father, Isaac. And God spoke unto Israel [4] in the visions of the night, and said: 'Jacob, Jacob.' [5] And he said: 'Here am I.' And He said: 'I am God, [6] the God of thy father; fear not to go down into Egypt; for I will there make of thee a great nation. I will go down with thee into Egypt; and I will also surely bring thee up again. . . . '

When Joseph heard that his father was approaching, he prepared his chariot and rode to the Egyptian city of Goshen. Seeing his father, he fell upon his shoulders and wept a long time, as their reunion finally took place. Jacob felt that his life was now complete and he was ready to die a happy man. He was escorted to Pharaoh, who showed great pleasure in meeting the father of the man who had saved Egypt. Jacob blessed the monarch[7] and settled in Goshen with his family. There were seventy

---

[4]God addressed Jacob by this name because he was *Israel*, the name which implied that his descendants would one day rule over Canaan.

—SFORNO

[5]Although his children would ultimately triumph, the immediate consequence of the journey would be bondage; hence God addressed him by the name of Jacob, not Israel.

—NACHMANIDES

[6]God reassured him, because he was distressed at having to leave the Holy Land.

—RASHI

[7]All who take their leave of princes bless them and ask permission to retire. Jacob's blessing was that the Nile should rise toward Pharaoh, the rising and overflowing of the Nile being the source of Egypt's

members of the tribe of Israel at this time.

Since Egypt was able to withstand the years of famine yet to come—thanks to Joseph's preparations—there was plenty of food for their flocks and cattle. The Jews soon grew in numbers and in wealth.

Joseph continued to supervise the economy, and through his leadership Egypt became a mighty nation, selling food not only to its own population but to other countries as well.

Haftorah Va-Yigash

EZEKIEL XXXVII, 15–28

Ezekiel was one of the great leaders of the Babylonian exile. His calls to repentance and hope kept the spirit of the exiles alive until their return to the Land of Israel.

There is a great deal of symbolism in the messages of the Prophet. In this Haftorah, God tells him to take two sticks and unite them. One was to represent the northern kingdom of Israel and the other was to represent the southern kingdom of Judea. The symbolic joining of the sticks showed the people that the two kingdoms would someday be reunited. Carried a step further, it also indicated that all the Jewish People will again be united on their own Land in fellowship and harmony.

This links the Haftorah to the Sidrah where Joseph is reunited with his brothers who had sold him into slavery. Despite the hatred and jealousy which originally had separated them, they managed to live together again in brotherly love.

And they shall dwell in the land that I have given unto Jacob My servant, wherein your fathers dwelt; and they

---

fertility. From the time of that blessing, the Nile did rise toward him and water the land.

—RASHI

shall dwell therein, they, and their children, and their children's children, for ever; and David My servant shall be their prince for ever . . . And the nations shall know that I am the Lord that sanctify Israel, when My sanctuary shall be in the midst of them for ever.

וַיְחִי

Va-Y-Chi

JACOB LIVED SEVENTEEN years following his reunion with Joseph in the land of Goshen.

His life was now drawing to a close and he was anxious that he be buried in Canaan.

> *And the time drew near[1] that Israel must die; and he called his son Joseph,[2] and he said unto him: 'If now I have found favor in thy sight, put, I pray thee, thy hand under my thigh, and deal kindly and truly with me; bury me not, I pray thee, in Egypt. But when I sleep with my fathers, thou shalt carry me out of Egypt, and bury me in their buryingplace.' And he said: 'I will do as thou hast said.' And he said: 'Swear unto me,' And he swore unto him. And Israel bowed down upon the bed's head.*

Shortly afterward, Joseph was informed that his father was ill and everyone knew that the last days of the patriarch had arrived. Joseph took his two sons, Manasseh and Ephraim, and brought them to his father's bedside. Jacob told his son how happy he was that he had been able to see him again after so many years of tragic separation. He spoke of his joy at being together not only with his son, but with his grandchildren as well. He told Joseph that he was going to consider the

---

[1]The expression to "draw near" is employed where the dying man desires to give a charge to his children.

—RASHBAM

[2]Jacob called for his son Joseph because, being the viceroy of Egypt, he had the power to carry out Jacob's wishes.

—RASHI

two children as his own and that their inheritance would be the same as Joseph's brothers. This blessing was fulfilled when Manasseh and Ephraim became two of the Twelve Tribes of Israel.

Jacob asked that the two boys be brought to his side. He kissed and embraced them. He then placed his right hand on the head of Ephraim the younger of the two, and his left hand on the older, Manasseh, and he gave the following blessing:

> *The God before whom my fathers Abraham and Isaac did walk, the God who hath been my shepherd all my life long unto this day, the angel who hath redeemed me from all evil, bless the lads; and let my name be named in them, and the names of my fathers Abraham and Isaac; and let them grow into a multitude in the midst of the earth.*

When Joseph saw that his father's right hand was not on the head of the older brother, he tried to switch his hands, but Jacob would not change their position. He explained to Joseph that although Manasseh's future would be bright,[3] the younger Ephraim's would be even brighter.[4]

> *And he blessed them that day, saying: 'By thee shall Israel bless, saying: God make thee as Ephraim and as Manasseh. And he set Ephraim before Manasseh. And Israel said unto Joseph: 'Behold, I die; but God will be with you, and bring you back unto the land of your fathers. . . .'*

---

[3]Gideon was to descend from Manasseh, through whom God was to perform a miracle.

—RASHI

[4]Ephraim's descendant was to be Joshua, who was going to lead Israel into the Promised Land and teach them the Torah.

—RASHI

Now, for the last act of his life, Jacob assembled all his twelve sons around him to also bless them. First, he wanted to reveal to them what would happen in "the end of days,"[5] but then confined himself to the blessings, one for each son.[6] The blessing explained the character and nature of the son and alluded to what the future would hold for the descendants of each of them.

The sons who stood around the bed of their father at this fateful moment were Reuben, Simeon, Levi, Judah, Zebulun, Issachar, Dan, Gad, Asher, Naphtali, Joseph and Benjamin. These twelve sons constituted the original Twelve Tribes of Israel.

As soon as Jacob completed these blessings, he once more charged them to bury him in the Promised Land.

And he charged them and said unto them: 'I am to be gathered unto my people; bury me with my fathers in the cave that is in the field of Ephron the Hittite, in the cave

---

[5]Jacob intended to reveal the "end" (the coming of the Messiah) to them, but the Divine Presence departed from him, and he turned to other matters.

—RASHI

When the Divine Presence left Jacob, he said: "Perhaps, God forbid, there is some defect in me. My grandfather, Abraham, had a son named Ishmael who did not follow his father's faith. My father, Isaac, had a son named Esau who also did not follow the teachings of his father." Immediately, his sons said: "Hear Oh Israel, the Lord our God, the Lord is one." Thus, the Jewish people repeat this formula each morning and evening, affirming that we still observe the faith which Jacob taught us.

—PESACHIM 56a

[6]Jacob counselled all his sons to accept the way which he had taught them all his life. In so doing, they would be true sons of Israel, striving with God and man, and prevailing.

—SFORNO

*that is in the field of Machpelah which is before Mamre,
in the land of Canaan, which Abraham bought with the
field from Ephron the Hittite for a possession of a burying-
place. There they buried Abraham and Sarah his wife;
there they buried Isaac and Rebekah his wife; and there I
buried Leah. The field and the cave that is therein, which
was purchased from the children of Heth,' And when Jacob
made an end of charging his sons, he gathered up his feet
into the bed, and expired, and was gathered unto his people.*

With tears and sadness Joseph commanded the physicians
of Egypt to prepare his father's body for the trip to Canaan. The
Egyptians also mourned Jacob's death for a period of seventy
days. Joseph was granted permission by Pharaoh to escort his
father for burial, and a great procession left Egypt to bring Jacob
to the Cave of Machpelah in Canaan.

Once more, the brothers were frightened. They feared that
with their father dead Joseph might take revenge against them.
But they were again reassured by Joseph[7] that although their
original intentions were evil, it was through his coming to Egypt
that many lives were saved during the famine. The brothers
continued to live in peace.

The Book of Genesis closes with the death of Joseph. He,
too, exacted an oath that when the People of Israel would return
to the Promised Land, they would take his remains with them.
Many years later, during the great Exodus from Egypt, Moses
was to redeem this oath.

With the end of this book, the Jewish People are no longer
a tribe, but a nation.

---

[7]Rabbi Elazar said: "This teaches us that Joseph spoke to his
brothers in friendly and placating words. For example, he said, 'If ten
candles cannot extinguish one candle [Joseph], how would it be possible for one candle to extinguish ten?' "

—MEGILLAH 16B

Haftorah Va-Y-Chi

I KINGS II, 1–12

The Sidrah and the Haftorah describe the last days in the lives of two great leaders of the Jewish people.

In the Torah reading, Jacob blesses each of his sons prior to his death. The Haftorah describes the blessing which King David, at the close of his life, bestows upon his son Solomon. Like Jacob, the King was concerned about the future of his dynasty and that of the Jewish People. He advises Solomon to always live by the laws of God and to walk in His ways. If the leader of the nation sets such an example, the people will surely follow him.

I go the way of all the earth; be thou strong therefore, and show thyself a man; and keep the charge of the Lord, thy God, to walk in His ways, to keep His statutes, and His commandments . . . that the Lord may establish His word which He spoke concerning Me, saying: If thy children take heed to their way, to walk before Me in truth with all their heart and with all their soul, there shall not fail thee, said He, a man on the throne of Israel.

THE BOOK OF
EXODUS

ספר שׁמות

The second book of the Torah is called Shemot ("Names") in
Hebrew since it begins by listing the names of Jacob's sons who
entered Egypt. It is called Exodus in English because one of its
main subjects is the departure of the Children of Israel from
Egyptian bondage. When the Israelites entered Egypt, they were
merely a tribe whose leader, Jacob, had come to be reunited with
his long lost son Joseph. In Egypt, this tribe developed into the
Jewish People and was miraculously delivered from slavery. Then
they received the Ten Commandments at Mount Sinai. In this
book are also found some of the adventures of the Israelites in the
desert, many of the laws which Moses received on Mount Sinai,
and the establishment of their temporary House of Worship, the
Sanctuary.

שְׁמוֹת

Shemot

CHAPTERS I–VI, 1

Now these are the names of the sons of Israel, who came into Egypt with Jacob; every man came with his household: Reuben, Simeon, Levi, and Judah; Issachar, Zebulun and Benjamin; Dan and Naphtali, Gad and Asher. And all the souls that came out of the loins of Jacob were seventy souls; and Joseph was in Egypt already.[1] And Joseph died, and all his brethren, and all that generation. And the Children of Israel were fruitful, and increased abundantly, and multiplied, and waxed exceeding mighty; and the land was filled with them.

IT WAS AFTER these events that a new king ascended the throne of Egypt. This Pharaoh did not acknowledge the many great contributions of Joseph which had saved Egypt from destruction during the seven years of famine. Instead, he contrived to enslave the Hebrews and consequently take advantage of their wealth and industry. He began by arousing the suspicion and hatred of the Egyptians against this peaceful people[2] by declar-

---

[1]The Torah repeats this fact here, although it had been previously recorded, in order to stress that, it spite of his long residence in Egypt, Joseph remained loyal to his early home upbringing. His rise to fame did not cause him to drift from his family and religious traditions. He wanted to identify himself with the Hebrews, and that is why the text includes his name with the rest of the Hebrew tribe.

—RASHI

[2]When Joseph died, the Hebrews changed their loyalty to their religion, saying, "Let us be like the Egyptians!" In punishment, God changed the love which the Egyptians had toward the Israelites to hatred.

—SHEMOT RABBAH

ing that they were getting too numerous and, in case of war, might join Egypt's enemies. Pharaoh's constant pressure against them caused them to be enslaved, and they were forced to build entire cities for their task-masters.

However, despite the bitter persecution against the Hebrews, their spirit was not broken and they continued to multiply. Pharaoh then decreed that all boys born to the slaves were to be killed at birth by the midwives who delivered them. When these women refused to cooperate with this cruel command, the king declared that all male Hebrew babies must be thrown into the river. The female babies were permitted to live. In this manner, he hoped to fatally weaken the Hebrew people.

At this time, a baby boy was born to parents of the Tribe of Levi. The mother carefully hid the child, but when its cries grew louder after three months, she realized that further hiding was impossible. She prepared a basket of bulrushes, into which she placed her child. The basket was then placed at the edge of the Nile. The baby's sister, Miriam, stood nearby to see what would become of her brother.

The daughter of Pharaoh chose this moment to bathe in the river and saw the basket. When it was opened, she realized that it contained one of the children of the Hebrews and she took pity on him. Miriam ran forward and asked the princess if she wanted a nurse for him. When she was told to fetch one, she brought back the child's mother who became his nurse and future teacher. Pharaoh's daughter named the child Moses and he grew up as an Egyptian prince.

Although everyone considered Moses part of Egyptian royalty, he knew that he was a Hebrew. Apparently, his mother had taught him never to forget his heritage and his kinship with the Hebrew slaves. One day, when he saw an Egyptian beating one of these slaves, Moses became so enraged at this cruelty that he killed the Egyptian. Soon after this event, he noticed two slaves quarrelling. When he tried to restore peace among them, one of them accused Moses of meddling in their affairs and informed him that the killing of the Egyptian had been observed. The matter quickly reached Pharaoh's ears and he now wanted to take Moses' life. Moses quickly fled from Egypt to the plains of

Midian where he lodged with a Midianite priest, by the name of Jethro. One of his daughters, Zipporah, became Moses' wife.

In Midian, Moses became a shepherd. One day, as he was tending his father-in-law's sheep in the desert, he noticed a strange sight.

And the angel of the Lord appeared unto him in a flame of fire out of the midst of a bush;[3] and he looked, and, behold the bush burned with fire,[4] and the bush was not consumed.[5] And Moses said: 'I will turn aside now, and see this great sight, why the bush is not burnt.' And when the Lord saw that he turned aside to see, God called to him out of the midst of the bush, and said: 'Moses, Moses.' And he said: 'Here am I.'

God continued to tell Moses to remove the shoes from his feet for he was standing on holy ground. As God revealed Himself to Moses, He told him that He was the God of Abraham, Isaac, and Jacob who would surely redeem the Hebrews from their bondage as He had promised their forefathers, and that He would bring them back to the Promised Land.

God then informed Moses that he was to be the leader of this exodus from Egypt. Being a very meek and humble person,

---

[3]It was a thorn bush.—Ibn Ezra. God chose the lowliest of the trees as the place of His revelation to signify that He was with the Israelites in their sufferings and humiliation.

—RASHI

[4]The bush was enveloped by a flame of fire.—Nachmanides. The angel in the bush remained unhurt, and this was symbolic of the miraculous escape from destruction of the righteous in Israel. At this early stage God revealed Himself to Moses through symbols, but once he had seen God face to face, the Almighty revealed Himself directly to him.

—SFORNO

[5]The bush was not even singed despite the heat of the flame.

—RASHBAM

Moses, at first, declined this mission. He was afraid that people would not listen to him or follow him. Even after God showed him how he could perform some miraculous signs, Moses was still hesitant. Finally, God told him that his brother, Aaron, would be his spokesman.[6] Now Moses agreed to become the leader of the Hebrews.

The slaves were joyful when Aaron told them of their forthcoming liberation. Moses and Aaron then faced Pharaoh.

And afterwards Moses and Aaron came, and said unto Pharaoh: 'Thus saith the Lord, the God of Israel: Let My people go, that they may hold a feast unto Me in the wilderness'.[7]

Pharaoh refused this demand. In angry tones, he told the slaves that they must now produce the same amount of bricks as before without receiving the necessary straw to make them. Previously, this straw was supplied.

The mood of the enslaved Hebrews now changed to great disappointment and anger at Moses and Aaron. Instead of helping them, the people felt that their lot had been greatly worsened. Moses began to have serious doubts about the success of his mission.

The voice of God came to him.

And the Lord said unto Moses: 'Now shalt thou see what I will do to Pharaoh; for by a strong hand shall he let them go, and by a strong hand shall he drive them out of his land'.

---

[6]Aaron was able to give eloquent expression to Moses' thoughts (Nachmanides). Also, he had been reared in Egypt and was proficient in its language (Rashbam).

[7]Moses requested a feast of three days because in that period his People could have reached Sinai by the most direct route.

—IBN EZRA

Haftorah Shemot

ISAIAH XXVII, 6–XXVIII, 13 AND XXIX, 22, 23

The Book of Exodus introduces the Egyptian bondage endured by the Jews for many years. In the days of the prophet Isaiah, another empire threatened the existence of the Jewish People.

Assyria, a small province of Babylonia, became a great power and overthrew the northern kingdom of Israel in 721 B.C.E. Its Ten Tribes were dispersed in the exile which followed. The continuation of the Jewish tradition was now up to the tiny kingdom of Judah in the south. The survival of this small state and its capital city of Jerusalem was a miracle.

Isaiah preached during these turbulent years (740–701 B.C.E.). His primary message was that God makes Himself felt in the destinies of men and nations. History is a Divine evolution—not merely a series of disconnected events.

Just as Egypt was ultimately punished for its crimes against the Jewish People—so will be the fate of Assyria.

The lost tribes which were driven out of their land by this empire shall return, together with all the other Jewish exiles as was promised to them by God.

And it shall come to pass in that day,
That a great horn shall be blown;
And they shall come that were lost in the land of Assyria,
And they that were dispersed in the land of Egypt;
And they shall worship the Lord in the holy mountain at
  Jerusalem.

וארא

Va-Ayra

CHAPTERS VI, 2–IX

*M*OSES ACCEPTED THE leadership of the Israelites very reluctantly. He knew that it would be a very difficult mission. In fact, his first meeting with Pharaoh ended in disaster, since, because of it, the Israelite slaves were driven even more harshly.

The voice of God came to Moses to reassure him that his work was under divine guidance and that it would succeed:

> *And God spoke unto Moses and said unto him:*
> *'. . . . I have heard the groaning of the Children of Israel,*
> *whom the Egyptians keep in bondage; and I have remembered My covenant. Wherefore say unto the Children of*
> *Israel: I am the Lord, and I will bring you out from under*
> *the burdens of the Egyptians, and I will deliver you from*
> *their bondage, and I will redeem you with an outstretched*
> *arm,*[1] *and with great judgements; and I will take you to*
> *Me for a people, and I will be to you a God; and ye shall*
> *know that I am the Lord your God, who brought you out*
> *from under the burdens of the Egyptians.'*

This time, however, the slaves did not listen[2] to Moses' words of encouragement when he spoke to them. Because of their added burdens after their meeting with him, they no longer welcomed Moses. As a result, God told Moses to go to Pharaoh

---

[1]God's arm will be extended protectingly over Israel until He takes them out of Egypt.

—NACHMANIDES.

[2]Because of the weariness brought on by their work, the people refused to be comforted.

—RASHI.

directly and demand the release of the Jews from their bondage.

Once more, Moses and Aaron stood before Pharaoh, king of Egypt. Since Moses had a speech defect, Aaron, his older brother, was the spokesman.[3] When Pharaoh asked for a sign that they were really sent by God, Aaron cast a staff on the ground and it became a serpent. Sorcery was a great art in Egypt, and when Pharaoh turned to his magicians, they also changed their rods into serpents. Although Aaron's serpent swallowed theirs, the king remained unconvinced. God had foretold that Pharaoh would harden his heart[4] against permitting the Israelites to leave Egypt. Pharaoh decreed that the Hebrews were forbidden to leave Egypt even to worship in the desert for three days.

Moses was then commanded to wait for Pharaoh at the bank of the Nile the following morning. The king was to be warned that if he again refused to free the slaves, the waters of the Nile would turn to blood.[5] The fish, an important food product for Egypt, would die, and the water would not be fit to drink. When Pharaoh refused, Aaron stretched his staff over the waters and then struck them. The waters immediately turned to blood. To

---

[3]Moses was to repeat to Aaron every message as it reached him from God, and the latter was to put it into forceful language and address it to Pharaoh.

—RASHI.

[4]The difficulty is that if God hardened Pharaoh's heart, how could he justly be condemned for his refusal? God has endowed every man with superior wisdom and intelligence to enable him to rise above fate, but Pharaoh failed to make the attempt.

—IBN EZRA

Also, Pharaoh had already forfeited the chance of repentance by the wrongs he had perpetrated upon Israel.

—NACHMANIDES

[5]Since the Egyptians deified the Nile and worshipped it, the Nile was the first to feel the weight of God's might by its waters being turned into blood.

—RASHI

eke out enough water to stay alive, the Egyptians had to dig for it. Pharaoh's magicians again were able to turn some water to blood, so Pharaoh completely denied the divine origin of this plague.

Once more Moses was commanded to appear before Pharaoh and to caution him that if he did not permit the Jews to leave Egypt, frogs would appear throughout the land. Receiving no response, Aaron again stretched his staff over the waters of Egypt and frogs infested every part of the country except Goshen, the home of the Jews. The magicians were also able to make frogs appear, but they could not stop the plague. Pharaoh pleaded with Moses to stop the plague and agreed to let the Jews leave his land to worship God. Exactly at the time that Pharaoh had requested, the frogs perished and the plague came to an end.

When Pharaoh saw that the country had returned to normal, he again refused to let the Jews leave. At God's command, Aaron struck the ground, and this time gnats swarmed over the earth, attacking man and beast. But the magicians were unable to reproduce this plague.

Then the magicians said unto Pharaoh: 'This is the finger of God';[6] and Pharaoh's heart was hardened, and he hearkened not unto them; as the Lord had spoken.

God's punishment continued. He commanded Moses to demand of Pharaoh: "Let My people go, that they may serve Me". When Pharaoh refused, a horde of flies descended upon Egypt. This time, Pharaoh fervently promised to let the Jews leave the country, but as soon as the plague stopped, he again changed his mind and refused.

A heavy plague then struck the cattle of the Egyptians,

---

[6]The magicians admitted that the plague was not worked by the magical powers of Moses and Aaron, but was a visitation that came upon Egypt; otherwise they, too, would have performed it.

—RASHBAM

killing most of them, but not a single animal of the Jews perished. Despite all this, Pharaoh remained stubborn.

The fury of the plagues continued.

And the Lord said unto Moses and unto Aaron: 'Take to you handfuls of soot of the furnace, and let Moses throw it heavenward in the sight of Pharaoh. And it shall become small dust over all the land of Egypt, and shall be a boil breaking forth with blains upon man and upon beast, throughout all the land of Egypt'.

This skin disease spread throughout Egypt and even Pharaoh's magicians were badly afflicted, but the king of Egypt would not relent.

The next day, Moses stretched his hand toward heaven and a heavy hail came down on Egypt killing all the people, cattle,[7] and vegetation in the path of its lightening speed. Heeding Moses' warning, some Egyptians sheltered their cattle and saved them. The thunder, lightening, and hail badly frightened Pharaoh and he pleaded with Moses to intercede for him with God to bring an end to the hail. Moses again complied with Pharaoh's pleas, but when the hail stopped, Pharaoh's heart was once more hardened, and he refused to let the Jews leave his land.

---

[7]But has it not been recorded that the cattle of Egypt died [in the previous plague]! That plague, however, was directed only against the cattle "which are in the field" and the Egyptians who feared God removed their cattle into their houses where they escaped.

—RASHI

Haftorah Va-Ayra

 EZEKIEL XXVIII, 25-XXIX, 21

The Torah reading speaks of Egypt, the nation which enslaved the Jewish People and kept them in bondage for many generations, until they gained their freedom in the great Exodus.

Many centuries later, during the tenure of the prophet Ezekiel, Egypt again became a great threat to the Judeans. The Babylonians had overrun their country and laid the Holy Temple to waste in the year 586 B.C.E. Ezekiel kept the flagging hopes of the exiles awake in Babylon. He assured them that the same God who had brought about their downfall would return them to their national and spiritual Homeland. The Holy Temple, Ezekiel affirmed, would surely be rebuilt.

The Prophet also observed events in Judea with great anxiety. Egypt sought to form an alliance with the Judeans to overthrow Babylonia. Ezekiel was desperately opposed to this course of action. National salvation will not come about through military treaties, he taught, but only through repentance and a return to the ways of God.

The text of the Haftorah is an angry prophecy directed against Egypt, and predicting its destruction. Although its exiles will ultimately return to Egypt, the nation will never again achieve its former prominence as a great power.

בּא

Bo

*T*HE JEWS WERE a beloved people in Egypt in the time of Jacob and Joseph; they contributed greatly to the welfare of the country. Nevertheless, with the rise of a new Pharaoh, they came to be cruelly oppressed. Moses, who was sent by God to free his People, could not move Pharaoh, who refused to let them leave Egypt. Seven plagues had already come upon the land, but in the end, Pharaoh again hardened his heart and continued to deny God's command: "Let My people go, that they may serve Me".

The voice of God again came to Moses, telling him to appear before Pharaoh.

> *And the Lord said unto Moses: 'Go in unto Pharaoh for I have hardened his heart, and the heart of his servants, that I may show these My signs in the midst of them; and that thou mayest tell in the ears of thy son, and thy son's son, what I have wrought upon Egypt, and My signs which I have done among them; that ye may know that I am the Lord.'*

Since Pharaoh over and over again refused to do justice, God, Himself would now harden his heart, to demonstrate to the monarch and to all of Egypt the consequences of their continued enslavement of the Jewish people—as well as a lesson to mankind for all times.

Once more Moses and Aaron appeared before Pharaoh warning that if he would not relent, his entire country would be overrun by locusts,[1] destroying everything that man-

---

[1]Nachmanides, differing with other commentators, holds that the interval between the plague of hail and the plague of locusts was very

aged to survive the plague of hail.

Pharaoh's servants pleaded with him to permit the slaves to leave the land—at least to worship God for three days—for they realized that Egypt was on the verge of destruction. Shaken, but still stubborn, Pharaoh tried to bargain with Moses to permit only some of the Jews to leave but Moses was firm in his demand.

> *And Moses said: 'We will go with our young and with our old, with our sons and with our daughters, with our flocks and with our herds will we go; for we must hold a feast unto the Lord.'*

This demand infuriated Pharaoh, who wanted the young to remain behind in Egypt. Moses and Aaron were driven from Pharaoh's presence. In response, Moses stretched his staff over the land of Egypt. An east wind brought such great swarms of locusts that the land actually became dark.

As the king saw his country being devoured by these hordes of insects, he again pleaded with Moses to ask God to halt the plague.[2] Moses consented and the eighth plague came to an end.

But the Jews were not yet free.

> *And the Lord said unto Moses: 'Stretch out thy hand toward heaven, that there may be darkness over the land of Egypt, even darkness which may be felt.' And Moses stretched forth his hand toward heaven; and there was a thick darkness[3] in all the land of Egypt three days; they*

---

brief. According to a Rabbinic tradition, the Ten Plagues took place over a period of twelve months.

[2]Pharaoh sent for Moses and Aaron to save the roots of the wheat and spelt that survived the previous plagues from being devoured by the locusts.

—SFORNO

[3]Sforno interprets this phrase to mean that the usual darkness of night would be replaced by extraordinary darkness which the Egyptians would not be able to overcome even by artificial lighting.

saw not one another,[4] *neither rose any from his place for three days; but all the Children of Israel had light in their dwellings.*[5]

Pharaoh was now ready to let all the Jews leave Egypt, but he wanted their flocks and herds to remain. Moses would make no concessions. He demanded that the slaves be freed, and that they be permitted to take along all their belongings. Pharaoh was not to have any further gain from his injustice. But Pharaoh refused, thereby unleashing the last and most destructive of the Ten Plagues.

The people of Egypt, realizing that the Jews were about to leave their land, gave them jewels with gold and silver.[6] Apparently the Egyptians themselves had a warm regard for these people which were struggling so hard to be free. Moses himself was greatly admired by the Egyptians.

And Moses said: 'Thus saith the Lord: About midnight will I go out into the midst of Egypt, and all the first-born in the land of Egypt shall die, from the first-born of Pharaoh that sitteth upon his throne, even unto the first-born of the maid-servant that is behind the mill; and all the first-born of cattle . . .'[7]

---

[4]The darkness was not caused by the sun not shining, but by a thick fog which settled over Egypt.

—NACHMANIDES

[5]The plague of darkness did not affect any Jew even though he dwelt near the house of an Egyptian.

—RASHI

[6]The Egyptians will bear no grudge against the Jews because of the plagues they had suffered, but will readily acknowledge their guilt and freely shower them with gifts.

—NACHMANIDES

[7]Because the Egyptians worshipped cattle as gods.

—RASHI

Nisan, the month in which they gained their freedom, was to become the first month in the calendar of the Jewish people.[8] God commanded that on the tenth day of that month, a lamb was to be taken by each family, kept until the fourteenth day, and then sacrificed as the Paschal Lamb—the *Pesach.* The Israelites were further commanded to sprinkle some blood of the sacrifice on the door-posts of their homes,[9] after which the lamb was to be eaten. This annual feast was to be observed by future generations and, except for sprinkling blood on the door-posts, was repeated until the destruction of the Holy Temple. In our time it is commemorated by placing a shank-bone on the Seder Plate on the first and second night of *Pesach.*

On the night of the sacrifice—at midnight—the tenth plague struck: The first-born in every Egyptian home died. So frightened were the Egyptians for their own lives, that they urged the Israelites to leave immediately. The Jews left in such haste that the dough they prepared for bread had no time to rise.

Now, after generations of slavery, the Jewish People marched out of Egypt together as free nation. There were about six hundred thousand men, their families and many others who had joined them. The dough which did not have time to rise became *matzah,* and it is eaten instead of bread during the Passover festival.

The first-born of both man and beast were henceforth to be

---

[8]This was the first commandment bestowed upon Israel as a people.

—NACHMANIDES

[9]The mark of blood was designed as an atonement for those inside the house who partook of the paschal offering; and also was a sign for the destroying angel to pass by the house.

—IBN EZRA

While God had no need for a sign to guide Him, the mark of blood on the houses of the Jews would serve as proof of their readiness to obey God's commandments and so further render them worthy of being spared by the plague.

—RASHI

dedicated to God. Parents were instructed to tell their children, for all time to come, of the great events which occurred in Egypt when God led the children of Israel from slavery to freedom. It is this annual telling which is the essence of the *Seder*.

Haftorah Bo

JEREMIAH XLVI, 13–28

While Ezekiel was preaching to the exiles in Babylonia, Jeremiah was the spiritual leader of his people in Jerusalem. He had the sad task of prophesying during the last days of the Jewish State.

Many of his countrymen considered forming an alliance with Egypt, thereby hoping to gain enough strength to overthrow Babylonia and restore the kingdom. Jeremiah, condemning this course of action, thunders against Egypt, the same country which oppressed the Jewish people as described in the Sidrah. Not only will Egypt fall to the might of Babylonia, but all those nations which trusted in her will go down, as well.

Israel's salvation will come from their God. If they will walk in His ways, they need have no fears nor seek any national alliances.

> *But fear not thou, O Jacob My servant,*
> *Neither be dismayed, O Israel;*
> *For, lo, I will save thee from afar,*
> *And thy seed from the land of their captivity;*
> *And Jacob shall again be quiet and at ease,*
> *And none shall make him afraid.*

בשלח

B-Shalach

*T*HE TENTH PLAGUE had struck Egypt and, with it, the Exodus of the children of Israel from Egypt began.[1] The Paschal Lamb had been sacrificed and eaten.

The long journey into the desert now began. To prevent the Jews from rushing back to slavery at the first signs of danger or hunger, God led them through a confusing and roundabout way which brought them to the Red Sea.[2] The course of their travels was determined by a cloud during the day, and a pillar of fire by night.[3]

Just as Joseph had once taken his father Jacob to be buried in Canaan, Moses now carried Joseph's bones with him for burial in the Promised Land.[4] Many years earlier, Joseph had

---

[1]Israel was redeemed from Egypt because of four meritorious attitudes: they did not change their [Hebrew] names; they did not change their language; they did not reveal their national secrets; and they did not abrogate the covenant of circumcision.

—YALKUT SHIMONI

[2]The traveling time from Egypt to Canaan by the direct route was about ten days; had it been longer, Jacob's sons could not have managed so easily to make that journey so many times.

—IBN EZRA

[3]The Torah's way of expressing the idea that the power of God accompanied them.

—IBN EZRA

[4]As leader of the people, he realized his responsibility to honor the promise made to Joseph.

—SFORNO.

Together with Joseph's bones, the Jews also brought out the bones of his brothers.

—RASHI

foreseen that his descendants would leave Egypt and asked that his bones accompany the Jews on their way to the Holy Land. This promise was now being fulfilled.

But the Jews had not seen the last of the cruel Pharaoh.

And it was told the king of Egypt that the people were fled; and the heart of Pharaoh and of his servants were turned towards the people, and they said: 'What is this we have done, that we have let Israel go from serving us?' And he made ready his chariots, and took his people with him. And he took six hundred chosen chariots, and all the chariots of Egypt, and captains over all of them. And the Lord hardened the heart of Pharaoh king of Egypt,[5] and he pursued after the Children of Israel; for the Children of Israel went out with a high hand.

When the Jews saw the Egyptian forces approaching them, they were struck by fear. Their first reaction was to turn on Moses: They would have preferred to be slaves in Egypt than to be killed by their former taskmasters in the wilderness.

Moses reassured the people, and he prayed to God for help. God told Moses that crying and pleading were not now appropriate.

And the Lord said unto Moses: 'Wherefore criest thou unto Me? speak unto the Children of Israel, that they go forward. And lift thou up thy rod, and stretch out thy hand over the sea, and divide it; and the Children of Israel shall go into the midst of the sea on dry ground.'

As Moses raised his staff, a strong east wind roared toward

---

[5]After his sufferings as a result of the plagues, Pharaoh would not feel disposed to pursue the Israelites. Therefore God hardened his heart to move him to undertake the pursuit and meet his deserved fate.

—NACHMANIDES

the Red Sea, forcing back the waves and dividing the waters. When the dry land of the sea bottom appeared, the Jews marched through the path to the shore on the other side.

In the meantime, the Egyptian army was in hot pursuit. As the Jews reached the other shore, the Egyptians were in the middle of the sea. Once more, the voice of God came to Moses.

> *And the Lord said unto Moses: 'Stretch out thy hand over the sea, that the waters may come back upon the Egyptians, upon their chariots, and upon their horsemen.' And Moses stretched forth his hand over the sea, and the sea returned to its strength when the morning appeared; and the Egyptians fled against it; and the Lord overthrew the Egyptians in the midst of the sea. And the waters returned, and covered the chariots, and the horsemen, even all the host of Pharaoh that went in after them into the sea; there remained not so much as one of them. But the Children of Israel walked upon dry land in the midst of the sea; and the waters were a wall unto them on their right hand, and on their left.*

Seeing this great miracle, the Jews were strengthened in their belief in God and Moses His servant. With great joy, Moses and all the people sang a song of praise and thanksgiving to God.[6]

> *I will sing unto the Lord, for He is highly exalted;*
> *The horse and his rider hath He thrown into the sea.*
> *The Lord is my strength and song,*
> *And He is become my salvation;*
> *This is my God, and I will glorify Him;*
> *My father's God, and I will exalt Him.*

---

[6]Until then the Jews felt as slaves who fled from their masters, but now that they saw the Egyptians dead, they felt that they were free men.

—SFORNO

84

Moses' sister Miriam led the women in song and dance.

Sing ye to the Lord, for He is highly exalted:
The horse and his rider hath He thrown into the sea.

As the Jews continued their journey, they often did not have enough food or water. Whenever this happened, they grumbled against Moses. Only three days after the miracle of the Red Sea, they had no water to drink at Marah, where the water was bitter. Moses prayed and the waters became sweet and fit for drinking.

Again, when they reached the desert of Sin, it was hunger which caused a wave of angry murmurings. It was here that another great miracle began.

Then said the Lord unto Moses: 'Behold, I will cause to
rain bread from heaven for you; and the people shall go out
and gather a day's portion every day, that I may prove
them, whether they will walk in My law, or not.'

This "manna"[7] was not found on the Sabbath. The people were told to collect a double portion the day before. Those who searched for extra food on the Sabbath were severely rebuked.

From the wilderness of Sin they traveled to Rephidim. Again, they could find no water and began to murmur against Moses, and again God miraculously provided them with water.

An attack now took place against the children of Israel which was to be remembered throughout history as one of the most treacherous assaults of all time. As the Jews were encamped in Rephidim, the tribe of Amalek—without provocation —attacked the camp of Israel from behind, where the women and children were concentrated.

Moses charged Joshua, his second-in-command, with the

---

[7]When eaten whole, the manna had the taste of wafers made with honey, similar to the sweetness of nuts eaten whole; but when ground in a mill or beaten in a mortar, it resembled cake baked in oil, since one tastes the oil of nuts when eating them in crushed form.

—RASHBAM

task of defense. Then Moses climbed to a mountain-top where he raised his hand. As long as his hand was held high, the people took courage and gained the advantage of the battle. But when his hand was lowered, Amalek grew stronger.[8] In order to assure victory, Aaron and Hur, who were on the mountain-top with Moses, prepared a rock for their leader to sit on, and held up his hands.[9] Joshua and his army won the battle and Amalek was defeated.

This inexcusable act of inhumanity was recorded in the Torah as an eternal reminder to Israel to fight "Amalek" and all that they stood for.[10]

Haftorah B-Shalach

JUDGES IV, 4–V, 31

Both the Sidrah and Haftorah contain joyous songs of triumph. In the former, we read how the Jews were miraculously saved from their Egyptian bondage by the repeated interventions of God. As soon as they had crossed the Red Sea, Moses sang a happy song of triumph and thanksgiving to God.

After the death of Joshua, the Twelve Tribes of Israel were constantly threatened and attacked by the Canaanites who survived Isra-

---

[8]Moses held his staff in his hand and it was to Israel like a rallying flag. They were like soldiers who fight with bravery while they see their flag aloft; but on seeing it lowered, they flee in despair and are defeated.

—RASHBAM

[9]Moses, desiring to share his people's hardships, refused to be placed on a plush seat; therefore Aaron and Hur placed a stone for him to sit on.

—RASHI

[10]Amalek was the first of the nations to attack Israel.

—RASHI

el's entry into Canaan. Whenever the existence of the Jewish People was in peril, one of the Judges would arise and save his people.

The Haftorah describes a decisive battle which was fought against the Canaanites under the leadership and inspiration of Deborah, the prophetess. This successful struggle also saw most of the Tribes united for the first time, thereby setting the foundation for a future united Israel.

After the battle was won, Deborah, like Moses, sang a song of victory to God.

Then sang Deborah and Barak the son of Abinoam on that
day, saying:
. . . Hear, O ye kings; give ear, O ye princes;
I, unto the Lord will sing;
I will sing praise to the Lord, the God of Israel.

יִתְרוֹ

Yitro

Chapters XVIII–XX

$\mathcal{H}$AVING been saved from Egypt by the miracle at the Red Sea, the Jews camped in Rephidim, which is near Horeb—another name for Sinai. It was at a mountain, in this region of Sinai, that the Jewish People was destined to receive the Decalogue[1] and the balance of the text, now known as the Five Books of Moses.

When Moses was a fugitive from Pharoah's wrath in Midian, he married one of Jethro's daughters. Zipporah, his wife, bore him two sons, Gershom and Eliezer. When he went to Egypt to lead his people out of slavery, Moses had left his family with his father-in-law. Jethro now brought Zipporah and the two boys back to Moses, as the Jews were almost at the foot of Mount Sinai.

Moses welcomed his family with great joy. He treated Jethro with deep respect.[2] Not only was this man the father of his wife, he was also a respected religious leader in Midian. Moses told

---

[1] We have rejected the expression "Ten Commandments," which implies that these laws are binding, and other laws in the Torah are less important—a concept embraced by other faiths which claim to adhere to the "Old Testament." The Hebrew *"Asereth Ha'Dibros"* literally means "Ten Words," not "Ten Commandments." We therefore use the word "Decalogue" from the Greek *deka* (ten), and *logos* (words), a more precise translation which does not lend itself to the distorted notion referred to above. The Sages tell us that *all* the laws of the Torah derive from the "Ten Words." Rather than being a selection of commandments, the Decalogue is actually a condensation of all the laws of the Torah.

[2] Moses' action demonstrates the nobility of his character. Though he held such eminent rank, he did not deem it beneath his dignity to go out to meet the man who had befriended him in his time of distress.
—SFORNO

him of all the great miracles which had occurred in Egypt, at the Red Sea, and in the desert. Jethro rejoiced when he learned about these fateful events.[3] They all sat down to dine together.

Jethro soon began to notice how hard Moses was working as a judge for all the people, while also teaching them the will of God at the same time. He offered some sage advise by encouraging Moses to set up a system of lower and higher courts.

And Moses' father-in-law said unto him: 'The thing that thou doest is not good. Thou wilt surely wear away, both thou, and this people that is with thee; for the thing is too heavy for thee; thou art not able to perform it thyself alone. Hearken now unto my voice, I will give thee counsel, and God be with thee: be thou for the people before God, and bring thou the causes unto God. And thou shalt teach them the statutes and the laws, and shalt show them the way wherein they must walk, and the work that they must do.[4] Moreover thou shalt provide out of all the people able men, such as fear God, men of truth, hating unjust gain; and place such over them, to be rulers of thousands, rulers of hundreds, rulers of fifties, and rulers of tens. And let them judge the people at all seasons; and it shall be, that every great matter they shall bring unto thee, but every small matter they shall judge themselves; so shall they make it easier for thee and bear the burden with thee. If thou shalt do this thing, and God command thee

---

[3]Jethro rejoiced not for the destruction of the Egyptians, but for the deliverance of Israel.

—SFORNO

[4]To instruct the people in God's law was a responsibility which Moses could not delegate to others; but judging disputes involving money and property could be done by judges appointed for that purpose.

—NACHMANIDES

*so, then thou shalt be able to endure, and all this people
also shall go to their place in peace.* [5]

Moses followed this advise and then bade farewell to Jethro,
who returned to his own home in Midian.

It was now the third month since the Hebrews had left
Egypt and they had arrived at Mount Sinai. Moses ascended the
mountain where the voice of God came to him. He was told to
tell the people that if they would follow God's commandments,
as recorded in the Torah, they would always be a people dedicated to God—"a nation of priests and a holy people". When
they received this message, the people agreed to abide by all that
God would ask of them.

They were then told to prepare themselves for three days
to witness a revelation at Mount Sinai. During this period, the
people were not permitted to step on the mountain, or even
touch it, since it was to be holy and sanctified. As soon as this
great event was over, the mountain would revert to its previous
status. [6]

On the morning of the third day, a cloud was seen on top
of Mount Sinai which was enveloped with thunder and lightening. [7] The people began to tremble as they heard the shrill sound
of the *shofar,* the ram's horn. [8] In this setting, as the mountain
gave forth clouds of smoke, Moses led the Jews up to its very
foot. The voice of God then called Moses to the top of the

[5] The Jewish people will be a nation which would not perish, but
live forever.

[6] A long blast [of the ram's horn] would be the signal of the departure of the Divine Presence and the end of the Divine Communion.

—RASHI

[7] God came down early, even before the Jews expected Him,
though normally a teacher does not wait for the arrival of his pupils.

—RASHI

[8] The sound of the shofar was far louder than the sound of any
trumpet they had ever heard.

—IBN EZRA

mountain. As Moses, accompanied by Aaron, ascended Sinai, the voice of God was heard proclaiming the Decalogue.[9]

I am the Lord, thy God, who brought thee out of the land of Egypt, out of the house of bondage.[10]

Thou shalt have no other gods before Me.[11] *Thou shalt not make unto thee a graven image, nor any manner of likeness, of any thing that is in heaven above, or that is in the earth beneath, or that is in the water under the earth; thou shalt not bow down unto them, nor serve them; for I the Lord thy God am a jealous God, visiting the iniquity of the fathers upon the children unto the third and fourth generation of them that hate Me;*[12] *and showing mercy unto the thousandth generation of them that love Me and keep My commandments.*

---

[9]Said Rabbi Abbahi in the name of Rabbi Yochanan: "When the Holy One, blessed be He, gave the Torah, the birds did not chirp, the fowl did not take wing, the oxen did not low, the angels did not fly nor sing praises to God, the oceans did not roll, humans did not speak; but the world was silent and still as the Voice went forth and proclaimed, 'I am the Lord your God.' "

—TALMUD

[10]You have a direct approach to Me and need no mediator to intercede with Me on your behalf.

—SFORNO

[11]Not that other gods exist—to declare this would be blasphemous—but rather "gods of others", beings or objects which others have deified.

—RASHI

[12]Not that God visits the sins of the fathers upon their children, but He takes the sins of the former into account when punishing the children for the evil they have done in following the bad example of their parents.

—RASHI

Thou shalt not take the name of the Lord thy God in vain; for the Lord will not hold him guiltless that taketh His name in vain.

Remember the Sabbath day, to keep it holy.[13] *Six days shalt thou labor, and do all thy work; but the seventh day is a sabbath unto the Lord thy God, in it thou shalt not do any manner of work, thou, nor thy son, nor thy daughter, nor thy man-servant, nor thy maid-servant, nor thy cattle, nor thy stranger that is within thy gates;*[14] *for in six days the Lord made heaven and earth, the sea, and all that in them is, and rested on the seventh day; wherefore the Lord blessed the sabbath day, and hallowed it.*

Honor thy father and thy mother, that thy days may be long upon the land which the Lord thy God giveth thee.[15]

Thou shalt not murder.

Thou shalt not commit adultery.

Thou shalt not steal.

Thou shalt not bear false witness against thy neighbor.

---

[13]With the advent of the Sabbath, a man should consider that all his labors have been completed and drive any thought of work from his mind.

—RASHI

[14]A day to be devoted to religious service and the study of sacred works in an atmosphere of spiritual joy.

—SFORNO

[15]He will live to old age in this world and his days will be long in the World to Come.

—NACHMANIDES

Thou shalt not covet thy neighbor's house; thou shalt not covet thy neighbor's wife, nor his man-servant, nor his maid-servant, nor his ox, nor his ass, nor any thing that is thy neighbor's.

As the people heard these commandments, they became terrified by the smoke, the thunder, lightning, and the sounds of the *shofar.* They thought they would die if God continued to speak to them. They therefore asked Moses to receive God's teachings and then convey the laws of the Torah to them. Despite Moses' reassurances, the people refused to remain at the mountain. Moses then went up into the thick darkness by himself. God told Moses to remind the people that they had heard His voice themselves. They were never to have idols of gold or silver. They were to worship on an earthen or stone altar upon which they were to offer sacrifices—only to God. This altar was not to be constructed with metal tools, which were symbols of war. God's altar, as well as His people, were to be symbols and instruments of peace.

Haftorah Yitro

Isaiah VI–VII, 6 and IX, 5, 6

The Sidrah describes the revelation of God on Mount Sinai to the Jewish People when they received the Decalogue. So important was this event in the history of the Jews, that it changed the entire scope and destiny of the Nation.

A revelation of God to Isaiah, described in this Haftorah, also changed the life of this man who became a prophet and one of the great leaders of his people.

The generation to which Isaiah preached enjoyed prosperity and the material enjoyments of life. It was the period during which King Uzzia reigned (790–740 B.C.E.). Because of their general satisfaction, the People did not seek God nor follow his teachings.

Isaiah responds to his Divine mission by prophesying to the People and working to lead them back to the paths of justice and righteousness.

During his tenure, Isaiah became a close confidante to kings and common people. The depth and beauty of his teachings have made a deep impression upon the world throughout the generations.

מִשְׁפָּטִים

Mishpatim

*T*HE DECALOGUE HAD been given to the Children of Israel standing at Mount Sinai. Moses now approached the cloud of the Divine Presence which hovered on top of the mountain to receive the balance of the Torah. The basic legal and moral code of the Jewish faith now begins to unfold in detail. In the entire Torah, there are six hundred and thirteen commandments.

In biblical days, slavery still existed, even among the Jews. However, the Torah gives very specific laws for the protection and ultimate freeing of these slaves. A Jew became a slave if he owed money through a theft or debt which he could not return. There are many laws regarding the proper care of such a slave.[1] A Jewish slave was to serve for a maximum period of six years, and released in the seventh. A maid-servant had other means of winning her freedom. The Jubilee year—which occurred every fifty years—signaled the freedom of all Jewish slaves.

The punishment for wilful murder is death, but only if it is proven beyond the shadow of a doubt that the act was premeditated, intentional, and only if committed in the presence of witnesses. Anyone guilty of causing the death of another person by accident was protected by the law.

He that smiteth a man, so that he dieth, shall surely be put to death. And if a man lie not in wait, but God cause it

---

[1]While the Torah did not compel the master to maintain the wife and children of his Jewish slave, he did have a moral obligation to care for them. He was expected to give them food and shelter which they repaid by their services to him—but they had the right to leave whenever they wished.

—NACHMANIDES

*to come to hand; then I will appoint thee a place whither
he may flee.*[2]

Other crimes for which the Torah prescribes capital punishment are the striking or cursing of parents, and kidnapping.

Anything stolen must be returned, or the victim compen-
sated; and a fine must be paid by the thief, depending upon
the nature of the crime.

*If a fire break out, and catch in thorns, so that the shocks
of corn, or the standing corn, or the field are consumed;
he that kindled the fire shall surely make restitution.*[3]

One who guards someone's property without payment, has
no liability, as long as he had not made unauthorized use of what
he was guarding. However, if a person is paid to watch another's
property, and this property is stolen, lost, or harmed, the guardian must prove that the damage was in no way his fault. Otherwise, he must make restitution.

When a borrowed animal is hurt by accident or dies of
natural causes, compensation must be made to the owner. But,
should a person rent an animal, and it becomes lost, he receives
no compensation, since he was paid for the use of the animal,
and assumed that risk.

---

[2]When Israel possessed cities to dwell in.

—RASHBAM.

Even in the wilderness there was a place of refuge for those who
had killed by accident, and it was situated in the encampment of the
Levites.

—RASHI

[3]If a man lit a fire in his own field and did not take sufficient
precaution to prevent its spreading, even though the wind was normal.

—RASHBAM

A man must show great respect for a woman. If he fails to do this, there are various laws to safeguard her honor and security.

The Torah forbids the practice of witchcraft. All unnatural relations are also prohibited.

In keeping with the Decalogue, only sacrifices to God are permitted.

The love of the stranger, already taught by Abraham, the first Jew, is enforced by law.

And a stranger[4] shalt thou not wrong, neither shalt thou oppress him; for ye were strangers in the land of Egypt.[5] Ye shall not afflict any widow, or fatherless child. If thou afflict them in any wise—for if they cry at all unto Me, I will surely hear their cry—My wrath shall wax hot, and I will kill you with the sword; and your wives shall be widows, and your children fatherless.

Jews may not take interest on loans from each other. Great care had to be taken not to cause hardship to others by taking objects they need from day to day as pledges for loans.

The rulers of the nation must always be shown respect.

Certain parts of the harvest, as well as certain first-born animals, were to be offered to God. As a symbol of the holiness of the people, only specific meats, prepared in a certain manner, were permitted to be eaten.

A word given is sacred, and it may not be broken.

---

[4]The resident alien who undertakes not to indulge in idolatry is here classed with the orphan and the widow as weak and defenseless.

—IBN EZRA

[5]Do not think that you can oppress the weak with impunity. You were once helpless in Egypt; and as I, God, punished your oppressors, so will I defend those whom you oppress.

—NACHMANIDES

Thou shalt not utter a false report;[6] put not thy hand with the wicked to be an unrighteous witness. Thou shalt not follow a multitude to do evil; neither shalt thou bear witness in a cause to turn aside after a multitude to pervert justice; neither shalt thou favor a poor man in his cause.[7]

If a person sees someone's cattle going astray—even his enemy's—he must return it. If someone's animal is suffering under its burden, you must assist him, even if he is your enemy. Judges are also given stern warnings.

Thou shalt not wrest the judgement of thy poor in his cause. Keep thee far from a false matter; and the innocent and righteous slay thou not;[8] for I will not justify the wicked.[9] And thou shalt take no gift; for a gift blindeth them that have sight, and perverteth the words of the righteous. And a stranger shalt thou not oppress, for ye know the heart of the stranger, seeing ye were strangers in the land of Egypt.

The land was to be worked for six years and lie fallow during the seventh, just as the Jewish people were to work six days and rest on the seventh.

---

[6]This precept is a warning against listening to calumny, and instructs the judge not to hear a lawsuit except in the presence of all the parties concerned.

—RASHI

[7]Out of sympathy and consideration for him (Rashi) from a mistaken idea that you are helping him thereby (Ibn Ezra).

[8]Upon this clause the Rabbis based the ruling that if fresh evidence comes to light after a man has been condemned, a retrial takes place; but once a man has been acquitted, his case cannot be reopened.

—RASHI

[9]Should he escape punishment at the hand of the judges, God will deal with him through one of His many other agents.

—RASHI

Three annual festivals were to be celebrated,—Passover, (*Pesach*) commemorating the exodus from Egypt; the Feast of Pentacost (*Shavuot*), the season of the first-fruits; and the Feast of Tabernacles (*Succot*), the season of the ingathering of the crops. During these three festivals, the Jews must go up to the city of Jerusalem and rejoice in God's sanctuary.

The Torah then goes on to tell us that if the Children of Israel will faithfully observe these laws, they will enter the land of Canaan and live there in happiness and security.

After Moses transmitted these commandments to the people, God told him and Aaron to go up to Mount Sinai, together with Aaron's two sons, Nadab and Abihu, and the seventy elders. There, on the heights of this mountain, they saw a manifestation of God. After this vision, Moses built an altar at the foot of the mountain, together with twelve pillars, representing the Twelve Tribes of Israel. The people worshipped there and again committed themselves to carrying out the teachings of God.

Finally, Moses was once more commanded to come up to the mountain to receive the tablets of stone bearing the Decalogue, as well as the rest of the Torah, following which he was to teach and explain the laws and commandments to the people. Moses ordered the elders to remain with the camp, together with Aaron and Hur, to teach the people in his absence.

Joshua stood close to the top of the mountain as Moses went up to its very peak, where he entered into a cloud and remained for the next forty days and forty nights.

Haftorah Mishpatim

JEREMIAH XXXIV, 8–22 AND XXXIII, 25, 26

The Haftorah relates the anger of Jeremiah at the breach of trust by the ruling classes of the Jewish nation.

If a Jewish man was guilty of a theft which he could not repay, or if circumstances made it impossible for him to return a loan, he was sold into servitude for a maximum period of six years. The Sidrah explains the regulations governing this system.

In the days of Jeremiah, the owners of such servants had refused to release them after the prescribed six years. The nation was in imminent danger of being conquered by Babylonia. Jeremiah convinced the owners of the servants to release them, thereby petitioning the mercy of God and the deliverance of Judah.

Although the wealthy slave-owners originally complied with Jeremiah's request, they later changed their minds and took back the slaves when the danger to the nation had passed.

In the Haftorah, Jeremiah thunders against their oppression and perversion of justice. He predicts that the Babylonians will destroy Judah, Jerusalem, and the Holy Temple.

תרומה

Terumah

*A*FTER THE CHILDREN of Israel had received the Decalogue, and the first section of the Law, Moses again went up to Mount Sinai for forty days and forty nights to receive the Tablets and to be taught the rest of the Torah.

The time had now come for the preparations of the first formal House of Worship. The original commandment for its construction came from God.

And let them make Me a sanctuary[1] that I may dwell among them.

This temporary structure was to be a portable house of worship, which was to accompany the Jews during their wanderings in the desert, until the permanent Holy Temple was to be built in Jerusalem.

Moses received instructions from God to ask the people for voluntary offerings[2] of gold, silver, and brass. They were also requested to contribute different cloths, acacia wood,[3] olive oil, spices, and precious stones. All these items were to be used for

---

[1] A place of appointment or meeting where God is ever in readiness to reveal Himself to Israel and to speak with them.

—RASHBAM

[2] No compulsory levy was to be made, but voluntary gifts were requested. The people did not wait for the collection to be announced but brought more than enough, and all that remained for the princes to contribute was the precious stones and the oil.

—SFORNO

[3] According to tradition, Jacob planted the acacia in Egypt, and on their departure the Jews took the wood of this tree with them.

—RASHI

the construction of the Sanctuary and the worship. Through these deeds, the people would experience the Divine Presence. Everything was to be done according to God's specifications.

One part of this sanctuary, the Tabernacle, was to contain the ark.[4] The tablets upon which the Decalogue was written were to be placed into this Ark and its resting place was to be called the Holy of Holies. The Ark was to be constructed from acacia wood, overlaid on both sides with pure gold and a border in the shape of a golden crown extended around its entire rim.[5] Four golden rings were attached to the bottom of the ark, through which wooden poles were extended, permitting the ark to be carried by the wanderers. After the tablets had been placed inside, it was to be overlaid with pure gold. The figures of two angels, called cherubs, were to be fashioned on the cover of the Ark.

"And thou shalt make two cherubim of gold; of beaten work shalt thou make them, at the two ends of the ark-cover. And make one cherub at the one end, and one cherub at the other end; of one piece with ark-cover shall ye make the cherubim of the two ends thereof. And the cherubim shall spread out their wings on high, screening the ark-cover with their wings, with their faces one to another; toward the ark-cover shall the faces of the cherubim be. And thou shalt put the ark-cover above upon the ark; and in the ark thou shalt put the testimony that I shall give

---

[4]The Ark was made in the form of a chest without supporting legs. Bezalel, the architect, made three lidless arks, one of wood and two of gold. The wooden ark he fitted into one golden ark, and the other golden ark he fitted into the wooden one. Then he covered the upper rim of the wooden ark with gold so that it was overlaid with gold both within and without.

—RASHI

[5]A golden crown-like moulding was to be run around the Ark and symbolized the "Crown of Torah."

—RASHI

thee. And there I will meet with thee, and I will speak with thee from above the ark-cover, from between the two cherubim which are upon the ark of the testimony, of all things which I will give thee in commandment unto the Children of Israel.''

Another furnishing of the Tabernacle was to be a table, also to be constructed of acacia wood and covered with pure gold, whose rim was to be in the shape of a crown. Four golden rings were to be placed under the table, one on each of its legs, through which poles were extended for its transportation. Twelve loaves of bread[6] were to be displayed there at all times, from Sabbath to Sabbath.

A candelabrum,[7] (*Menorah*), was to be forged for the Tabernacle out of pure gold. It was to have a base out of which a centerpiece rose, with three branches extending from both its sides. Altogether, there were seven almond-shaped cups, which were filled with pure olive oil and kindled. One of these cups was designated as the Eternal Light since its flame was to burn continually.

The entire Tabernacle[8] was to be covered with a curtain of

---

[6]The literal translation of showbread is "bread of faces". It received its name from the fact that it was baked in a mould with two sides open. Hence the bread was said to have two "faces" or surfaces, directed to the two sides of the Sanctuary.

—RASHI

[7]The candelabrum was situated in that place to light up the table.

—RASHBAM

[8]The curtains when joined together gave the appearance of a single whole.

—RASHBAM.

The Tabernacle, comprising all the various objects, is called "one". Similarly, a body is not a single thing but consists of various parts. Thus God is One but comprehends all. So should the smaller world (Israel) and the larger world (Mankind) endeavor to be one.

—IBN EZRA

linen, supported by wooden boards. Inside, a hanging veil was to form two rooms. The first room, called "Holy", contained the Table of Bread, the Candelabra, and an Altar for Incense. The inner room, called the Holy of Holies, contained the Ark with the two tablets.

Outside the Tabernacle, the Altar for the Sacrifices was to be constructed of acacia wood overlaid with brass. The four corners of the altar were elevated to resemble horns. All the vessels necessary for the offerings were also forged from brass. A network of brass was to be built under the altar into which four rings of brass were placed to support the poles extending through them for carrying from place to place.

Finally, a court was to be established for the Tabernacle by an enclosure of curtains. Surrounding the altar and Sanctuary, these hanging curtains were supported by wooden pillars, overlaid with silver. The curtain-hooks were made of silver and all the sockets were constructed of brass.

The many detailed rules regarding the construction of the Sanctuary were to demonstrate to the people that they were building their house of worship exactly as God had ordained and each section and part had deep significance.

Haftorah Terumah

I KINGS V, 26–VI, 13

The Sidrah describes the first temporary Sanctuary in which the Jewish People worshipped and offered their sacrifices. Both its construction and maintenance had to follow very specific regulations as listed in the Torah.

Similar sanctuaries continued to be erected in a number of places until the nation enjoyed a period of peace and prosperity under the reign of King Solomon.

The Haftorah depicts Solomon, in his great wisdom, setting about to build the Holy Temple in Jerusalem. He organized a large army of laborers to hew the stones and prepare the timber brought from Lebanon.

A treaty was concluded with Hiram, King of Tyre, to supply the wood and skilled workmen for the construction of the Temple. Solomon, in return, supplied him with wheat and oil.

When the great structure was completed, the voice of God came to King Solomon and expressed approval of all the work which had been accomplished.

And the word of the Lord came to Solomon, saying: 'As for this house which thou art building, if thou wilt walk in My statutes, and execute Mine ordinances, and keep My commandments to walk in them; then will I establish My word with thee, which I spoke unto David thy father; in that I will dwell therein among the children of Israel, and will not forsake My people Israel.'

תְּצַוֶּה

Tetzaveh

*W*ITH THE COMPLETION of the detailed description of how the Sanctuary was to be built, and how the many articles it was to contain were to be fashioned, the Torah now instructs the men who were to minister in it. Moses received these commandments to convey to the people, during the forty days and forty nights he spent on Mount Sinai, where he received the entire Torah.

The *Menorah* (candelabrum), was one of the major Sanctuary furnishings to be constructed. The people were commanded to bring pure olive-oil[1] for an eternal light, known in Hebrew as the *Ner Tamid.*

> *In the tent of meeting, without the veil which is before the testimony, Aaron and his sons shall set it in order, to burn from evening to morning before the Lord; it shall be a statute forever throughout their generations on behalf of the Children of Israel.*

This constant flame burned in the center[2] of the seven-pronged candelabrum and always provided light in the Sanctuary. After the Holy Temple was built in Jerusalem, the Eternal Light glowed there. Even now, many years after the destruction of the Holy Temple, an Eternal Light shines over the Holy Ark in every synagogue.

---

[1]Supplying this oil was to remain a communal responsibility for all generations.

—IBN EZRA

[2]The central light was to burn continually, and from it the others were kindled each evening.

—NACHMANIDES

The priesthood was now established. The Hebrew word for priest is *kohain,* and his function was to offer sacrifices and prayers in the Sanctuary. Moses' brother, Aaron, and his four sons, were charged with the responsibilities of this office.[3]

And bring thou near unto thee Aaron thy brother, and his sons with him, from among the Children of Israel, that they may minister unto Me in the priest's office, even Aaron, Nadab and Abihu, Eleazar and Ithamar, Aaron's sons.

The priesthood is hereditary, continuing to pass down to the descendants of Aaron. To this day, the rank of *Kohain, Levi,* or *Yisrael,* is passed from father to son.

The priest wore special garments fashioned by skillful artisans: the *ephod,* a coat made of gold and beautiful linen; two shoulder-pieces to hold up the *ephod;* and a band to circle the *kohain's* waist. Two onyx-stones were attached to each of the two shoulder-straps. The symbols of six of the Tribes of Israel were to be inscribed on each of these two stones, so that all the Twelve Tribes were represented before God when Aaron appeared in the Sanctuary.[4]

The *Kohain Gadol* (High Priest), wore these garments with these additions: a golden breastplate, with attached blue, purple, and scarlet linen; in rows of four, twelve precious stones set into the breastplate, each bearing the name of a Tribe of Israel; and a gold setting for each row.[5] Blue threads were attached to

---

[3]Moses, as the first priest, formally announced God's choice of Aaron. That Moses did not himself undertake the office did not mean that he sought to evade its responsibilities. He had heavy duties to perform as teacher and judge of Israel.

—IBN EZRA

[4]Reuben, Simeon, Levi, Judah, Dan and Naphtali were represented on one stone; Gad, Asher, Issachar, Zebulun, Joseph and Benjamin on the other. This made a total of twenty-five letters on each stone, Benjamin's name being spelled with an additional *yud.*

—RASHI

[5]So that the names of The Twelve tribes shall be visible before

four golden rings which were sewn onto the breastplate and shoulder-pieces, and kept the breastplate in place. In this manner, Aaron had the names of all the Children of Israel represented by the Twelve Tribes near his heart when he offered up his prayers to God. This breastplate was the medium for requesting divine guidance in matters too difficult to resolve by man.

> *And thou shalt put in the breastplate of judgement the Urim and the Thummim;*[6] *and they shall be upon Aaron's heart, when he goeth in before the Lord; and Aaron shall bear the judgement of the Children of Israel upon his heart before the Lord continually.*[7]

Another garment which the High priest wore during worship was a blue robe, with the figures of pomegranates and bells of gold woven on the lower border. When the bells sounded, the people knew that the High Priest had entered the room where he began the Holy service.

A type of turban was wound about Aaron's forehead, carrying a golden plate with the inscription: "Holy Unto the Lord".

The rest of Aaron's garments consisted of a tunic going

God and He will remember their righteousness.

—RASHI.

He will show mercy to Israel for the merit of the founders of the tribes.

—SFORNO

[6]The Ineffable Name of God was inscribed on some (unknown) material and placed in the fold of the breastplate. By means of it the Divine will was revealed in clear terms (like the 'light') and its promises were verified ('made perfect'). Hence the name *Urim* and *Thummim*, meaning 'lights' and 'perfection'. In the Second Temple the High Priest wore the breastplate, but it lacked the *Urim* and the *Thummim*.

—RASHI

[7]Through this medium Aaron was to seek and obtain Divine guidance and judgement for Israel.

—RASHI

down to his feet; the sleeves were connected with a sash, and he wore breeches which came down to his knees.

Similar garments were worn by Aaron's sons, the ordinary priests, but they were not as elaborate. Both in the Sanctuary and, later, in the Holy Temple in Jerusalem, these garments were worn by the High Priest and the ordinary priests whenever they performed the divine service.

Each of the garments had a specific reason and meaning, and they greatly enhanced the beauty and inspiration of the worship.[8] During the *Yom Kipur* services we read in our prayer-books "Happy is the eye that beheld the appearance of the *kohain*."

Aaron was initiated into his office with sacrifices and the annointing of oil at the door of the Tent of Meeting. A seven-day ceremony[9] took place for the induction of Aaron and his sons into their office. The priesthood was established as an everlasting institution for Aaron's descendants. There are men today who trace their ancestry to Aaron and are therefore known as *kohanim*.

Two communal sacrifices were offered each day: one in the morning; the other at dusk. Our daily *Shacharis* (Morning) and *Mincha* (Afternoon) prayers are based on these two sacrifices.

Finally, instructions were given for building the Altar of Incense: it was assembled of acacia wood, overlaid with pure gold; horn-like elevations rose from its corners; and a gold rim resembling a crown was set around it. Two golden rings were placed under this crown through which poles were placed to carry the altar. It rested before the veil of the Holy of Holies. Each morning and evening, Aaron offered sweet spices on it. Once a year, on the Day of Atonement, this altar had a prominent place in the special atonement service.

---

[8]These vestments correspond to the royal garments of a king, and elevated the wearer above the rest of the people in dignity.

—NACHMANIDES

[9]During these seven days, Moses alone officiated; but on the eighth day Aaron and his sons assumed their duties.

—RASHBAM

Haftorah Tetzaveh

EZEKIEL XLIII, 10-27

The Sidrah continues to list the detailed laws of the Tabernacle, the temporary place of worship for the Jewish People in the desert.

This portable sanctuary was finally converted into the Holy Temple in Jerusalem. It remained there for many years as the central point of religious worship for the Jewish People. In the year 586 B.C.E., it was destroyed by the Babylonians.

Ezekiel was one of the most famous of the prophets to preach to the exiles in Babylon. He assured them that God would cause the Holy Temple to be rebuilt and bring an end to the exile.

In the last portion of his book, the Prophet describes a vision of the new and rebuilt Jerusalem which would arise at the conclusion of the Babylonian dispersion. He also saw the new Temple in all its detailed particulars.

Since public worship of God, as taught in the Torah, had to follow very precise regulations, the laws of the Tabernacle and Ezekiel's description of the new Holy Temple form the link between the Sidrah and the Haftorah.

כִּי תִשָּׂא

Ki Tissa

*M*OSES WAS STILL on Mount Sinai as he continued to receive
the laws of the Torah from God. A census[1] was to be taken to
determine how many men would be eligible for military service.
A contribution of half a shekel was to be made by each man, to
avoid an actual count, which was forbidden.

> *Every one that passeth among them that are numbered, from
> twenty years old [2] and upward, shall give the offering of the
> Lord. The rich shall not give more, and the poor shall not
> give less,[3] than the half shekel,[4] when they give the offering
> of the Lord, to make atonement for your souls. And thou
> shalt take the atonement money from the Children of Israel
> before the Lord, to make atonement for your souls.*

Later, this half shekel was to be collected as a tax for the
daily sacrifices in the Holy Temple in Jerusalem, and to keep the

---

[1]The method of taking a census here described was not to be
confined to this occasion, but was to be followed whenever a census was
to be taken.

—NACHMANIDES

[2]The inference is that a male under twenty years was not eligible for
military service and did not come within the category of "man."

—RASHI

[3]Since the half-shekel was a "ransom for a soul" [and before God
all are equal], the rich may not give more, nor the poor less.

—IBN EZRA

[4]Moses, as Israel's ruler, introduced this coin, which derived its
name from the fact that it was made of pure metal and was full of
'weight'.

—NACHMANIDES

structure in good condition. By simply counting these coins, the total population of military-age men was determined.

Moses was now told how to build another furnishing for the Sanctuary: a brass basin with a brass base, to be placed between the Tent of Meeting and the Altar. This wash basin was to be filled with water so that Aaron and his sons could wash themselves before they entered the Tent of Meeting.

Oil was mixed with the finest spices and used to annoint the Tent of Meeting, the Ark, the Table with its vessels, the Candelabrum, the Incense Altar, the Sacrificial Altar, and the Wash Basin and its base. With the oil being placed[5] on these furnishings, they became sanctified for their specific holy services.

Incense was produced from sweet spices, and placed before the Ark during divine services.

The entire work of the construction of the Tent of Meeting and the Sanctuary, with all their contents, was delegated to a man from the tribe of Judah.

And the Lord spoke unto Moses, saying: "See, I have called by name Bezalel [6] the son of Uri, the son of Hur, of the tribe of Judah; and I have filled him with the spirit of God, in wisdom, and in understanding, and in knowledge,[7]

---

[5]Whenever annointing is mentioned in Scriptures, it was done in the form of an X—except at the coronation of a king, when it was done in a circle round the head.

—RASHI

[6]Considering that the Jews had been humbled by their rigorous labors in Egypt and had no opportunity to develop proficiency in artistic work, it is extraordinary that they should have produced a master artist of the calibre of Bezalel, who—in addition to designing the Tabernacle and its vessels—also understood the symbolism of every object he designed.

—NACHMANIDES

[7]"Wisdom" means learning from others and making the knowledge his own. "Understanding" is the ability to draw deductions from what one has already learned. "Knowledge" comes from Divine inspiration.

—RASHI

and in all manner of workmanship, to devise skillful works, to work in gold, and in silver, and in brass, and in cutting of stones for setting, and in carving of wood, to work in all manner of workmanship."

Prior to the beginning of the actual labor of construction of the Sanctuary, Moses was again told by God that the sanctity of the Sabbath was supreme, and therefore no work could be done on this project on the Sabbath.[8]

And He gave unto Moses, when He had made an end of speaking with him upon Mount Sinai, the two tables of the testimony, tables of stone, written with the finger of God.

As these great events were taking place on top of the mountain, a terrible tragedy was unfolding below.

And when the people saw that Moses delayed [9] to come down from the mount, the people gathered themselves together unto Aaron, and said unto him: 'Make us a god who shall go before us; for as for this Moses—the man that brought us up out of the land of Egypt—we know not what is become of him.'

Aaron collected golden jewelry from which he forged the figure of a calf, and the people proclaimed the golden calf to be

---

[8]The Sabbath is a sign of God's choice of Israel.—Rashi. If Israel desecrates this sign, [the Sabbath] the whole purpose of building a Sanctuary to Him is lost.

—SFORNO

[9]Before ascending the mount, Moses informed the Jews that he would return after forty days, meaning after forty complete days (each day with the preceding night). They understood the period to be inclusive of the day of his ascent; and when they found that he did not return the day they expected him, they concluded that he was dead and became disheartened.

—RASHI

their new god. They built an altar in front of the idol and offered sacrifices and announced a great feast for the next day.

The conversation between God and Moses was suddenly interrupted, and Moses was ordered to leave the Divine Presence, since his people had rebelled. As God was about to destroy the Jews, Moses intervened with a fervent prayer.

And Moses besought the Lord his God, and said, 'Lord, why doth Thy wrath wax hot against Thy people, that Thou hast brought forth out of the land of Egypt with great power and with a mighty hand? Wherefore should the Egyptians speak, saying: For evil did He bring them forth, to slay them in the mountains, and to consume them from the face of the earth? Turn from Thy fierce wrath, and repent of this evil against Thy people. Remember Abraham, Isaac, and Israel,[10] Thy servants, to whom Thou didst swear by Thine own self, and said unto them: I will multiply your seed as the stars of heaven, and all this land that I have spoken of will I give unto your seed, and they shall inherit it for ever.'

And the Lord repented of the evil which He said He would do unto His people.

When Moses had come down from the mountain far enough to see the golden calf and the people dancing, he grew very angry and smashed to the ground the two tablets he had been carrying. He then destroyed the idol and burned it to ashes. After scattering these ashes into the water,[11] Moses made the shocked people drink the mixture. He strongly rebuked

---

[10]To each of these, merit was due for some act of faith. Let it stand in favor of their offspring.

—RASHI

[11]Moses did all this to discredit the idol in the eyes of the worshippers.

—NACHMANIDES

Aaron for his part in this great sin. Then, Moses summoned the people who were loyal to God to rally to his side. All the men of the tribe of Levi responded to his call. Moses ordered them to prepare for war and slay all those who persisted in their rebellion against God.[12] Friends and brothers had to rise against each other in this tragic civil war.

When the battle was over and the forces of Moses were victorious, he went back up to Mount Sinai to receive God's pardon for the people.

> *And Moses returned unto the Lord, and said: 'Oh, this people have sinned a great sin, and have made them a god of gold. Yet now, if Thou wilt forgive their sin—and if not, blot me, I pray Thee, out of Thy book which Thou hast written.' And the Lord said unto Moses: 'Whosoever hath sinned against Me, him will I blot out of My book.[13] And now go, lead the people unto the place of which I have spoken unto thee; behold, Mine angel shall go before thee; nevertheless in the day when I visit, I will visit their sin upon them.'*

At this time, Moses was permitted to experience some of the mystical aspects of God.[14] He was then told to hew new tab-

---

[12]In this exceptional circumstance, the Levites carried out these directions, since the culprits were too numerous to be dealt with by the judges.

—NACHMANIDES

[13]God's judgment is that each man must bear the punishment for *his* deeds and receive the reward of *his* merits. Consequently, Moses' request could not be granted.

—SFORNO

[14]God told Moses that the moment had now come for him to be taught His attributes, which he was to invoke in prayer. Not that the petition would always be granted—at times God would display His graciousness and mercy, and at times He would not—but to invoke the

lets[15] out of the stone on which the words of the Decalogue were again inscribed. God again promised that the Jews would be led into the land of Canaan which was later to be known as the Land of Israel. They were warned, however, never again to fall into the idol-worshipping ways of the inhabitants of Canaan.

Moses spent another forty days on Mount Sinai, preparing the second set of tablets and receiving further instructions for the Torah. When he came down, he was so inspired that a radiance[16] came forth from his face. When the people became frightened, he placed a veil over his face. Moses continued to speak with God and teach the people.

Haftorah Ki Tissa

I KINGS XVIII, 1–39

Throughout history, there were periods when the Jewish People turned away from the teachings of God to engage in idol-worship and various other forms of religious rebellion.

The Sidrah describes the terrible events surrounding the Golden Calf when the Jews adopted a primitive form of paganism shortly after they witnessed the revelation of God on Mount Sinai.

In the Haftorah, another tragic episode in the history of the Jewish People is described. This event occurred during the leadership of the great prophet Elijah.

Ahab was a weak-willed king who was dominated by Jezebel, his

---

attributes in the hour of need would never be altogether without efficacy.

—RASHI

[15]Moses had broken the first tablets and must now hew others for himself.

—RASHI

[16]There was an appearance of majestic splendor on his face.

—RASHBAM

wicked Phoenician wife. She worshipped the idol Baal, and murdered the prophets who tried to teach the people the Torah and its way of life.

Left all alone, Elijah confronted King Ahab on Mount Carmel and challenged him to a public contest. The priests of Baal were to construct an altar to their idol, upon which they were to place an offering. They were then to pray to Baal, petitioning him to send a fire which will consume the sacrifice.

Elijah told the King that he too would build an altar of twelve stones to represent the Twelve Tribes of Israel. He would also place a sacrifice on this altar and pray to God that He produce a flame to consume the offering.

When the preparations for this great contest had been completed, four hundred and fifty of Baal's priests prayed, danced and tried in every conceivable manner to have their idol bring forth a flame—but to no avail.

When the time for the evening sacrifice came, Elijah prayed to God to reestablish His sovereignty over the Jewish People.

> *And it came to pass at the time of the offering of the evening offering, that Elijah the prophet came near, and said: 'O Lord, the God of Abraham, of Isaac, and of Israel, let it be known this day that Thou art God in Israel, and that I am Thy servant, and that I have done all these things at Thy word. Hear me, O Lord, hear me, that this people may know that Thou, Lord, art God, for Thou didst turn their heart backward.' Then the fire of the Lord fell, and consumed the burnt-offering, and the wood, and the stones, and the dust, and licked up the water that was in the trench. And when all the people saw it, they fell on their faces; and they said: 'The Lord, He is God; the Lord, He is God'.*

וַיַּקְהֵל

Va-Yak-Hel

CHAPTERS XXXV–XXXVIII, 20

*A*FTER THE DETAILED instructions had been given to Moses for the construction of the Sanctuary, the actual building is described. Having gathered the people together,[1] Moses once more reviews the laws of the Sabbath and their purpose.

And Moses assembled all the congregation of the Children of Israel, and said unto them: 'These are the words which the Lord hath commanded, that ye should do them. Six days[2] shall work be done, but on the seventh day there shall be to you a holy day, a Sabbath of solemn rest to the Lord; whosoever doeth any work therein shall be put to death. Ye shall kindle no fire[3] throughout your habitations upon the Sabbath day.'

The material for the work of building the Sanctuary was to be freely donated by the people. Much was needed: gold, silver and brass; all types of linen; skins and wood; oil for light; spices;

---

[1]The object of the assembly was to ask the people to make freewill-offerings for the tabernacle.

—IBN EZRA.

. . . And also to demand the payment of the half-shekel.

—RASHBAM

[2]Moses prefaced his instructions with the warning that though he asked them to undertake work for the Sanctuary, they were not to violate the Sabbath in the process.

—RASHI

[3]Although during a Festival which falls on a week-day kindling fire for the preparation of food required solely for that day is permissible, on the Sabbath it is forbidden.

—IBN EZRA

incense; and precious stones. By freely giving these materials, every Jew had a share in this house of worship.

The same procedure was applied to the actual construction work which was done by volunteers.

And all the congregation of the Children of Israel departed from the presence of Moses. And they came, every one whose heart stirred him up, and every one whom his spirit made willing, and brought the Lord's offering, for the work of the tent of meeting, and for all the service thereof, and for the holy garments.

So wholehearted and complete was the response of the people, that all the necessary supplies and skills were readily made available.[4] While the men did the construction work, the women spun the blue, purple and scarlet strands and goat's hair.

And Moses said unto the Children of Israel: 'See, the Lord hath called by name Bezalel the son of Uri, the son of Hur, of the tribe of Judah. And He hath filled him with the spirit of God, in wisdom, in understanding, and in knowledge, and in all manner of workmanship. And to devise skillful works, to work in gold, and in silver, and in brass, and in cutting of stones for setting, and in carving of wood, to work in all manner of skillful workmanship. And He hath put in his heart that he may teach,[5] both he, and

---

[4]Both the men and the women responded. The husbands accompanied their wives to declare that the gifts which they brought had their approval.

—SFORNO

The women in particular wore golden ornaments and so had a valuable contribution to make.

—NACHMANIDES

[5]Bezalel and Oholiab were not only skilled workers, but also had the ability to instruct others.

—IBN EZRA

Oholiab,[6] the son of Ahisamach, of the tribe of Dan. Them hath He filled with wisdom of heart, to work all manner of workmanship of the craftsman, and of the skillful workman, and of the weaver in colors, in blue, and in purple, in scarlet, and in fine linen, and of the weaver, even of them that do any workmanship, and of those that devise skillful works.'

So much was brought by the people that Moses had to put a halt to their gifts. From that which was collected, the workers began to choose the necessary materials.

The curtains were prepared first—ten of them enclosed the Tabernacle. They were blue, purple and scarlet, and lined with images of angels, called "cherubim." Then a tent over the Tabernacle was woven of eleven curtains of goats' hair.

Upright boards were fashioned of acacia wood to support the walls, and they were covered with gold. The door of the Tabernacle was made of screen.

The Ark was built[7] of acacia wood overlaid with pure gold, and surrounded by a golden crown. The Candelabrum, (*Menorah*) was also constructed of pure gold, with seven branches, one of which remained lit at all times. The Incense Altar was built of acacia wood and its edges protruded in a horned shape. The entire surface was overlaid with pure gold.

The Altar for the burnt offerings was constructed of acacia wood with horned edges overlaid with brass. All the vessels required for this service were also made of brass. There were mirrors at the door of the tent for those women who brought sacrifices.[8]

---

[6]Although a member of one of the smaller tribes, Dan, God involved him in the work with Bezalel—who belonged to the leading tribe of Judah—to indicate that before Him all are equal.

—RASHI

[7]Bezalel personally made the ark because of its exceptional sanctity. He also made all the sacred vessels.

—IBN EZRA

[8]These were made of burnished copper. Moses was at first hesitant

All the garments to be worn by Aaron, the High Priest, and his sons, were fashioned in accordance with the instructions received by Moses. Then, the court was staked out with pillars and hanging curtains of twisted linen.

Haftorah Va-Yak-Hel

I KINGS VII, 40–50

The Sidrah describes how the Tabernacle was carefully constructed to conform to all the regulations and specifications which God had commanded Moses.

In the same manner, the Haftorah renders a detailed account of how Hiram of Tyre constructed every section of the Holy Temple. Each one of them conformed to the same pattern and detail originally prescribed in the Torah.

All these plans and labor were reviewed by King Solomon who had knowledge of the traditions and precise measurements required.

As a result, when the construction of the Holy Temple was completed, both its form, as well as its contents, conformed to the original commandments of God.

---

to accept the mirrors, as they ministered to the vanity of women. But God commanded him to take them as particularly acceptable to Him, because the Jewish women had encouraged their husbands to beget children in Egypt despite their being in slavery.

—RASHI

פְקוּדֵי

Pekudey

*These are the accounts[1] of the tabernacle,[2] even the taber-
nacle of the testimony, as they were rendered according to
the commandment of Moses, through the service of the
Levites,[3] by the hand of Ithamar, the son of Aaron the
priest. —And Bezalel the son of Uri, the son of Hur, of
the tribe of Judah, made all that the Lord commanded
Moses. And with him was Oholiab, the son of Ahisamach,
of the tribe of Dan, a craftsman, and a skillful workman,
and weaver in colors, in blue, and in purple, and in scarlet,
and fine linen.[4]*

----

[1]In this section is listed the total quantity of gold, silver and brass
used for the construction of the Tabernacle; and the sacred vessels are
also enumerated.

—RASHI

[2]The Hebrew word *mishkan* is a general term for the Sanctuary and
its contents. It is defined here as "the Tabernacle of Testimony"
because the Tables of Testimony were deposited in it.

—IBN EZRA

Also, the Tabernacle was testimony of God's pardon of Israel for
making the Calf.

—RASHI

[3]The Levites had the Sanctuary and its contents in their charge
during the journeying in the wilderness.

—RASHI

[4]They are mentioned honorably for the excellent work they have
done.

—IBN EZRA

So skilled was Bezalel, that even when Moses did not give him full

𝒥T SHOULD BE remembered that all the precious metals and stones, as well as all the other materials and craftsmanship came from the free-offering of the people. In this manner, the Sanctuary became the property of the entire people, whose possessions and skills made it possible.

After the metals which were employed are enumerated,[5] an account is given of the manner in which the garments for Aaron and his sons were fashioned, and the materials of which they were made. It is important to note that all the specific details of these garments, and the work done in the construction of the Sanctuary and all its contents, were exactly in conformity with the manner in which God had commanded Moses.

It was the task of Aaron and his sons to perform the religious services in the Sanctuary. This responsibility was to continue with their descendants for the future when the sacrifices will once again be offered in the Holy Temple in Jerusalem.

Thus was finished all the work of the Tabernacle of the Tent of Meeting; and the Children of Israel did according to all that the Lord had commanded Moses, so did they.

When Moses saw that everything had been constructed in exactly the way he had been commanded by God, he was pleased, and he blessed the people.[6]

---

details, he fashioned such objects exactly in the manner Moses had been commanded to make them.

—RASHI

[5]The quantities of precious metals are given to show how insignificant they were in comparison with the [future] Temples of Solomon and Herod. *Nevertheless:* the Divine Presence was more consistently found in the humbler structure, demonstrating that the expenditure of abundant wealth for a Sanctuary does not draw the Presence to it, but it is rather the obedience of the people to His will.

—SFORNO

[6]With the words, "May it be God's will that His Presence rest upon the work of your hands. 'And let the graciousness of the Lord our God

On the first day of the month[7] after all the various parts of the Sanctuary had been completed, its assembly took place.[8] Having been properly set up, the various furnishings were placed in the exact places which God had specified. To sanctify them for their holy use, they were annointed with oil. Then Aaron, who was to be the High Priest, and his sons, stood at the door of the Tent. They washed to be spiritually pure and their special garments were placed upon them. After this, they were annointed with oil in the same manner as the holy vessels.

All the descendants of Aaron were to minister in the Holy Temple and have certain religious duties. Even today, the *kohain* blesses the congregation during religious services, "redeems" the first-born sons, and has certain religious restrictions and obligations. The lineage of a *kohain* is determined by the status of his father.

The tablets which Moses brought down from Mount Sinai were then placed into the Ark, after which Moses lit the lamps of the candelabrum, and the incense made of spices.[9] He also offered sacrifices upon the Altar. Water was poured into the special basin to permit Moses, Aaron, and his sons to wash. The work of the Sanctuary was now completed and the divine services had begun.

---

be upon us; establish Thou also upon us the work of our hands; yea, the work of our hands establish Thou it.' " (Psalms xc. 17, one of the eleven psalms attributed to Moses.)

—RASHI

[7]Of the month Nisan which was the eighth day of consecration.
—IBN EZRA

[8]The actual work of assembling the parts of the Tabernacle and of placing the sacred vessels in position was reserved by the command of God for Moses; no one of the other workers being permitted to do it.

—RASHI

[9]Moses, as the first officiating priest, performed the ceremony of burning the incense, morning and evening, during the seven days of consecration.

—NACHMANIDES

*Then the cloud covered the tent of meeting, and the glory
of the Lord filled the Tabernacle. And Moses was not
able*[10] *to enter into the Tent of Meeting, because the cloud
abode thereon, and the glory of the Lord filled the Tabernacle. —And whenever the cloud was taken up from over the
Tabernacle, the Children of Israel went onward, throughout all their journeys. But if the cloud was not taken up,
then they journeyed not till the day that it was taken up.
For the cloud of the Lord was upon the Tabernacle by day,
and there was fire therein by night, in the sight of all the
house of Israel, throughout all their journeys.*[11]

Haftorah Pekudey

I KINGS VII, 51–VIII, 21

The Sidrah recounts the conclusion of the construction of the Sanctuary in the Wilderness. A similar theme is struck in the Haftorah as we
read about the events which transpired when the building of the Holy
Temple and all its accompanying work came to a conclusion.

A great dedication ceremony took place in Jerusalem in the presence of the elders and all the people of Israel. The Ark, containing
the two tablets Moses had received on Mount Sinai, together with all
the vessels for the service, were brought to the Temple by the Priests
and Levites. Amid great festivity, many sacrifices were offered to
God.

During this inspiring ceremony, King Solomon turned to the people, and blessed the whole congregation, saying:

---

[10]He had to wait for the cloud to drift away before he could enter
and speak with God.

—RASHI

[11]At every place they halted, the cloud rested upon the tabernacle.

RASHI

Blessed be the Lord, the God of Israel, who spoke with His mouth unto David, my father, and hath with His hand fulfilled it. . . . and the Lord hath established His word that He spoke; for I am risen up in the room of David my father, and sit on the throne of Israel, as the Lord promised, and have built the house for the name of the Lord, the God of Israel. And there have I set a place for the Ark, wherein is the covenant of the Lord, which He made with our fathers, when He brought them out of the land of Egypt.

THE BOOK OF LEVITICUS

ספר ויקרא

The third book of the Torah, Leviticus, is also known as the "Torah of the Kohanim" (priests) since a large part of this book deals with the sacrifices which were offered by a group within the Tribe of Levi—the descendants of Aaron—during the service in the Sanctuary. Although sacrifices ceased with the destruction of the Holy Temple, an understanding of these laws is very important if one is to appreciate our prayers which have replaced the sacrifices.

Containing very little history, this book teaches many of the laws regarding permitted and forbidden foods, religious purity and purification, rules of marriage, social behavior, and a description of the Jewish holidays.

In this book's teaching of how man can and should live at peace with his fellow-man, we find the Guiding Rule (Chapter 19: verse 18) "And thou shalt love thy neighbor as thyself".

וִיקְרָא

Va-Yikra

CHAPTERS I–V

THE BOOK OF Exodus closed with a description of the detailed laws regarding the construction of the Sanctuary and all its furnishings. Now, the Torah turns its attention to the specific type of worship which was to take place in its confines. These instructions are related to Moses by God at the Tent of Meeting.

There were two types of sacrifices.[1] One was communal and offered in the name of all Israel. The other was of a personal nature, offered by the individual. These were voluntary offerings,[2] donated on special occasions in the life of a person.

The first such sacrifice described is the burnt-offering, known in Hebrew as an *olah*. This offering was brought by any person who, through some unintentional misdeed or similar circumstances, felt removed from God and wanted to again be close to Him. The sacrifice had to be accompanied by a confession of the sin to God, coupled with sincere repentance. Domestic cattle[3] were chosen for this offering, either from the herd or

---

[1]Before giving Israel the other commandments enumerated in this Book, God stipulated that the laws regulating sacrifices must be strictly observed.

—IBN EZRA

[2]Literally,—'of his free will'. The sacrifice was not acceptable unless the owner spontaneously declared, 'I choose of my free will to bring this offering.' In extreme cases, the *Beth Din* (Court) had the power to force a man to make this declaration in order that he should not escape bringing an offer.

—RASHI

[3]Domestic animals only are to be used, as these alone represent a real sacrifice to whoever offers any of them. Wild animals, costing nothing, are excluded; and the bringing of a stolen animal constitutes a desecration. Clean and domesticated animals, furthermore, neither

from the flock.[4] Only a male animal without any blemish could
be employed. The donor placed his hands on the animal's head
at the entrance of the Sanctuary,[5] after which Aaron and his sons
performed the sacrifice. The entire animal then was offered on
the altar.

If someone could not afford cattle, sheep or goats, he could
bring turtle-doves or young pigeons. The Torah strongly suggests that it is not the value of the sacrifice which determines its
worth, but the sincerity with which it is given. Both types of
sacrifices are described as being a "sweet savor to God". This
expression indicates that God is pleased with the repentance of
the person offering the sacrifice, regardless of its monetary
value.

Those who wished to bring this type of sacrifice but could
not afford either cattle or fowl, were able to offer a *mincha*
sacrifice,[6] known as a meal-offering. This was composed of a
preparation of fine flour, mixed with oil and a spice called frankincense. The preparation was not permitted to become leavened. Honey, which the pagans considered to be a food for the
gods, was not to be used. This sacrifice, as well as all others, had
to be seasoned with salt.[7] Whereas the animal sacrifices de-

---

prey on other creatures nor live by killing.

—HERTZ

[4]The offerings are to be brought only from cattle, herd, or flock;
and he who brings them of other species is guilty of transgression.

—NACHMANIDES

[5]The owner of the sacrifice was to bring the animal right up to the
forecourt where it was handed over to the priest, whose duties then
began.

—RASHI

[6]The literal translation is: *'and when a soul bringeth'*. The Rabbis
explain why the use of the word *nefesh* (soul) occurs only in connection
with the meal-offering: Who usually brings a meal-offering?—the poor
man. His offering is accepted as if he had offered himself (his soul) as
a sacrifice.

—RASHI, FROM THE THE TALMUD

[7]God had brought Israel into a covenant with Himself, and com-

scribed were completely burned on the altar, part of this meal-offering remained as food for the priests. It was also possible to bring a meal-offering of first fruits.

The next sacrifice discussed is the peace-offering,[8] know in Hebrew as the *shelamim* which consisted of either a male or female from the herd. It was offered as an expression of thanksgiving or to fulfill a vow. This sacrifice was only partially burned on the altar. Part of it was given to the priest and the rest was eaten at a meal prepared by the donor of the offering and his guests. During the description of the peace-offering, the Torah also teaches that neither blood, nor the fat of the stomach and the intestines of the animal may be eaten.[9]

The sin-offering, known in Hebrew as the *chatot* is described next. It was to be brought by those who had mistakenly or unknowingly committed some trespass. Even if a sin is committed in apparent error, it is assumed there was some negligence. This sacrifice varied according to the station of the offender. It had to be accompanied by confession and repentance.

If the person who committed such a sin was either the High Priest,[10] or if it was the elders of a community who had collectively sinned, the sacrifice had to be a young bullock. If the ruler

---

manded that no saltless offering shall be brought upon the altar because it is a mark of contempt.

—IBN EZRA

Since the dining table is compared to an altar, a pinch of salt is strewn upon the bread of blessing (*motzi*) prior to the meal.

[8]They are called *shelamim* because they bring peace (*shalom*) to the world.

—RASHI

[9]As the Rabbis explained, the prohibition against fat and blood is independent of time and place, and is always and everywhere binding.

—RASHI

[10]Since it is the duty of the High Priest to know the Torah thoroughly, his error in judgement is regarded as more serious than that of an ordinary priest.

—IBN EZRA

of the nation[11] had sinned, he was commanded to bring a male goat. Should an ordinary Jew have been guilty of such an inadvertant sin, he was to offer a female goat or lamb. All these animals had to be without blemish.

There are certain sins which the Torah enumerates for which a sin-offering had to be brought: failure to give testimony when required; being spiritually unclean by having touched certain impure objects; or uttering an unnecessary oath. Should such a violator be unable to afford the required animal, he could offer two turtle-doves or two pigeons. Should even this be a burden to him, his sacrifice could be half a measure of fine flour.

If a person mistakenly took holy objects from the Sanctuary for his personal use, he had to offer a ram. This sacrifice is known as a guilt-offering, an *asham* in Hebrew. Prior to this offering, however, restitution had to be made by the return of the object, plus a fine of one fifth of its value.[12]

A ram was also sacrificed as a guilt-offering by a person who was in doubt as to whether or not he committed a specific sin.

Finally, we learn that an individual was also to sacrifice a ram if he dealt falsely with another person's property, deposits, pledges, or robbed goods. The same applies to someone who withheld property—such as wages—who denied having found an article; or who rendered a false oath. But before bringing this sacrifice, the value of the goods had to be returned with the payment of a fine of one fifth of the amount.

If confession and repentance accompanied these sacrifices, the sinner was forgiven.

---

[11]Happy is the generation whose ruler is concerned to bring a sacrifice for a sin committed in error, for then he will certainly do penance for any sin committed willfully.

—RASHI

[12]No sacrifice atones unless he first contemplated the claimant. The *asham* can only be brought after he had given back what was stolen.

—SFORNO

Haftorah Va-Yikra

ISAIAH XLIII, 21–XLIV, 23

The Book of Leviticus details the services to be observed in the Sanctuary and later in the Holy Temple. Because of the People's neglect of this service, coupled with a general abandonment of God's commandments, the Holy Temple was destroyed.

The prophet Isaiah chastises the exiles on this account. Not only was their relationship to the Temple sorely lacking when they were still in Jerusalem, but even in Babylonia—where no sacrifices were required—the People exhibited apathy and a lack of faith.

Isaiah nevertheless predicts that God will have compassion on His people and return them from the Babylonian exile to the Promised Land. There they will again rebuild the Holy Temple and once more have the opportunity to worship God as prescribed in the Torah.

Remember these things, O Jacob,
And Israel, for thou art My servant,
I have formed thee, thou art Mine own servant;
O Israel, thou shouldest not forget Me.

צו

Tzav

Chapters VI–VIII

IN THE BOOK of Exodus it was taught that a communal sacrifice, known in Hebrew as the *tamid*, had to be brought each morning and evening. Since the fire on the sacrificial altar had to be kept burning continually, the flames of the evening sacrifice had to be kept alive until the fire could be used to kindle the wood for the morning offering. Each morning, the priest dressed in all the garments of his office and would remove the ashes from the previous night, offer the morning sacrifice, and then feed the flames throughout the day.[1]

Accompanying these two daily sacrifices of lambs, there was a meal-offering composed of flour, oil, frankincense, and a measure of wine. Part of this mixture was burned on the altar and the rest was eaten by the priests.

Moses had prepared Aaron and his sons for their new office of service in the Sanctuary. On the day that Aaron was to be annointed as High Priest (*Kohain Gadol*), he was to offer a meal-offering composed of flour soaked in oil. The High Priest was to offer this sacrifice every day of his ministry—half in the morning and the other half in the evening. An ordinary priest was only required to bring such a sacrifice on the day on which he was initiated. These sacrifices had to be entirely burned on the altar—they could not be eaten.

The Torah now gives some more instructions regarding those sacrifices previously discussed. The sin-offering, the guilt-offering, and the meal-offering, were only partially consumed on the altar. The balance of the food was eaten by the priests. These foods which were reserved for the priests were very im-

---

[1]The officiating priests had to see that there was always sufficient wood on the altar to keep the fire burning perpetually; not to do so meant violating a negative command of the Torah.

—NACHMANIDES

portant to them, since they were eaten by themselves and their immediate families and represented an important part of their livelihood.

We also read a review of the peace-offering which was brought by a person who wanted to express thanksgiving for being saved from some danger or illness; by a person who made a vow to bring such a sacrifice for reasons of his own; or by an individual who wanted to express his general gratitude to God.[2] In the cases of all these sacrifices, after a portion was offered to God on the altar, the balance was consumed by the donor and his guests at a special meal,[3] as well as by the priests.

Once more, the law forbidding the Jewish people to eat any blood is repeated, as well as the prohibition against eating certain fats of the ox, sheep, and goat.[4]

The Torah now begins to list the steps to be followed in the initiation ceremony in which Aaron and his sons were to participate, prior to the beginning of their functions in the Sanctuary. Aaron was to be the first High Priest and his sons were to assume the position of ordinary priests. This sacrificial service continued throughout the existence of both Holy Temples in Jerusalem. Even to this day, a Jew's status of priest, Levite, or Israelite, follows that of his father.

-----

[2]It was the custom of those who had returned from a voyage on the sea or through the wilderness, or had been released from prison, or had recovered from some illness, to offer thanks to God for their safety.

—RASHI

Today, a special blessing of thanksgiving (*gomel*) is recited.

[3]After he had presented one cake of each of the four kinds to the officiating priest, the owner may eat the rest.

—RASHI

[4]The prohibition of eating the flesh of an animal which died of itself, or of one torn by wild beasts, is an additional prohibition to that of eating fat. He who eats the fat of the latter class of animals transgresses two commands.

—RASHI

The time had come for the ceremonies which were to consecrate Aaron and his sons to their new offices.

And the Lord spoke unto Moses, saying: 'Take Aaron and his sons with him, and the garments, and the annointing oil, and the bullock of the sin-offering, and the two rams, and the basket of unleavened bread; and assemble thou all the congregation at the door of the tent of meeting'.

Aaron and his sons were washed to purify them for the rituals. They wore the garments which they were commanded in the book of Exodus. The entire Tabernacle and all its contents were sprinkled with oil by Moses as an annointment for the sacred services which were to be held there. After this task had been completed, Aaron was also annointed and thereby sanctified for his new station. This entire procedure was then repeated for his sons.[5]

Then, the sacrifices for the ceremony commenced. First, a bullock was brought as a sin-offering upon whose head Aaron and his sons placed their hands. Part of this sacrifice was offered on the altar and the rest was burned outside the camp. Then, Aaron and his sons placed their hands upon the head of a ram which was offered as a burnt-offering. This ram was entirely consumed upon the altar.

The second ram which was sacrificed was dedicated exclusively for the consecration of Aaron and his sons. This ram, together with unleavened cake, oiled bread, and wafers, was partially burned on the altar. The rest was eaten on that day by Aaron, his sons and guests, one of whom was Moses.

This ceremony was repeated each day for a period of seven days. Aaron and his sons had to remain within the confines of the Tent of Meeting which was the period of time stipulated

---

[5]Contrary to the view of Rashi that, though no mention is made here concerning the sons of Aaron, it is to be understood that what was done to their father was also done to them. Nachmanides contends that this annointing was only performed on Aaron.

prior to the conclusion of the consecration. This waiting period was in obedience to the command of God, as related by Moses.

> . . . *"And ye shall not go out from the door of the Tent of Meeting seven days,[6] until the days of your consecration be fulfilled; for He shall consecrate you seven days. As hath been done this day, so the Lord hath commanded to do, to make atonement for you. And at the door of the Tent of Meeting shall ye abide day and night seven days, and keep the charge of the Lord, that ye die not; for so I am commanded." And Aaron and his sons did all the things which the Lord commanded by the hand of Moses.[7]*

Haftorah Tzav

JEREMIAH VII, 21–VIII, 3; IX, 22, 23

The sad task of Jeremiah was to foretell the coming downfall of the Jewish State and the destruction of the Holy Temple in Jerusalem.

The Prophet explains how the commandments concerning sacrifices—which continue to be described in the Sidrah—are merely rungs upon the spiritual ladder which each Jew must climb. Simply to offer sacrifices and go through the motions of the Temple service without repentance and sincerity are empty and meaningless acts.

---

[6]A precaution against contracting impurity, and to prevent their diversion by wordly matters. Throughout the week of consecration, mind and heart were to be concentrated upon the solemnity and importance of the office they were entering.

—HERTZ

[7]The verse recounts the merit of Aaron and his sons who did exactly as they were commanded, turning neither to the right nor to the left.

—RASHI

To worsen the situation, many Jews had fallen into actual idol-worship, and all the evils which accompany these pagan cults.

As a result, the Prophet predicts, a terrible doom will strike the Jewish people, with numerous disasters followed by exile.

Only by the ultimate recognition of the supremacy of God and total allegiance to His teachings will the Jewish People finally be redeemed.

Thus saith the Lord:
Let not the wise man glory in his wisdom,
Neither let the mighty man glory in his might,
Let not the rich man glory in his riches;

But let him that glorieth glory in this,
That he understandeth, and knoweth Me,
That I am the Lord who exercise mercy,

Justice, and righteousness, in the earth;
For in these things I delight,
Saith the Lord.

שְׁמִינִי

Shemini

CHAPTERS IX–XI

*F*OR SEVEN DAYS Aaron and his sons had remained at the door of the Tent of Meeting in anticipation of their initiation to the priesthood. The eighth day of their vigil had now arrived,[1] which marked the time for the conclusion of the ceremony investing Aaron with the office of High Priest, and his sons as the ordinary priests. It began with Aaron, his sons, and the elders of Israel being called together by Moses. Sacrifices were offered for the priests and the people: sin-offerings, burnt-offerings, and peace and meal sacrifices. After these sacrifices were completed, Aaron and Moses raised their hands and blessed the people.[2]

In the midst of this time of joy and pride for Aaron and the whole congregation, a great tragedy occurred.

And Nadab and Abihu,[3] the sons of Aaron, took each of them his censer, and put fire therein, and laid incense

---

[1]In the opinion of Ibn Ezra it was the eighth day of (the Hebrew month) *Nisan;* but according to tradition it was the first of the month, and during the seven days of consecration, Moses had the Sanctuary set up and taken down daily for the sake of practice.

[2]Nachmanides disagrees with Rashi and Ibn Ezra that the blessing was the priestly benediction (Numbers VI-24), since that had not yet been communicated to Aaron. He argues that it was a blessing similar in nature to that pronounced by Solomon at the dedication of the Temple he was later to build. (I Kings VIII-55).

[3]The Rabbis offered varying explanations of the offense committed by Nadab and Abihu: they decided religious matters in the presence of their master Moses; they entered the Sanctuary while in a state of intoxication. In support of the latter is the exhortation addressed to the priests in verse 9.

—RASHI

thereon, and offered a strange fire before the Lord, which He had not commanded them. And there came forth fire from before the Lord, and devoured them, and they died before the Lord.[4]

Aaron and the rest of his sons, despite their terrible grief, understood the lesson they had just learned regarding unauthorized acts and bowed to the will of God. The bodies of the two men were removed by others, since Aaron and his sons were commanded not to publicly display their grief and mourning.[5]

Immediately after this incident, Aaron and his descendants are commanded never to be intoxicated when officiating at the divine services. (See note number 3)

To conclude the ceremony—which began so joyously and was then so tragically marred—Aaron and his remaining two sons were to eat that part of the ram of the sin-offering which had not been burned on the altar. When Moses could not find this food, he inquired and learned that Aaron and his sons had burned the entire ram on the altar. In response to Moses' demand for an explanation of this second infraction of the commands of God, Aaron explained that it would not have been pleasing to God for them to sit down at a banquet in the midst of their tragedy. Moses agreed with his brother.

The Torah now turns to laws which play a major role in contemporary Jewish life.[6] Animals may be used as food, but

---

[4]As soon as Aaron learned of the tragedy, his first thought was to leave the Sanctuary and go into mourning for his sons; but Moses informed him of God's purpose.

—RASHBAM

[5]Moses exhorted Aaron not to mourn or interrupt his priestly functions. God wished to be sanctified by priests who were nigh unto Him to serve Him, and His service must not be desecrated through them. For this reason regulations concerning their behavior follow.

—RASHBAM

[6]Hitherto the laws mainly concerned the Sanctuary and were ap-

only selectively and only after specified preparations.[7] Such foods are known as *kosher*, or, permitted. Animals, to be counted as permitted food, must have split hooves and chew their cuds. If they have only one of these essential qualifications, they are not permitted.

Fish must also have two characteristics in order to be permissable food for Jewish people. A *kosher* fish must have fins and scales and the absence of one of these qualifications makes the fish unfit for food. As a result, all sea animals which do not have scales and fins—whether swimming, crawling or creeping—are not considered *kosher* and may not be eaten.

In the case of birds for food, the Torah lists forbidden fowl, all of which are birds of prey,[8] and states that these rules apply to others of their kind. These species of birds, then, became the basis upon which other birds may or may not be eaten. It was thus learned that a *kosher* fowl must also have a food crop.

While these laws only list the types of living creatures which are *kosher*, there is a large body of Jewish tradition governing the preparation of animals for food.

---

plicable to the priests; but the dietary laws were the concern of the whole people who had to be taught what they may eat and what was forbidden to them.

—NACHMANIDES

[7]The Midrash understands the phrase in the Torah as: 'This, O living [nation], is what ye may eat'; and it is illustrated by a parable. A doctor had two patients: one was critically ill, and the other had a chance to recover. While the first one was allowed to eat whatever he wished, the second was placed on a restricted diet. . . . From the use of the expression 'these are' we learn that Moses illustrated the laws concerning the animals, fish and birds by displaying a specimen of each species to the Jewish people.

—RASHI

[8]The prohibited species are birds of prey which are cruel; they are therefore regarded as injurious to the humane feelings of those who eat their flesh.

—NACHMANIDES

As taught previously in the Torah, all blood and certain animal fats are forbidden even from the permitted species. The method of slaughter removes the maximum amount of blood from the animal and causes it the least pain. It must be done by someone specially trained. To assure the removal of any remaining blood, salting or broiling is required before the meat is ready for eating.

Finally, dairy foods and meat foods are always separated. The Torah sums up the laws governing the foods we may eat:

For I am the Lord your God; sanctify yourselves therefore, and be holy; for I am holy; neither shall ye defile yourselves[9] with any manner of swarming things that moveth upon the earth. For I am the Lord that brought you up out of the land of Egypt,[10] to be your God; ye shall therefore be holy, for I am holy. This is the law of the beast, and of the fowl, and of every living creature that moveth in the waters, and of every creature that swarmeth upon the earth; to differentiate between the unclean and the clean, and between the living thing that may be eaten and the living thing that may not be eaten.

---

[9]This prohibition is repeated to warn us that by eating unclean creatures we violate many negative commandments.

—RASHI

[10]It was on condition that Israel would observe these laws that God brought them out of Egypt. The Hebrew verb *ma'aleh* (to bring up) indicates that these laws have the effect of elevating Israel above the people of Egypt who were steeped in abominations.

—RASHI

To be Godlike one must observe these laws.

—SFORNO

Haftorah Shemini

II SAMUEL VI, 1–VII, 17

As the Consecration of the Sanctuary is described in the Sidrah reading, so the Haftorah describes the procession in which the Ark of the Covenant was brought to Jerusalem.

After uniting the nation, David established its capital in Jerusalem. The King then gathered thirty thousand chosen men, and in a great procession escorted the Ark to its intended resting place at Mount Zion.

Unlike the accounts in the book of Numbers (Chapter 3, verse 29), the Levites did not carry the Ark on their shoulders—it was placed on a wagon pulled by oxen. At one point, the animals stumbled and Uzzah held the Ark to prevent it from falling. As he did so, he died. David was very upset and decided to halt the parade. He left the Ark in the home of Obed-edom for three months.

After this period of time, David resumed the procession and entered Jerusalem with great joy and festivity. The King himself danced and leaped in the ecstasy he experienced in bringing the Ark to Jerusalem.

After the festivities, Michal, David's wife, who was King Saul's daughter, severely criticized him for acting with such levity before his subjects. The King rebuked her by saying that he was glad to dance and be merry before God. The Haftorah relates that Michal never had any children—perhaps as punishment for her unwarranted criticism of King David.

When the wars of David ended, the King summoned the prophet Nathan. He expressed a wish to build a Temple in which the Ark could be properly housed. David felt it was wrong for him to live in a beautiful palace while the Ark rested in a mere tent.

But the prophet Nathan revealed God's will to David: the Holy Temple would not be built until David's son, Solomon, ascends the throne. His reign would be an era of peace and prosperity which will be a fitting period for the emergence of the Temple—itself a symbol of peace.

תַזְרִיעַ

Tazria

CHAPTERS XII and XIII

THE LAWS OF the Torah which are to govern the lives of the Jewish People not only encompass matters which we would consider 'religious', but cover every phase of life. This chapter, for example, deals with commandments relating to a woman who has given birth to a child.

If the child was a boy, the Torah again instructs that he be circumcised on the eighth[1] day, as described in the book of Genesis when Abraham was commanded to circumcise himself and his sons. Since the eighth day was specified by the Torah, this means that even if this day coincides with the Sabbath or any of the holy days, the circumcision must nevertheless take place on the eighth day, providing that the child is in good health.

If the child was a male, the mother was spiritually impure for seven days, after which she could not enter the Sanctuary for another period of thirty-three days. If the child was a girl, the mother would be spiritually impure for two weeks[2] and would then be prohibited from entering the Sanctuary for another sixty-six days. The total duration of spiritual impurity for the mother of a boy would be forty days, and of a girl a period of eighty days.

---

[1]By then, the impure blood, from which the child received its nourishment while in the womb, has been eliminated and he is fit to enter the Holy Covenant of circumcision.

—SFORNO

[2]The time is doubled in length, because the after-effects are prolonged owing to the difference in the physical constitution of a female child as compared with a male.

—NACHMANIDES

As soon as either of these two period of impurity ended, the mother brought two separate offerings[3] to the Sanctuary, in a spirit of thanksgiving and rededication to God.

The laws of spiritual purity and impurity are complex and many of them can only be observed when the Holy Temple stands in Jerusalem.

The health of the Community is next discussed through the diagnosis and treatment of certain communicable diseases, such as leprosy. It seems quite clear from reading the Torah that the High Priest, as well as the other priests were well versed in the detection and treatment of these sicknesses.[4] Commandments regarding these maladies, as well as all the other laws of the Torah, are rendered as religious precepts.[5] The physical benefits were so apparent, however, that Jewish communities seldom became infected by plagues and similar epidemics even long before modern medicine developed.

First, we read of people who developed skin infections. Such persons had to be examined by Aaron or one of his priestly sons. If it was clear that leprosy had been contracted,[6] the person was immediately declared to be unclean. The clothing he

---

[3]One was a burnt-offering (*olah*) which some say was brought in case evil words 'went up' (*alah*) from her mouth during the pains of child-birth, and she may have rashly vowed to keep apart from her husband so as not to conceive again.

—IBN EZRA

[4]Only the priest, the teacher of the people, could pronounce judgement on such a matter. His duty was to admonish the sinner, and add his prayer to that of the afflicted person for his recovery.

—SFORNO

[5]For an understanding of the laws that follow, we must not depend upon the literal interpretation of the text or human expertness, but upon the explanations of our Sages.

—RASHBAM

[6]Since, in the view of the Sages, leprosy was a medium of atonement for sin committed, the patient was confined in a solitary place to reflect and thereby arouse a feeling of penitence.

—SFORNO

was wearing had to be destroyed[7] and he was not permitted to keep his sickness a secret, but had to openly admit it in order to prevent others from coming too close to him. He had to be isolated outside the camp until it was certain that he was fully recovered.[8]

If at the first examination there was a doubt if the rash was a contagious disease, the person was quarantined outside the camp for a period of seven days.[9] If the symptoms subsided during that week, his clothing were thoroughly washed and he was returned to the camp. If the sickness did not subside during this week, the previous rules were reapplied.

The garments were washed because they had become contaminated through contact with a sick person, or by a parasite making its home in them. Such suspected apparel was closely inspected by the priest and then isolated for seven days. If after a week the decay had spread, the garments had to be burned. Should there still have been doubt after the first seven days, the clothing were washed and put away for another week. If the spreading of the decay then stopped, only the decayed portion had to be cut out. Otherwise, the entire garment had to be burned.

----

[7]To distinguish him from other people. It was also a sign of mourning for the sins which had reduced him to this state.

—IBN EZRA

[8]The Rabbis asked, 'Why is the leper—unlike other defiled persons—required to dwell alone? Because by his slander (that being considered the sin of which leprosy was the punishment) he parted husband and wife, or a man and his friend; he too must suffer separation from all'.

—RASHI

[9]Most illnesses take a decisive turn by the seventh day.

—IBN EZRA

The symptoms after that period determine whether he is unclean.

—RASHI

Haftorah Tazria

II KINGS IV, 42–V, 19

Elisha was the disciple of the great prophet Elijah and the Haftorah relates two incidents in his life. The second deals with a case of leprosy, forming the link with the Sidrah which describes procedures for the containment and cure of this and other contagious diseases.

In the first event, which took place during a famine, twenty loaves of bread and some fresh ears of corn were brought to Elisha by a generous person. Elisha's camp consisted of a hundred prophets. His servant, to whom the gift had been presented, did not want to leave such a small amount of food in front of that great a number. Elisha assured him, however, that God had promised to multiply the food so that there would be enough for all, even with some left over. The food was placed before the prophets, and, as promised, there was more than enough for all.

The second event concerns Naaman, a famous Syrian general, who was afflicted with leprosy. The reputed healing powers of Elisha were brought to his attention. With a great entourage, the general approached the house of the Prophet, who merely sent word that he bathe in the Jordon River seven times.

The general was infuriated at the Prophet's apparent lack of respect by not coming out to greet him and affecting a dramatic cure. He was further incensed because the waters of his native Damascus run deeper and purer than those of the more shallow Jordan. But Naaman's servant convinced him to follow the Prophet's advise. Upon doing so, the general was completely cured.

When the soldier returned to Elisha's home to offer him all sorts of riches, the Prophet would take nothing. Naaman then affirmed that he would henceforth only recognize God as the Supreme Being of the Universe.

מְצוֹרָע

Metzora

CHAPTERS XIV–XV

$\mathcal{T}$HE PREVENTION OF contagious skin diseases, as well as the treatment of clothing which had become contaminated, continues to occupy the Torah in this section. Since the welfare of the entire community is affected by these diseases, very specific laws are taught by which their victims had to be isolated, to be returned only when they were completely cured.

When the leper was thought to be healed, the priest was called to examine him outside the camp.[1] If the marks of infection had disappeared, a ceremony outside the camp was performed. Two birds[2] were brought: one was sacrificed; the other was permitted to fly away freely. The person who had suffered the sickness now washed his clothing, shaved and bathed, after which the priest declared him cured. Since his state of contagion was over, his isolation also ended and he could again return to the community. As an added precaution, however, he had to live outside his tent for another seven days. If he remained healthy during this week, he once more washed his clothing, shaved and bathed and was then declared completely healthy and healed.

On the eighth day of the person's cure, the priest who had supervised his cleansing sacrificed three offerings on his behalf at the door of the Tent of Meeting. If the required lambs for the sacrifices were too costly, he could bring turtle-doves and pi-

---

[1]Though pronounced clean, the cured man was not allowed to enter the camp or a city before his sacrifices had been offered.

—IBN EZRA

[2]The Rabbis declared that since leprosy was a punishment for slander, the offering consisted of birds which twitter.

—RASHI

geons. These sacrifices were intended to formally restore him to the community and to express his gratitude and thanksgiving to God for his recovery.[3]

Today, when sacrifices cannot be offered, a person who survived a serious illness or a dangerous experience offers a special prayer of thanksgiving in the synagogue when called to the reading of the Torah.

Through these laws which strictly isolated all persons suffering or even suspected of having contracted contagious diseases, the camp of Israel was able to travel through the desert without fear of epidemics. These regulations also assured the future health of the entire society. While these are public health laws, they are based upon religious belief and ceremony.

Prior to entering the Promised Land,[4] other laws were set down for the communal well-being of the Jewish people. Moses and Aaron are taught, at this point, that when the people enter their new homes in Canaan, rot and decay may infest these structures[5] in the same manner that malignant diseases may afflict a human being. The occupant of such a building must

---

[3]One was a guilt-offering of the class which had to be brought when one trespassed in connection with holy things. By being slanderous and haughty—and in consequence smitten with leprosy—he had offended against what was holy.

—SFORNO

[4]This law was enacted for the Land on account of its sanctity as the location of the Temple in which the Divine Presence abode.

—IBN EZRA

[5]According to the Midrash the Amorites concealed treasures of gold in the walls of their houses during the forty years of Israel's wanderings in the wilderness, in order that when the Israelites conquered the land they would not be able to lay their hands on these valuables. God, therefore, smote the houses with the plague so that the Israelites should demolish them and so discover the hidden treasures.

—RASHI

summon the priest for an examination.[6] Prior to his entry into the house, all the contents had to be removed. This prevented the furnishings from being considered unclean if the priest found it necessary to condemn the house.[7]

If upon inspection the priest found corrosion in the house, the entire building was shut up for a period of seven days. If the decay continued to spread during these seven days, all the affected stones and bricks had to be removed to a special isolated area outside the city, together with all the attached cement. If the decay began again,[8] the entire edifice had to be condemned and torn down, after which it was removed from the city. All the people who lived in the house were considered unclean until that evening. Those who ate[9] or slept[10] in the house had to wash their clothing.

---

[6]The time before the priest's arrival was to be used as an occasion by the owner for prayer and penitence.

—SFORNO

Until the arrival of the priest, the law of uncleanliness did not apply.

—RASHI

[7]Once the priest has come and pronounced that there is a plague in the house, all the contents are unclean, and so removal is commanded. The Torah shows consideration for a person's property, especially for earthenware vessels which had to be broken since there was no method of cleansing them.

—RASHI

[8]This does not mean the reappearance of the original infection, as with the leprosy of a man, but a different outbreak.

—NACHMANIDES

[9]By a person's mere entry into a house his garments do not become unclean. Only if he remains there a sufficient time in which he could eat half a loaf are his garments defiled.

—RASHI

[10]His contamination is of a stricter nature; so he must wash his garments and bathe his body, and he remains unclean until the evening.

—IBN EZRA

Should the decay have ceased after the second waiting period, the house was pronounced clean and safe, after which a sacrifice of two birds was brought as in the case of the cured leper.

Finally, the Torah discusses the cases of those who had any discharge or bleeding. Anyone who touched them or anything with which they had been in contact had to bathe and wash his clothing. He was considered unclean until that evening. Objects touched by those who had a discharge or bleeding had to be discarded or needed special processing. When the discharge stopped, the afflicted person had to count seven normal or healthy days, after which he washed his clothing, bathed in running water, and was again considered healthy and clean. On the eighth day, he offered sacrifices at the door of the Tent of Meeting.

Because the Holy Temple is yet to be rebuilt and the necessary sacrifices cannot be brought, many of these laws of quarantine and purification are not applicable today, although some are. The underlying principle of these regulations is the isolation of the diseased for their own protection, and the safety of the community.

Haftorah Metzora

II KINGS VII, 3–20

The diagnosis and cure of the dread disease of leprosy is the theme of the Sidrah. In the Haftorah, a desperate situation of a besieged Samaria is brought to an end through the report of four lepers.

Syria had laid siege to Samaria whose inhabitants were at the point of starvation. Elisha had counselled the people to continue the battle. When the siege reached a crisis point, the King blamed Elisha for the catastrophe which was befalling them.

Despite the apparent hopelessness of the situation, Elisha assured the King that the siege would be broken on the next day when food would again be available.

The four lepers, on the verge of starvation, decided to enter the Syrian camp. They reasoned that if the enemy would take them alive, they would be fed. Should the enemy slay them—they would have died anyway.

To their amazement, the entire Syrian camp was abandoned. God had caused loud chariot-like noises to be heard. The Syrians, thinking that Samaria had solicited the aid of other armies, beat a hasty retreat, leaving behind their food and supplies.

The lepers informed the besieged city of their good fortune and Samaria was saved.

אחרי מות

Acharey Mot

CHAPERS XVI–XVIII

*A*LTHOUGH MAN MAY confess his sins to God and seek divine pardon every day of the year, the Day of Atonement (*Yom Kipur*), has been specifically set aside for penitence. The detailed and inspiring ceremonies which took place in the Sanctuary on this solemn day—and later in the Holy Temple in Jerusalem—are described in this chapter. A great part of the synagogue service on the Day of Atonement is based upon these practices.

It was only on the Day of Atonement that the High Priest was permitted to enter the room in the Sanctuary known as the Holy of Holies. The sole furnishings in this chamber were the Ark and its Cover, which contained the Tablets that Moses had brought down from Mount Sinai.

Prior to his entry into this room, Aaron had to bathe and don simple white linen garments. The color of this clothing symbolizes humility, purity and the hope for Divine forgiveness. He then presented a young bullock[1] which was to serve as a sin-offering for his own transgressions, and those of his family and the other priests.

Two male goats[2] were then placed before the door of the Tent of Meeting. By the casting of lots,[3] one was designated to

---

[1]Not that he was to bring the animal into the Holy of Holies, but that he must first offer up a bullock of his own as an atonement for himself and the other priests, but not including the Levites who were reckoned as Israelites in this regard.

—IBN EZRA

[2]One to atone for sins committed in connection with the Sanctuary, and the second to be sent away to atone for the sins of the community.

—SFORNO

[3]One goat he placed on his right hand, the other on his left. He

be sacrificed to God and the other was sent away into the wilderness to symbolically carry away the sins of those Jews who had repented their sins.

Aaron now sacrificed the bullock which he had chosen as a personal sin-offering, and then kindled a golden censer which formed a cloud of incense. Following this moving cloud, he entered the Holy of Holies to ask for God's pardon for his own sins, and for those of his family and the other priests.

When he emerged from the Holy of Holies, he sacrificed the goat which he had chosen as the sin-offering for the people, and returned to the Holy of Holies to pray for God's forgiveness of all the people. Forgiveness was also asked at the golden incense altar for all those people who might have transgressed in matters pertaining to the Sanctuary. During these ceremonies, only the High Priest was permitted to be in the Tent of Meeting.

Upon coming out of the Holy of Holies for the second time, Aaron placed his hands upon the head of the other goat and confessed the general sins of the people. The goat was then led away into the wilderness, symbolically bearing away the sins of all the people.[4]

Finally, the High Priest removed his white garments, bathed, and put on his golden vestments in which he sacrificed two more rams; one for himself and one for the people.

This ceremony had to be performed each year in the seventh Hebrew month (*Tishrei*) on the tenth day as long as the Holy Temple stood in Jerusalem. The Day of Atonement is of course still observed today, but we can only read about the sacrifices and Temple service in our prayer-books. No work is

---

then put both hands in the urn, took one lot in each hand and placed it upon the corresponding goat. One of the lots was inscribed "for the Lord" and the other "for Azazel".

—RASHI

[4]The sins having departed from Israel, were figuratively placed on the head of the goat which went to a remote place where they would no more be remembered.

—IBN EZRA

permitted on this day and it is to be spent in fasting, prayer, and repentance.

> *And it shall be a statute forever unto you; in the seventh month, on the tenth day of the month, ye shall afflict your souls,[5] and shall do no manner of work, the home-born, or the stranger that sojourneth among you. For on this day shall atonement be made for you, to cleanse you; from all your sins shall ye be clean before the Lord.[6] It is a sabbath of solemn rest unto you, and ye shall afflict your souls; it is a statute for ever.[7]*

The Torah then teaches that sacrifices may only be offered at God's chosen altar and to no other but God.[8]

At that time, only those meats were permitted to be eaten which had been left over from a sacrifice. Later, other meats were made permissible, but only from certain animals and prepared in a specific manner.[9]

---

[5]This phrase, when used in Scripture, denotes fasting.

—NACHMANIDES

[6]Although the priest officiates, it is only from God that purification from sin can come as the effect of confession and penitence, since He alone knows their sincerity.

—SFORNO

[7]To fast on the Day of Atonement.

—IBN EZRA

Even when the Temple no longer stands, the Sabbath of solemn rest and fasting must still be observed, for even without the Temple and its service, the Day of Atonement can be the occasion of purification from sin by means of repentance.

—SFORNO

[8]Not to sacrifice to demons even though they are not regarded as gods, but even merely to seek their help.

—SFORNO

[9]Ibn Ezra attacks those who declare that flesh must not be eaten in the diaspora since sacrifices have now ceased. According to Nachma-

The Torah again forbids the eating of blood.

And whatsoever man there be of the house of Israel, or of the strangers that sojourn among them, that eateth any manner of blood,[10] *I will set My face against that soul that eateth blood, and will cut him off from among his people. For the life of the flesh is in the blood; and I have given it to you upon the altar to make atonement for your souls; for it is the blood that maketh atonement by reason of the life.*

Flesh of animals which died a natural death or were killed are also prohibited.

The final section of this chapter deals with permissible and forbidden marriages.[11] Marital union between all blood relatives is forbidden, and since such unions are incest they are not deemed marriage. This prohibition extends to the wives of

---

nides, the purpose of the chapter is to emphasize that the slaughtering of animals as sacrifices must take place only within the confines of the Sanctuary. While the Jews were in the wilderness, the only flesh allowed them was from the peace-offerings brought on the altar. The ox, the lamb, and the goat were sacrificed as peace-offerings in the Tent of Meeting and their fat and blood offered on the altar. Only when that had been done could the flesh be eaten. But when their borders were extended, the Jews were permitted to eat non-sacrificial meat because they dwelt far from the Temple.

[10]Nachmanides maintains that the prohibition stemmed from the fact that those who eat the blood in time become imbued with the same bestial passions which the animal possessed. The Jews must accordingly pour the blood on the altar as an atonement, as it is not right that one creature (man) should devour the life-blood of another creature. To emphasize the fact that the blood must not be eaten, it was ordained that following slaughter the blood of a beast or fowl must be covered over with earth.

[11]These are laws which coincide with human reason and should be instituted had they not already been ordained by the Torah.

—RASHI

blood relations and to the close relatives of a man's wife. The specific rules regulating these relations are listed in this chapter.

There are other male-female unions and relationships which the Torah forbids. By honoring these moral codes and marrying in a healthy and sanctified circumstance, the People are assured that they will live happily in their land and serve God according to His will.

Haftorah Acharey Mot

EZEKIEL XXII, 1–19

Many commandments of morality, justice and righteousness are enumerated in the Sidrah.

The violation of these commandments seems to have been the order of the day in Judah prior to its destruction in 586 B.C.E.

In a terrible and ominous denouncement, Ezekiel condemns the inhabitants of Jerusalem. He labels the capital of Judah a "bloody city". The Prophet accuses the populace of bloodshed, immorality, idolatry, oppression and violation of the Sabbaths.

As a result, the Prophet warns that the end of the kingdom is at hand. Only through destruction, suffering and exile will the people finally repent. Then, and only then, will God's gates of mercy be opened again, and His People will return to their ancient homeland.

קְדשִׁים

Kedoshim

CHAPTERS XIX–XX

*T*HE FUNDAMENTAL ETHICAL concepts of Judaism are outlined in the following chapters of the Torah. The Hebrew name of this section is *Kedoshim* which means "holy". Living by these principles, the People are assured they will be a holy and sanctified nation.

> *And the Lord spoke unto Moses, saying. Speak unto all the congregation*[1] *of the children of Israel, and say unto them: Ye shall be holy;*[2] *for I the Lord your God am holy. Ye shall fear every man his mother, and his father,*[3] *and ye shall keep My sabbaths;*[4] *I am the Lord your God. Turn ye not*

---

[1]The laws in this chapter, being so fundamental, are directed to all Israel.

—RASHI

[2]After God had caused His Presence to abide in the midst of Israel and warned them against what would defile them, the Torah states that the purpose is that the people should imitate God so far as that is humanly possible.

—SFORNO

[3]Because the child is apt to fear his father more, the mother is mentioned first. In the matter of honor, however, the father receives priority because the child naturally honors his mother more, since she is more affectionate to him.

—RASHI

[4]This law follows immediately to indicate that if a child is ordered by his father to desecrate the Sabbath, the father is not to be obeyed, and similarly with the other commandments.

—RASHI

*unto the idols, nor make to yourselves molten gods: I am
the Lord your God.*[5]

Sacrifices were the basic form of worship at that time. To
make them acceptable to God, they had to be offered precisely
as prescribed in the Torah.

No community can live in happiness and tranquility if there
is poverty in its midst. Those who work the land were therefore
instructed not to harvest the corners of their fields but to leave
them for the poor.[6] Similarly, when some of their produce
dropped to the ground, they were not to retrieve it, but leave
it for those in want of food.[7]

*Ye shall not steal; neither shall ye deal falsely, nor lie one
to another. And ye shall not swear by My name falsely, so
that thou profane the name of thy God: I am the Lord.
Thou shalt not oppress thy neighbor, nor rob him; the
wages of a hired servant shall not abide with thee all night
until morning.*[8]

Outside of family, our closest relationships are with our
neighbors, with whom we are commanded to deal as we would
want others to deal with us. Thievery and oppression are sinful
regardless of who the victims may be.

---

[5]Do as I did. As I rested on the Sabbath, so should you.

—IBN EZRA

[6]The last corner to be reaped.

—RASHI

[7]The ears of corn which fall from the hand of the reaper. One or
two ears, but not three, come within this law.

—RASHI

[8]The wages of a laborer employed during the day must be paid
to him before the break of the following day.

—RASHI

The Torah now lists additional commandments which must govern a just and harmonious society.

Thou shalt not curse the deaf,[9] nor put a stumbling-block before the blind,[10] but thou shalt fear thy God: I am the Lord.

Ye shall do no unrighteousness in judgement; thou shalt not respect the person of the poor, nor favor the person of the mighty; but in righteousness shalt thou judge thy neighbor.

Thou shalt not go up and down as a talebearer among thy people; neither shalt thou stand idly by the blood of thy neighbor: I am the Lord.

Thou shalt not hate thy neighbor in thy heart;[11] thou shalt surely rebuke thy neighbor: I am the Lord.

Thou shalt not take vengeance, nor bear any grudge against the children of thy people, but thou shalt love thy fellow as thyself:[12] I am the Lord.

Although most of the commandments of the Torah are quite logical, the reasons for some of the laws are not quite apparent. Nevertheless, we are taught to observe all the commandments as an act of faith in God. Thus, we learn that a field

---

[9]Since the deaf, who cannot hear and be incensed by what is said, may not be cursed, how much less those who can hear and feel the insult!

—NACHMANIDES

[10]The word 'blind' is metaphorical for any unsuspecting person.

—RASHI

[11]All these commands relate to the feelings of the heart. Upon this obedience depends a secure social life; for was not the Second Temple destroyed on account of vain hatred?

—IBN EZRA

[12]Rabbi Akiba described this as a fundamental law of the Torah.

—RASHI

may not be planted with different kinds of seeds,[13] nor should clothing be worn that contain a mixture of wool and linen.[14]

Relations between man and woman must be based upon respect and purity.

Once the Jewish People had reached the Promised Land, the first fruits of new trees could not be eaten for the first three years. During the fourth year, the fruits are considered holy and could be eaten only in Jerusalem. After that, they are permitted to be eaten by everyone at all times and places.

> *Ye shall not eat with the blood; neither shall ye practice divination*[15] *nor soothsaying.*[16]

The corners of the head and beard may not be shaven with a blade, nor may incisions or markings be made upon the skin to mourn the dead—a practice common among the pagan people. In the same manner, all types of witchcraft and fortune-telling are forbidden.

> *Profane not thy daughter, to make her a harlot, lest the land fall into harlotry, and the land become full of lewdness.*
> *Ye shall keep My sabbaths,*[17] *and reverence My sanctuary:*

---

[13]As at Creation God commanded each species to reproduce itself after its kind, one may not mix them.

—NACHMANIDES

[14]Nachmanides quotes Maimonides that the priests of antiquity used to wear garments of two kinds of stuff mingled together in their idolatrous worship.

[15]Discovering omens in the cry of a weasel, the twittering of birds, bread falling from one's mouth, or a stag crossing one's path.

—RASHI

[16]One must not say, "This day is propitious for beginning a task and this day is not".

—RASHI

[17]The plural includes the festivals.

—SFORNO

I am the Lord.
Turn ye not unto the ghosts, nor unto familiar spirits; seek
them not out, to be defiled by them: I am the Lord your God.
Thou shalt rise up before the hoary head, and honor the face
of the old man, and thou shalt fear thy God: I am the Lord.

The stranger in the land must always be loved and treated
as an equal. Because the Jewish People were once strangers in
Egypt, they must forever remember their own bondage and
never impose oppression upon others.

In all business dealings, weights and balances must be measured honestly and justly.

We read of the need to separate clean and unclean animals,
birds and sea-life used for food.[18]

These commandments were given to set the Jewish People
apart from the many perverse and corrupt ways in which the
people of the land of Canaan were living. The Divine assurance
that the People would live a happy life in the Promised Land is
tied to their determination to lead a Godly life, in which case the
Torah promises:

Ye shall inherit their land, a land flowing with milk and
honey.

Haftorah Kedoshim

Amos IX, 7–15

As the Sidrah lays the foundations for a life of righteousness, so does
the Prophet of this Haftorah proclaim that the only way Israel can

---

[18]One must make a distinction between an animal which is permitted as food and one which is not; also between an animal which has
been correctly slaughtered and one which was not.

—RASHI

achieve its special relationship with God is by living up to His commandments and way of life.

Israel must not expect any special privileges in the fulfilment of its obligations. All nations are composed of individuals equally important to God.

The wicked shall perish regardless of their national identity. All righteous people shall ultimately achieve their reward.

If Israel will heed God's call, they will live in their land in happiness, prosperity and security.

Behold, the days come, saith the Lord,
That the plowman shall overtake the reaper,
And the treader of grapes him that soweth seed;
And all the hills shall melt.

And I will turn the captivity of My people Israel,
And they shall build the waste cities, and inhabit them;
And they shall plant vineyards, and drink the wine thereof;
They shall also make gardens, and eat the fruit of them.

And I will plant them upon their land,
And they shall no more be plucked up
Out of their land which I have given them,
Saith the Lord thy God.

אמר

Emor

THE TORAH DEVOTES many chapters to the description of the construction of the Sanctuary and the sacrifices which were to be offered within it. Attention is now focused on the priests, *kohanim,* who were to officiate at these services.[1]

A priest, to this very day, is forbidden to be within proximity of a corpse,[2] since this would render him spiritually impure and not eligible to serve in the Sanctuary.[3] He however assists in the burial of seven close relatives: his mother, father, son, daughter, brother, unmarried sister and wife, since it is his responsibility to see that they are properly buried.

It is forbidden for him, as for others, to shave his head, the corners of his beard, or to cut himself while mourning for his dead, as was the custom of the pagans. The priests are governed by the same marriage regulations as ordinary Jews, with the exception that they may not marry a woman who has been divorced, or is known to be immoral.

The same general rules apply to the High Priest, the *Kohain*

---

[1]After having warned Israel and the priests included that they must strive for holiness, Scripture turns once more to the priests who have to be particularly careful, as custodians of the Torah, not to become unclean.

—IBN EZRA

[2]As long as there are Israelites who can devote themselves to this task, the priests must not defile themselves to bury the dead. Should there be a corpse lying in a place where there are no Israelites, and no relatives are known (*met mitzvah*) the priest should occupy himself with the burial.

—RASHI

[3]He must not enter a tent (or house) where there is a corpse. Contact with blood renders men and vessels in the same tent unclean.

—RASHI

Gadol who was the highest ranking priest. In some respects however, he was more restricted. He was not allowed to approach any corpse or mourn for them by letting his hair grow and by tearing his clothing, even for the seven close kin mentioned above. Also, he could only marry a woman who was never previously married.

In order to officiate in the Sanctuary, the priest had to be of sound mind and body. A serious physical defect rendered him unfit to offer the sacrifices, although he could still partake of the sacrificial foods. The only times that he could not eat these sanctified meals was when he was unclean in some specified way. All members of his family dependent on him for their support could also partake of the food offered in the Sanctuary.

Just as the priest had to be healthy and whole for priestly service, the animals used for the sacrifices had to be perfect. An animal designated as an offering was not to be removed from its mother[4] until the eighth day after its birth, and it could not be offered on the same day as its mother.

A review of the Jewish festivals and holy days is presented next, beginning with the Sabbath, which is designated as a holy day on which no work is permitted.

And the Lord spoke unto Moses, saying: Speak unto the children of Israel,[5] and say unto them:
The appointed seasons[6] of the Lord, which ye shall proclaim to be holy convocations, even these are My appointed

---

[4]When the male parent is definitely known the law applies to him.
—IBN EZRA

[5]Moses is told to make such regulations concerning the festivals that all Israel should become instructed in their observance.
—RASHI

[6]The Sabbath is not included among the appointed seasons of the Lord, and so the next verse repeats the phrase, since the Sabbath is a day fixed by God, whereas the actual date for the observance of the festivals had to await the proclamation of the Sanhedrin.
—NACHMANIDES

*seasons. Six days shall work be done; but on the seventh
day is a sabbath of solemn rest, a holy convocation; ye shall
do no manner of work; it is a sabbath unto the Lord[7] in
all your dwellings.*

The festival of Passover is to take place on the eve of the
fifteenth day of Nisan, the first month, and it commemorates the
exodus of Israel from their Egyptian bondage. It is a seven day
festival: the first and last are "holy convocations",[9] and the other
days a partial holiday. In countries outside of Israel, an extra day
has been added. No leavened foods may be eaten throughout
the week of Passover.

On the sixteenth day of Nisan, after the first day[10] of Passover has passed, a sheaf of barley, an *omer,* was presented as an
offering which represented the Springtime harvest. This offering was brought with the other holiday sacrifices and the
people then counted forty-nine days. This was the span of time
between the children of Israel leaving Egypt and receiving the
Decalogue and the Law at Mount Sinai.

The Feast of Weeks, *Shavuot,* took place on the fiftieth day
of this seven week cycle. The first fruits were presented on this
festival amid other sacrifices.

The New Year, Rosh Hashana, was set on the first day of
Tishrei, the seventh month. This holy day, later extended to two
days, was to be a solemn gathering of the people, who were to
hear the sound of the Shofar, the Ram's Horn.

---

[7]God Who created light and darkness, fixed the Sabbath for all
your places of residence, i.e. the time of its beginning and ending is
determined by local conditions of longitude and latitude.

—SFORNO

[9]The only work permitted is the preparation of food to be eaten
on the day (provided the festival does not fall on a Sabbath).

—NACHMANIDES

[10]Ibn Ezra and Nachmanides take great pain to refute the Sad-
ducees and others who contend, contrary to Rabbinic teaching, that
the phrase means the first day of the week.

The tenth day of this month is *Yom Kipur*, the Day of Atonement.

Howbeit on the tenth day of this seventh month is a day of atonement; there shall be a holy convocation unto you, and ye shall afflict your souls; and ye shall bring an offering made by fire unto the Lord. And ye shall do no manner of work in that same day;[12] *for it is a day of atonement, to make atonement for you before the Lord your God.*

The Feast of Tabernacles, *Succot*, takes place on the fifteenth day of Tishrei, four days after Yom Kipur. The Torah proclaims a seven day festival: the first and last are to be holy days of sanctity and rest. In countries outside of Israel, an extra day has been added.

Howbeit on the fifteenth day of the seventh month, when ye have gathered in the fruits of the land, ye shall keep the feast of the Lord seven days; on the first day shall be a solemn rest, and on the eighth day shall be a solemn rest. And ye shall take you on the first day the fruit of goodly trees, branches of palm-trees, and boughs of thick trees, and willows of the brook, and ye shall rejoice before the Lord your God seven days. And ye shall keep it a feast unto the Lord seven days in the year; it is a statute forever in your generations; ye shall keep it in the seventh month. Ye shall dwell in booths seven days; all that are home-born in Israel shall dwell in booths; that your generations may know[13] *that I made the children of Israel to dwell in booths, when*

---

[12]The intention of the phrase is that, apart from the atonement effected through the ritual of sacrifice, the day itself is holy as an occasion for the afflicting of souls and purification of sin, and consequently no work must be done.

—NACHMANIDES

[13]The literal explanation is that the Israelites dwelt in actual booths; and Tabernacles was ordained to be observed at harvest-time

I brought them out of the land of Egypt: I am the Lord your God.
And Moses declared unto the children of Israel the appointed seasons of the Lord.

After the holidays were explained, the priests are commanded to always keep an Eternal Light burning in the Sanctuary.

And the Lord spoke unto Moses, saying: Command the children of Israel, that they bring unto thee pure olive oil beaten for the light, to cause a lamp to burn continually. Without the veil of testimony, in the tent of meeting, shall Aaron order it from evening to morning before the Lord continually; it shall be a statute for ever throughout your generations. He shall order the lamps upon the pure candlestick before the Lord continually.

Twelve loaves of bread had to be placed in two rows of six on a special table in the Sanctuary, with a small cup of incense at the end of each of the two rows. These loaves were placed there each Sabbath, remaining there during the week, and replaced with new ones on the following Sabbath.

An incident is related at this point in which a man was put to death for cursing God. Publicly defaming the name of God is a grave sin.

Finally, the regulations of restitution are outlined. The deliberate taking of human life cannot be expiated except by taking of the life of the murderer. This happened very rarely, but a life taken could not be repaid with money. The unlawful killing of an animal requires payment of its full value. It is in this manner that the phrase "eye for eye, tooth for tooth" was applied by the Jewish courts. Harm inflicted on a human being

---

to deter man from feeling excessive pride at the sight of his abundance and induce in him a sense of dependence upon God.

—RASHBAM

required payment coming as close as possible to covering all aspects of the damage done, including medical costs and time lost from earning a livelihood.

Haftorah Emor

EZEKIEL XLIV, 15–31

The Sidrah outlines the duties of the priests who are the descendants of Aaron and ministered in the Sanctuary and the Holy Temple.

Ezekiel, who lived through the period of the destruction of the Holy Temple and foretold its rebuilding, had a clear vision of the New Jerusalem and the Holy Temple.

He decreed that only those priests who are descendants of Zadok may offer the sacrifices in the new Temple. It was Zadok and his family who remained loyal to God during the destruction, when all others rebelled.

By specifying all the details of the forthcoming responsibilities of the priests, Ezekiel not only reviewed the laws which were about to be in effect again, but he also makes the Return from Babylonia an imminent reality.

בהר

Behar

CHAPTERS XXV–XXVI, 2

*T*URNING FROM THE Sanctuary, the Sabbath and the festivals, the Torah now focuses upon social justice and the assurance of a sound economy for the nation. Upon entering the Promised Land, the Jewish People were to observe a number of agricultural commandments.

> *And the Lord spoke unto Moses in Mount Sinai,[1] saying:*
> *Speak unto the children of Israel, and say unto them:*
> *When ye come into the land which I give you, then shall*
> *the land keep a sabbath[2] unto the Lord.[3] Six years thou*
> *shalt sow thy field, and in six years thou shalt prune the*
> *vineyard, and gather in the products thereof. But in the*
> *seventh year shall be a sabbath of solemn rest for the land,*
> *a sabbath unto the Lord; thou shalt neither sow thy field,*
> *nor prune thy vineyard. That which groweth of itself of thy*
> *harvest thou shalt not reap,[4] and the grapes of thy un-*

---

[1]Why is it recorded of the sabbatical year that it was communicated on the mount? To teach that as this law was ordained there with its general rules and its minute details, so is it with all the commandments of the Torah.

—RASHI

[2]A gentile may not sow the land on behalf of a Jew in that year.

—IBN EZRA

[3]During this year of rest landowners will have an opportunity to seek the Lord.

—SFORNO

[4]It is not the exclusive property of the owner, but is free for others as well as himself to reap.

—RASHI

dressed vine thou shalt not gather; it shall be a year of solemn rest for the land. And the sabbath-produce of the land shall be for food for you: for thee, and for thy servant and for thy maid, and for thy hired servant and for the settler by thy side that sojourn with thee; and for thy cattle, and for the beasts that are in thy land, shall all the increase thereof be for food.

It is not sufficient to merely rest on the Sabbath, but one should also sanctify this day through prayer and study. So it was with the seventh year. It was to be utilized by the otherwise hard working farmer for the study and deeper understanding of his faith. Through it, the people came to realize that the land was not their ultimate property. Also, the land was not to be sapped of its strength. Because all the people thus had the opportunity to engage in religious study and service, no clergy class ever developed among the Jewish people who were entirely in charge of religion. The Law of God was the possession of all Israel.

After seven such cycles had been counted and forty-nine years had passed, a Jubilee year, *Yovel* was proclaimed on the Day of Atonement. The advent of the Jubilee year was heralded by the sound of the *Shofar*,[5] the ram's horn. One of the reasons why we sound the *Shofar* at the conclusion of *Yom Kipur* is to remind us of the way in which the Jubilee year was announced.

During this fiftieth Jubilee year, the land was not to be worked, in the same manner as this work was forbidden in the seventh year. Also, all land which had changed hands over the previous forty-nine years reverted back to the original owners. In this manner no small group could ever control the vast majority of the national wealth. There was always to be an equal distribution.

When land was sold, it was not its actual value which was paid for, but the price of the number of harvests until the next

---

[5]As a sign of joy at the emancipation of slaves and return of the fields to their original owners.

—SFORNO

Jubilee. In this way, fair amounts could be established and the purchaser would not be the loser when he had to return the land at the time of the Jubilee.

Man must realize that he is a stranger and pilgrim[6] upon the earth which belongs to God. Never being able to buy land forever makes each Jew conscious of this fact.

We also read that if the Jubilee arrived during the six year tenure of a servant, he automatically became a free man.

*And ye shall hallow the fiftieth year, and proclaim liberty[7]
throughout the land unto all the inhabitants thereof; it
shall be a jubilee unto you; and ye shall return every man
unto his possession, and ye shall return every man unto his
family.*

The relatives of a person who became poor should, whenever possible, buy back any land which the needy individual was forced to sell.[8] If one had no such relatives and had to sell his land to repay debts, he was able to redeem it as soon as he had the means. Otherwise, it reverted back to him at the Jubilee.[9]

The laws regarding the sale of a house differed slightly. If the house sold was within a walled city,[10] the seller had the right

---

[6]Therefore do not resent these laws: the land is not the property of any man.

—RASHI

[7]The Hebrew word *dror* is the name of the swallow which sings while free, but, when captive, refuses to eat and then dies.

—IBN EZRA

[8]Only under such pressure of poverty should a man sell his property.

—RASHI

[9]Should the Jubilee fall in the first year of the sale, the house does not go back to its owner.

—RASHI, QUOTING RABBI SAPHRA

[10]Surrounded by a wall since the time of Joshua.

—RASHI

to buy the house back within a year. Otherwise, he lost that right. A house in an open city was governed by the same rules as land.

The Levites,[11] who did not receive an allocation of land when they settled in Canaan, could always buy their houses back, even if they were in a walled city. The fields around these cities which belonged to the Levites were their permanent possession and could never be sold.

Instead of simply doling out charity to the poor, the Torah outlines a program for assisting them and alleviating their poverty.

> *And if thy brother be waxen poor, and his means fail with thee; then thou shalt uphold him:*[12] *as a stranger and a settler shall he live with thee.*[13] *Take thou no interest*[14] *of him or increase; but fear thy God; that thy brother may live with thee.*[15] *Thou shalt not give him thy money upon*

---

[11]Forty-eight cities were given to them. Cities other than those assigned to the Levites, or houses possessed by them in cities inhabited by Israelites, do not come under this law.

—RASHI

[12]Help him as soon as he shows signs of falling.

—RASHI

[13]It is a positive command of the Torah to sustain him.

—NACHMANIDES

[14]The best way to help him is to make him a loan without interest.

—SFORNO

[15]Provided you have sufficient for your own needs and to make him a loan; for the Rabbis declared, 'Your life comes before your fellow-man's life'.

—SFORNO

Nachmanides refers to the problem raised in the Midrash of two men on a journey who have only sufficient water to keep one of them alive. Ben Paturi held that they should both drink even though both will die. Rabbi Akiba held that whoever had the water had the right to save his life by drinking alone. He based his opinion on the passage: —*let thy brother live with thee*—which means: save his life together with your own, otherwise your own life takes precedence over his.

interest, nor give him thy victuals for increase. I am the Lord your God, who brought you forth out of the land of Egypt, to give you the land of Canaan, to be your God.[16]

In those days, a Jew who was poor could sell himself into servitude.[17] The person who bought him had to treat him as a hired laborer and could not impose any indignities or hardships upon him. If the poor man was sold to a stranger away from his people, he could always be redeemed by others and was automatically released from his debt and term of work after six years or when the Jubilee fell during his six years of servitude.

Slavery has existed since ancient times and slaves have been cruelly treated among most people. But the Jew who owned a slave had clearly defined responsibilities toward both alien as well as Jewish slaves.

The section closes with the oft-repeated warning against idol-worship and the commandment of observing the Sabbath.

Ye shall make no idols, neither shall ye rear you up a graven image, or a pillar, neither shall ye place any figured stone in your land, to bow down unto it;[18] *for I am the Lord your God. You shall keep My sabbaths, and reverence My sanctuary:*[19] *I am the Lord.*

---

[16]To the Jews who dwell in Canaan I am God; but he who voluntarily leaves the land is as though he worshipped idols.

—RASHI

The purpose of the Divine laws is that you live together in mutual aid.

—SFORNO

[17]Either of his own accord, or by order of the court for the crime of theft.

—IBN EZRA

[18]He may not do so even to God; for outside the Temple, prostration which involved stretching forth the hands and feet is forbidden.

—RASHI

[19]The noun (in Hebrew) is plural and includes the synagogues and

Haftorah Behar

JEREMIAH XXXII, 6–27

The Sidrah explains that land was to remain as a family inheritance and how a relative could repurchase sold land, to assure it remaining within the family estate.

The Haftorah describes one of the most critical periods in Jewish history. It was 587 B.C.E., just before the Babylonian conquest and destruction.

One of the great prophets of that day, Jeremiah, was approached by a nephew with an offer to purchase a parcel of land in Judah. This purchase would "redeem" the land for Jeremiah's family property.

Since the country was about to fall to the Babylonians, it seemed almost foolish for Jeremiah to expend money on such a transaction. Nevertheless, the Prophet saw this as a God-given opportunity to demonstrate to the Jewish People that the ensuing exile was only going to be temporary and that the People would surely return to their homeland. Therefore he purchased the parcel of land for the full amount of the required seventeen shekels of silver, accompanied by a legal deed.

At the conclusion of the sale, Jeremiah spoke these words of hope:

> *For thus saith the Lord of hosts, the God of Israel: 'Houses and fields and vineyards shall yet again be bought in this land.'*

---

houses of study set up in place of the Temple when the people is in captivity.

—SFORNO

בְּחֻקֹּתַי

Bechukotai

CHAPTERS XXVI, 3–XXVII

*J*HE BOOK OF Leviticus, so rich in moral codes, rules of Sanctuary worship, history, and assorted laws of Judaism comes to a close with a choice offered by God to the Jewish People.

If ye walk in My statues, and keep My commandments,[1] and do them; then I will give you rains[2] in their season, and the land shall yield her produce, and the trees of the field shall yield their fruit. And your threshing shall reach unto the vintage, and the vintage shall reach unto the sowing time; and ye shall eat your bread until you have enough, and dwell in your land safely.[3] And I will give peace in the land,[4] and ye shall lie down, and none shall make you afraid; and I will cause evil beasts to cease out of the land, neither shall the sword go through your land. And ye shall chase your enemies, and they shall fall before you by the sword. . . . And I will have respect unto you,

---

[1]The aim of the study of the commandments must be performance.

—RASHI

It denotes scrupulous performance from the motive of love. Only then can it be said that you—"do them".

—SFORNO

[2]This is given first place, because all depends upon the rain in its proper season: physical health, good harvests and fruitful cattle.

—NACHMANIDES

[3]Famine is the cause of people migrating from their land.

—IBN EZRA

[4]Peace surpasses all other blessings.

—NACHMANIDES

and make you fruitful, and multiply you; and will establish
My covenant[5] with you[6] . . . And I will walk among
you,[7] and will be your God, and ye shall be My people.

Coupled with this promise, however, is a devastating and
detailed warning that if the people should refuse to walk in the
commandments of God,[8] horrible disasters would befall them.[9]
In clear and terrible sentences, the Torah outlines how the rains
will cease and the land will no longer yield its produce; how the
nation will suffer within, and then fall prey to enemies from
without: finally to be driven out of their Land into a long and
dismal exile.

This Divine warning is not spoken in a spirit of hatred which
is alien to God, but out of love for His chosen people.[10] Even

---

[5]That you will be numerous like the stars and the dust of the earth.
(Genesis XIII 16, XV 5).

—IBN EZRA

[6]Because of your own merit—apart from what I promised the
Patriarchs.

—SFORNO

[7]My treatment of you will be like that of a king who mingles with
his people in their camp and sees after their needs.

—NACHMANIDES

The Hebrew verb signifies to 'walk from place to place', so where-
ever Israel may be, God's glory will be with them—where the righteous
are found, that place is holy as though the Temple stood there.

—SFORNO

[8]Denying the cardinal principal of God's existence.

—RASHI

To be like the heathens without the yoke of the Torah.

—SFORNO.

[9]Since they planned to break God's covenant, it will also be
broken on God's side.

—SFORNO

[10]God's purpose is only to chasten them until their hearts are
humbled.

—IBN EZRA.

when the Jews will have been exiled into strange and foreign
lands, torn away from their native soil and Holy Temple, God
will never forget them.[11] Even when the Jews are delivered into
the hands of their enemies, they will not be rejected or hated by
God. Had God indeed ever abandoned them, this tiny nation
would immediately have been destroyed.

Regardless of the sins of the People, and the consequent
retribution, the Covenant between God and the Jewish People
will never be broken. Sooner or later, they will return to their
ancient homeland, rebuild their cities, and live in peace.

The book of Leviticus closes with some of the regulations
of the Sanctuary, one of the major concerns of the Book. Besides
the communal offerings, a person could bring a private and
individual sacrifice. The Torah now teaches that individual gifts
could also be made to the Sanctuary.

If, for example, a person vowed to offer his "entire being"
to the Sanctuary,[12] an estimate of his value was made, the sum
of which he was then obligated to donate. This amount was
determined by an evaluation of the labor a person could produce. It therefore differed for male and female, and on the basis
of age.[13] The amount in the Torah was estimated by the current
unit of currency known as the *shekel*. If the estimated value of the
person was more than he could afford to pay, the priest would
adjust the figure in keeping with his financial means.[14]

---

[11]Nachmanides gives the later historical background to this promise, and quotes the Sages who declare that even in the times of Alex-
ander of Macedon and Vespasian God did not forget His people.

[12]It is customary for a man to vow that if God grants him his
request, he will devote to the Temple the monetary value of his life,
or of his child, or of his cattle.

—IBN EZRA.

[13]Not the market-price which varies, but the value attached to the
age-group.

—RASHI

[14]The priest shall assess him according to what he possesses,

If a person made a vow to offer one of his animals to the Sanctuary, he could not replace it with another one—even a better animal. As soon as the vow is spoken, that specific animal becomes the property of the Sanctuary. If it was an animal which was unfit for Temple use, it was redeemed for money, with the addition of one fifth of its value.

The same rules hold true regarding a house which was offered to the Sanctuary. The priest assessed the value of the building, and this amount was given by the donor, with the addition of one fifth the value of the house.

The price of land which a person could dedicate to the Sanctuary was based on the cost of the seed necessary to sow it until the next Jubilee year. As a result, the value was determined by the proximity of the time the vow was made to the Jubilee. If the donor decides to redeem the land, he could donate the money instead, with the additional one fifth of its value. Otherwise, it would revert to the Sanctuary at the time of the Jubilee.

All first-born animals became the property of the Sanctuary. Therefore, they could not be offered to the Sanctuary by the owner a second time. Should a first-born animal be unfit for Temple use, it was redeemed and its value, plus one fifth of the amount, was given to the Sanctuary. If a person was condemned to death by the courts for a capital crime and wished to donate his value to the Sanctuary, it was rejected since no benefit could be derived from a person's death.

There were also a number of offerings from crops and fruits which had to be tithed for use by the Sanctuary. Either the actual produce was given, or it could be redeemed for money, with the additional one fifth of its value. Each tenth animal of the flock or herd also was to be included in this tithe.

These are the commandments which the Lord commanded Moses for the children of Israel in Mount Sinai.

---

taking care to leave him the necessities of life and what is required for his employment.

—RASHI

Haftorah Bechukotai

JEREMIAH XVI, 19–XVII, 14

The Book of Leviticus closes with a solemn warning to the People to live according to God's ways in order to enjoy a good and happy life. Failure to do so would result in national and personal disaster and exile.

Jeremiah saw the tragic results of the Nation's disobedience to the commandments of God. Having fallen into corruption and idolatry, Judea was conquered and the Holy Temple was destroyed.

The Prophet foresaw this impending doom and desperately tried to steer the people away from this path of calamity.

As soon as the exile was a reality, however, Jeremiah stirred the People with words of comfort and hope.

Blessed is the man that trusteth in the Lord,
And whose trust the Lord is,
For he shall be as a tree planted by the waters,
And that spreadeth out its roots by the river,
And shall not see when heat cometh,
But its foliage shall be luxuriant;
And shall not be anxious in the year of drought,
Neither shall cease from yielding fruit.

Heal me, O Lord, and I shall be healed;
Save me, and I shall be saved;
For Thou art my praise.

THE BOOK OF
NUMBERS

ספר במדבר

The Book of Numbers, known in Hebrew as Bemidbar, is the
fourth book of the Pentateuch. The English title derives from the
fact that twice in this book the Jewish People were "numbered"
when a census was taken. Bemidbar means "in the desert"—the
central theme of the text. We read about what happened to the
People as they made their way from Egypt to Canaan, later to be
known as the Land of Israel. We learn of God guiding them
through their tribulations, and the punishment they suffered when
they rebelled against God and Moses' leadership.

This book also has chapters devoted to laws of the Sanctuary,
spiritual purity and other commandments.

בְּמִדְבַּר

Bemidbar

A YEAR HAD passed since the Jewish People had left Egyptian
bondage and the construction of the Tabernacle had been completed. It was in the second month of that year that Moses
received the command of God to conduct a census.

> *And the Lord spoke unto Moses in the wilderness of Sinai,*[1]
> *in the Tent of Meeting, on the first day of the second month,*
> *in the second year after they were come out of the land of*
> *Egypt, saying: Take ye the sum*[2] *of all the congregation of*
> *the children of Israel, by their families, by their fathers'*
> *houses,*[3] *according to the number of names, every male, by*
> *their polls; from twenty years old and upward, all that are*
> *able to go forth in war in Israel: ye shall number them by*
> *their hosts, even thou and Aaron.*

It must be rembered that there were many thousands of
men, women and children in this moving camp. Since no regular
army had been organized to protect the Jews from attack by the
nations and tribes through which they passed during their wanderings, this census was now imperative.

---

[1]The emphasis is on *in the wilderness,* i.e., this as well as all other
revelations after the setting up of the Tabernacle took place there,
whereas prior revelations came to Moses on Mount Sinai.

—IBN EZRA

[2]The purpose of this census was to determine the number of men
twenty years of age who were to be recruited for the forthcoming battle
for the Promised Land.

—RASHBAM

[3]Descent from the father and not the mother determined the
child's relationship.

—RASHI

Moses was to be assisted in conducting this count by his brother Aaron, as well as the prince of each of the Twelve Tribes. The sum revealed that the total number able to serve in the army was six hundred and three thousand and five hundred and fifty men.

The only group exempt from military service was the tribe of Levi.

And the Lord spoke unto Moses, saying: 'Howbeit the tribe of Levi thou shalt not number,[4] neither shalt thou take the sum of them among the children of Israel;[5] but appoint thou the Levites over the tabernacle of the testimony, and over all the furnishings thereof, and over all that belongeth to it; they shall bear the tabernacle, and all the furnishings thereof; and they shall minister unto it, and shall encamp round about the tabernacle.'

The tribe of Levi was delegated to serve in the Tabernacle, and all others were forbidden to engage in these tasks.

The order in which the various tribes were to march through the wilderness is also described in the Torah. Each tribe had its own flag[6] with its specific ensign.[7] Under these banners,

---

[4]The Levites were exempt from military service—they were therefore numbered separately for the purpose of taking up service at the Sanctuary.

—NACHMANIDES

[5]As the servants of God, the Levites were worthy of being numbered separately from the rest of the Jewish People.

—RASHI

[6]The color of each of the four standards was the same as the corresponding stone for each of the four tribes in the breast-plate of the High Priest.

—RASHI

Ibn Ezra notes that the standard of Reuben had the figure of a man, the standard of Judah that of a lion, the standard of Ephraim that of an ox, and the standard of Dan the figure of an eagle.

[7]The tribe under one specific standard would not take its place

the tribes were divided into four groups. On the east marched the tribes of Judah, Issachar and Zebulun. This unit of three tribes always led the rest of the camp.

The southern flank was composed of the tribes of Reuben, Simeon and Gad.

After these two groups had begun the march, the Tent of Meeting was lifted and carried by the Levites in the midst of the moving camp.[8]

On the west were the tribes of Ephraim, Manasseh and Benjamin, and the tribes of Dan, Asher and Naftali marched on the northern side.

God chose to have the Levites minister the sacred functions, originally the role of the first-born.

And the Lord spoke unto Moses, saying: 'And I, behold, I have taken the Levites from among the children of Israel instead of every first-born[9] that openeth the womb among the children of Israel; and the Levites shall be Mine. . . .'

A special census was now taken of the Levites. Every male of this tribe from the age of one month[10] was to be counted, since all the first-born had to be redeemed at this age. There

---

under another standard.

—IBN EZRA.

[8]The Levites were to be stationed round about the Tabernacle to prevent unauthorized Israelites from interfering with the services, because such interference would incur Divine displeasure.

—IBN EZRA

[9]The firstborn, who originally performed holy functions, were removed from their office on account of their worship of the Golden Calf. They were replaced by the Levites who had remained innocent on that occasion.

—SFORNO.

[10]Since every Levite was a substitute for an Israelite firstborn,—whose duty to be redeemed began at the age of one month—the census of the Levites had to cover the same age group.

—RASHBAM.

were twenty-two thousand Levites in this count, exclusive of the first-born Levites who were not included in the tally.

The redemption of the first-born (*Pid-yon Haben*) is still practiced today. It is performed on the thirty-first weekday after the birth of a male child, if neither of his parents is a member of the priestly *Kohain* or Levite families. The *Kohain* redeems the infant through an exchange of five units of coinage based on the *shekel*,[11] an ancient Israeli coin.

The Levites were divided into four groups. Each of these units marched on a different side of the Tabernacle. Their tasks were determined through another census of those Levites between the ages of thirty and fifty years.[12] This was the age span during which the Levites were expected to carry out their active duties.

One task, however, could be done only by Aaron and his sons: taking apart the objects of the Sanctuary prior to a new march. No other Levites were permitted to perform this sacred duty.

---

[11]The ransom of the firstborn was to atone for the crime against Joseph who was the firstborn of his mother. Hence the sum of *five shekels* was appointed, equal to the twenty pieces of silver for which Joseph was sold. (Genesis xxxvii 28)

—RASHI.

[12]The age group between thirty and fifty was adopted since this is the age when physical strength is at its height, and the service of the Levites consisted mainly in the work of carrying the parts of the Tabernacle and its equipment.

—IBN EZRA.

Haftorah Bemidbar

HOSEA II, 1–22

The Sidrah records the sum of Jews who traveled in the Wilderness on their journey to the Promised Land. At the outset of the Haftorah, Hosea takes up this theme by stating that "The Children of Israel shall be as the sand of the sea, which cannot be measured nor numbered . . ."

The Prophet denounces Israel for its unfaithfulness to God and warns of the punishment which would result from such a course. But since God's love for Israel is unending, God will always take His people back as His own.

Since Hosea had an unfaithful wife, Gomer, whom he deeply loved, he cites his relationship with her as a parallel to God's anger. He will ultimately pardon the Jewish People.

In the end, the intimate relationship which exists between God and the Jewish People will be restored.

And I will betroth thee unto Me for ever;
Yea, I will betroth thee unto Me in righteousness, and in
  justice,
And in lovingkindness, and in compassion.
And I will betroth thee unto Me in faithfulness;
And thou shalt know the Lord.

נשֹׂא

Naso

*A*FTER THE SANCTUARY had been completed, Moses was assigned to organize the tribes to march through the Wilderness
in an orderly fashion and to instruct the Levites in the proper
care of all the articles used in divine worship. The Levites
camped and marched around the Tent of Meeting in the middle
of the camp, with the other tribes around this inner circle.

The religious duties of the Levites continue to be enumerated. Each Levitical family was assigned to carry and care for
specific parts of the Sanctuary. The men called upon to perform
these physical tasks were between thirty and fifty years of age.

Once more, Moses was commanded to remove all the people from the camp who were spiritually unclean or suffered from
contagious disease:

> *And the Lord spoke unto Moses, saying: 'Command the
> children of Israel, that they put out*[1] *of the camp*[2] *every
> leper, and every one that hath an issue, and whosoever is
> unclean by the dead; both male and female shall ye put out,
> without the camp shall ye put them; that they defile not*

---

[1]The setting up of the Tabernacle and the fixing of the holy
boundaries necessitated the removal of ritually unclean persons from
the enclosure.

—NACHMANIDES.

[2]There were three camps: the Tabernacle area within the hang-
ings of the surrounding court constituted the 'camp of the Shechina';
the encampment of the Levites round about this area was the 'camp
of the Levites'; and extending from there to the limits of the Israelite
division on all four sides was the 'camp of the Israelites'.

—RASHI.

their camp, in the midst whereof I dwell.' And the children of Israel did so, and put them without the camp; as the Lord spoke unto Moses, so did the children of Israel.

In this manner, the traveling Israelites remained spiritually and physically pure and healthy. As soon as those who were quarantined had returned to their normal condition, they rejoined the camp.[3]

Religious and civil courts functioned, and all wrongs committed against God or man had to be properly atoned for.

And the Lord spoke unto Moses, saying: Speak unto the children of Israel: When a man or woman shall commit any sin that men commit, to commit a tresspass[4] against the Lord, and that soul be guilty; then they shall confess their sin which they have done; and he shall make restitution for his guilt in full, and add unto it the fifth part thereof and give it unto him in respect of whom he hath been guilty.

If neither the thief nor the victim or his kinsman survived, the property reverted to the priest. If the theft was from holy objects, the value of the object, plus a fifth had to be returned to the Sanctuary.

If a man accused his wife of infidelity and there was no

---

[3]All three classes of unclean persons specified here had this in common: the duration of their uncleanliness was seven days, and their defilement could be passed on to others.

—IBN EZRA.

[4]This law concerning robbery by violence and swearing falsely is repeated here (it appears earlier in Leviticus v. 25) to add two new points: a person was only liable to pay the added fifth part and to bring a guilt-offering if he confessed his guilt; and if the claimant was a proselyte who had died, the restitution was to be handed over to the priests.

—RASHBAM.

proof,[5] the Torah makes provision for testing her guilt or innocence.

First, she was brought to the priest who offered a sacrifice. Then, the wife was requested to drink a potion[6] specially prepared for this purpose. Prior to drinking it, she had to indicate that she understood exactly what was taking place by answering *amen* to an oath which was administered describing the event. This oath was read by the priest from a scroll and clearly outlined the dire physical effects she would suffer if she were indeed guilty. If she was innocent, there would be no adverse effects. This procedure was done away with after the destruction of the second Holy Temple. From that time, if a husband suspected his wife of unfaithfulness and was jealous, provisions were made for divorce.

A person could, if he or she so wished, take on obligations not imposed by the Torah through the vow of a Nazirite,[7] consecrating himself to the service of God in a more disciplined way than the general community. He pledged himself to abstain from all wine[8] and other intoxicating beverages; not to cut his hair;[9] nor to approach a dead body,[10] even if it were of his

---

[5]As regards adultery; but there must be witnesses who saw her with a man in suspicious circumstances.

—RASHI.

[6]Water that became holy through being in the laver used by the priests.

—RASHBAM.

[7]The word *nazir* means 'keeping away from something'. In this instance he abstains from wine and other pleasures.

—IBN EZRA.

[8]Rashi, quoting Onkelos, renders: 'from new wine and old wine'. He must not, however, indulge in excessive fasting or practice flagellation.

—SFORNO.

[9]The prohibition of cutting his hair divert his thoughts from his physical beauty, and keeps him from indulging in vanity.

—SFORNO.

[10]As in the case with the High Priest, the Nazirite must not defile

closest kin. Such a vow could be binding for a minimum of thirty days or for longer periods. Some were even designated to be Nazirites for their entire lives. When his term was completed, the Nazirite had to bring a number of sacrifices, after which these added restrictions were no longer binding.

Blessings have a great significance in the Torah. God blessed His creations; the fathers of the Jewish People blessed their children; and now the priests are commanded to convey[11] the blessings of God to the people. The text of this blessing is simple and beautiful.

> *The Lord bless thee,[12] and keep thee;[13]*
> *The Lord make His face to shine upon thee,*
> *and be gracious unto thee;*
> *The Lord lift up His countenance upon thee*
> *and give thee peace.[14]*

When the Holy Temple stood, this blessing was delivered by the priests twice daily from a platform called the *duchan*. It is still recited daily in the Holy Land during public morning prayers. In countries outside of Israel, the priests deliver this blessing at various times according to the specific custom of each community.

---

his state of holiness by coming in contact with a corpse.

—SFORNO.

[11]By blessing them in God's name, as worded in the following verses, and not by expressing their own good wishes.

—RASHBAM.

[12]With long life and wealth.

—RASHI.

[13]That is: May He guard thee from robbery of your possessions.

—RASHI.

[14]By guarding you against accidents and the designs of your enemies.

—IBN EZRA.

Sforno understands it as the everlasting peace of the Hereafter.

The Torah reading concludes with the offering of gifts by the princes of each of the Twelve Tribes on the occasion of the dedication of the altar.[15] One gift was brought each day for a total of twelve days. These gifts were accompanied by a daily sacrifice, offered by the prince who made the presentation each day. Six covered wagons, representing one wagon for each two princes, were donated. Each prince further gave one ox, making a total gift of a dozen oxen. The articles of the disassembled Sanctuary were placed in these wagons when the camp moved. The holiest objects, however, were carried on the shoulders of the sons of Kohath, supported by poles which were inserted through rings. Besides these gifts, the princes also donated gold and silver vessels which were used for incense and meal offerings.

Haftorah Naso

JUDGES XII, 2–25

The laws of Nazirite vows are outlined in the Sidrah. One who takes such an oath may not eat grapes or any of its products, such as wine. He is also forbidden to cut his hair during the period that he is a Nazirite.

The Haftorah relates the mystical events leading to the birth of Samson, one of the Judges, who was consecrated as a Nazirite by his parents even before his birth.

An angel appeared to Samson's mother, informing her that she was to bear a son. She was told that the child would grow to be a savior of the Jewish People, rescuing them from their Philistine oppressors.

---

[15]The first of Nisan.

—RASHI.

The section dealing with the priestly blessing is immediately followed by that of the consecration of the altar, because both events took place on the same day in the order here recorded.

—IBN EZRA.

When she related these events to her husband, Manoah, he prayed to God, pleading for a second appearance of the angel. Once more, the angel came and charged the parents with the responsibility of making their son a Nazirite.

Manoah offered a sacrifice to God in thanksgiving. The prayers of the parents were answered when Samson was born. He became a mighty warrior, battling the Philistines who were oppressing the Jewish People.

בְּהַעֲלֹתְךָ

Beha-A-Lotcha

CHAPTERS VIII–XII

*T*HE ORIGINAL DIVINE commandment concerning the lighting of
the candelabra, known as the *menorah* was spoken to Aaron.

> *And the Lord spoke unto Moses, saying: 'Speak unto
> Aaron,[1] and say into him: When thou lightest the lamps,
> the seven lamps shall give light in front of the candlestick.'
> And Aaron did so:[2] he lighted the lamps thereof so as to
> give light in front of the candlestick, as the Lord com-
> manded Moses. And this was the work of the candlestick,
> beaten work of gold;[3] unto the base thereof, and unto the
> flowers thereof, it was beaten work; according unto the
> pattern which the Lord had shown Moses, so he made the
> candlestick.[4]*

---

[1]Since Aaron was charged with the task of attending to the sacred
lamp, it was appropriate that he should receive the instruction concerning it.

—IBN EZRA.

[2]Although Aaron and his sons were called up to attend to the
candelabrum, Aaron in his zeal always performed this important function himself.

—NACHMANIDES.

[3]The entire candlestick with all its projecting parts was beaten and
fashioned from one solid block of gold. It was not to be made of
separate parts and welded together.

—RASHI.

[4]The subject *he* refers to the one who made all the other articles,
viz. Bezalel.

—RASHI.

Ibn Ezra takes it to allude to Moses.

This *menorah* of the Holy Temple has remained as one of the most important religious symbols of the Jewish people. It is symbolized in every Jewish house of worship by the Eternal Light suspended over the Holy Ark.

The dedication of the Levites to their service of God now takes place. The Levites were entrusted with this sacred work replacing the first-born, who were originally assigned this task, because they took part in the worship of the Golden Calf. Only the tribe of Levi, unlike the first-born, refused to participate in this rebellion against God.

Thus did Moses, and Aaron, and all the congregation of the children of Israel, unto the Levites; according unto all that the Lord commanded Moses touching the Levites, so did the children of Israel unto them.[5] And the Levites purified themselves, and they washed their clothes; and Aaron offered them for a sacred gift before the Lord; and Aaron made atonement for them to cleanse them. And after that went the Levites in to do their service in the Tent of Meeting before Aaron, and before his sons; as the Lord had commanded Moses concerning the Levites, so did they unto them.

The major tasks of the Levites were the care and carrying of the Tabernacle with its contents, and the chanting of the hymns.

And the Lord spoke unto Moses, saying: 'This is that which pertaineth unto the Levites:[6] from twenty and five

---

[5]They were eager to carry out the Diviner instructions concerning the Levites.

—SFORNO.

[6]What follows is a new ordinance concerning the Levites. The census of Levites between the ages of 30 and 50, described above, was taken for the purpose of recruiting all those Levites who were fit to carry the parts of the Tabernacle. The age-group of 25 mentioned here

*years old and upward they shall go in to perform the service
in the work of the Tent of Meeting; and from the age of
fifty years they shall return from the service of work and
shall serve no more;[7] but shall minister with their brethren
in the Tent of Meeting, to keep the charge, but they shall
do no manner of service. Thus shalt thou do unto the
Levites touching their charges.*

After the Levites had cleansed themselves, they were presented at the Tent of Meeting. The other Israelites placed their
hands on the heads of the Levites to show that they consented
to their being raised to this high office. Amid the offering of
sacrifices, the ceremony was concluded.

As long as the Holy Temple stood in Jerusalem, the Jewish
People were commanded to sacrifice a lamb on the eve of the
fourteenth day of the month of *Nisan.* They were to eat this
offering roasted, together with unleavened bread and bitter
herbs.

When this procedure was celebrated for the first time after
the Exodus, a number of men who were spiritually impure and
could not enter the Sanctuary, asked Moses how they could offer
the Paschal Lamb. After inquiring of God, Moses fixed the "Second Passover" on the eve of the fourteenth day of *Iyar,* exactly
one month after *Nisan.* All those who were spiritually unclean
or far away on a journey and could not offer the Passover sacrifice at the fixed time, could now bring this offering one month
later. Naturally, those who were able to, had to sacrifice the lamb
at the appointed time.

The Torah now tells us that the movement of the camp
through the desert was determined by a cloud which rested over
the Tabernacle in the day, and a fiery cloud by night. Whenever

---

was charged with the duty of guarding the Tabernacle and its contents.
—RASHBAM.

[7] At the age of 50 they retired from the duty of carrying loads
during the transport, but could still serve as gate-keeper and assistant.
—RASHI.

the cloud rose, the people moved after it.[8] When it stood still, the Jews encamped in that place.[9]

> *Whether it were two days, or a month, or a year, that the cloud tarried upon the tabernacle, abiding thereon, the children of Israel remained encamped, and journeyed not; but when it was taken up, they journeyed. At the command-ment of the Lord they journeyed; they kept the charge of the Lord, at the commandment of the Lord by the hand of Moses.*

In order to alert and assemble the people, Moses was com-manded to make two trumpets of silver. These instruments were also used to summon the princes before resuming the journey, and to sound the alarm of war. They were likewise used during the holidays when the sons of Aaron sounded them at the time of the sacrifices.

Ten months and nineteen days after the People had camped at Mount Sinai, the cloud over the Tabernacle rose and the march toward the Promised Land was resumed. Moses asked his father-in-law, Jethro, to accompany them and be their guide in the desert which was familiar to him.

Whenever the Ark was lifted or again placed to rest, Moses offered a prayer to God which is still recited in the syna-gogue when the Torah is removed from the Holy Ark and re-placed.

> *And it came to pass, when the ark set forward, that Moses said: 'Rise up, O Lord, and let Thine enemies be scattered: and let them that hate Thee flee before Thee.'*

---

[8]Though they were quite happy there, they left as soon as the cloud moved on.

—SFORNO.

[9]In their trust in God, Israel halted wherever the cloud stopped, even if the place was most desolate and infested with wild beasts.

—SFORNO.

And when it rested, he said: 'Return, O Lord, unto the ten thousands of the families of Israel.'

And the people were as murmurers,[10] *speaking evil in the ears of the Lord; and when the Lord heard it, His anger was kindled; and the fire of the Lord burnt among them, and devoured in the uttermost part of the camp. And the people cried unto Moses; and Moses prayed unto the Lord, and the fire abated. And the name of that place was called "Taberah" ("Burning"), because the fire of the Lord burnt among them.*

Again, the people began to complain and bemoan the fact that they no longer had the food which they had eaten in Egypt, but only the mannah which came down from heaven. Moses, in despair, told God that he could not possibly lead the people by himself because of their constant complaints and grumblings.

In answer to Moses' appeal, God asked him to assemble seventy elders[11] at the Tent of Meeting. These seventy men[12] were to become leaders to assist Moses in his work. Moses was not jealous of these people: when told that Eldad and Medad were prophesying, he said,

---

[10]When they left the Sinai region which was adjacent to inhabited land and penetrated deeper into the *great and dreadful wilderness* (Deuteronomy i-19) they became restless and began complaining. The wilderness appeared to them as a death-trap.

—NACHMANIDES.

[11]With the transmission of Moses' prophetic powers to the seventy elders, Moses' own powers did not diminish, even as a candle may kindle other candles without losing its own power of illumination.

—IBN EZRA.

[12]The Rabbis explain that, in order to avoid jealousy, Moses registered six elders from each of the twelve tribes, a total of 72 men, and by means of a ballot chose the prescribed number of 70, thus excluding two candidates.

—RASHI.

"Would that all the people be prophets of God."

When the people continued to lust after other food, hoards of quail came flying into the camp. The people ate these birds with no restraint. Soon, a plague broke out among them and many perished in that place which was named *Kibroth-Hataavah* ("The Graves of Lust") to commemorate the unhappy results of their lust.

Another great and personal tragedy came into Moses' life when his own sister and brother , Miriam[13] and Aaron, rebelled against him. They complained about the Ethiopian woman[14] their brother had married. Using this as a pretext to find fault with him, they said that Moses was not the only prophet, but that they, too, communicated with God. Moses did nothing to defend himself against them. Soon, God called all three to the Tent of Meeting. Aaron and Miriam were called forward.[15]

And He said: Hear now My words: if there by a prophet among you, I the Lord do make Myself known unto him in a vision, I do speak with him in a dream. My servant Moses is not so; he is trusted in all My house;[16] with him

---

[13]Miriam is mentioned first because she was the major offender.

—IBN EZRA.

[14]A woman of Ethiopian origin. Their complaint was that he had married an Ethiopian woman. Legend tells that Moses married the queen of Ethiopia and reigned over the country for forty years.

—RASHBAM.

Ibn Ezra identifies the Cushite woman with Zipporah who was a native of Midian. The Midianites, who were tent-dwellers and dark-skinned, were also known as *Kushim.*

[15]Moses was excluded at this stage because God praised him to them. A man's total praise may be spoken only in his absence.

—NACHMANIDES.

[16]He is like a member of the household who enters the house at all times without specific authorization.

—IBN EZRA.

do I speak mouth to mouth,[17] *even manifestly, and not in dark speeches; and the similitude of the Lord doth he behold; wherefore then were ye not afraid to speak again My servant, against Moses?*

The cloud of God then departed and Miriam, who had instigated the attack, saw that she had turned into a leper. Aaron pleaded with Moses to pray for their sister, admitting how wrong they had been. Moses immediately prayed and Miriam was healed. However, she had to remain isolated, like other cured lepers, for a period of seven days.

And the Lord said unto Moses: 'If her father had but spit in her face, should she not hide in shame seven days? Let her be shut up without the camp seven days, and after that she shall be brought in again.' And Miriam was shut up without the camp seven days; and the people journeyed not till Miriam was brought in again.[18] *And afterward the people journeyed from Hazeroth, and pitched in the wilderness of Paran.*

Haftorah Beha-A-Lotcha

ZECHARIAH II, 14–IV, 7

The opening commandment of the Sidrah concerns the *Menorah*, the Candelabrum which was an essential part of the Sanctuary and Temple service.

---

[17]Without an intermediary.

—IBN EZRA.

[18]This honor was shown to Miriam as a reward for her waiting at the time when Moses was thrown into the Nile. (Exodus ii-4).

—RASHI.

Zechariah had a vision of the Golden *Menorah* which would be placed in the second Holy Temple. He was one of the exiles who returned from Babylonia in 537 B.C.E. to rebuild the Land of Israel.

Many setbacks had discouraged the returned exiles from rebuilding the Holy Temple. They were faced with so many handicaps that the work of reconstruction had stopped for many years.

Zachariah and the prophet Haggai revived the flagging hopes and spirits of the People and provided the impetus for the work of rebuilding the Holy Temple to resume.

The Prophet taught that regardless of the strength of the enemy, the Will of God shall remain supreme.

"Not by might nor by power, but by My spirit, saith the Lord of Hosts."

שְׁלַח

Shelach Lecha

*M*OSES HAD FACED many challenges as leader of the Jewish People. Whenever the people did not have enough food or water, they murmured against God and Moses. Only a few chapters ago the Torah related how Moses' own brother and sister had spoken against him.

The lack of faith by the Jews now reaches a disaster point. So serious was the breach of trust in God that it kept the entire generation from entering the Promised Land.

The People were encamped in Kadesh, which was south of and quite close to the land of Canaan. The time had come for the conquest of the Land. Prior to the battle, however, Moses sent twelve men, one from each of the Twelve Tribes of Israel, to secretly search out the Land.

> *And the Lord spoke unto Moses, saying: 'Send thou men,*[1] *that they may spy out the land of Canaan, which I give unto the children of Israel; of every tribe of their fathers shall we send a man, every one a prince among them.'*

Moses assumed that these spies would be courageous and bring back a report which would give the people confidence and strength. They were told to report on the type of people living in Canaan; the strength of the cities; and the type of crops the land produced.

When the spies returned to Kadesh, after a forty day search of the Land, the report of ten of them was so negative that great calamities followed.

---

[1] It is evident from Deuteronomy i 21ff. that the people first asked for the sending of spies. This is not God's command but a concession to their clamor.

—IBN EZRA.

*And they returned from spying out the land at the end of forty
days. And they went and came to Moses, and to Aaron, and to
all the congregation of the children of Israel, unto the wilderness of Paran, to Kadesh; and brought back word unto them,
and unto all the congregation, and showed them the fruit of
the land. And they told him, and said: 'We came unto the land
whither thou sentest us, and surely it floweth with milk and
honey; and this is the fruit of it. Howbeit[2] the people that
dwell in the land are fierce, and the cities are fortified, and
very great. . . . We are not able to go up against the people; for
they are stronger than we.' And they spread an evil report[3] of
the land which they had spied out unto the children of Israel,[4]
saying: 'The land through which we have passed to spy it out,
is a land that eateth up the inhabitants thereof; and all the
people that we saw in it are men of great stature[5] . . . and we
were in our own sight as grasshoppers, and so we were in their
sight.'*

---

[2]The Hebrew term *ephes* denotes human impossibility. This one
word revealed their unpardonable offence. Had they simply said that the
people of the country were mighty and the cities fortified, they would
merely have stated a fact and thus discharged their duty. But in that one
word *ephes,* and in describing the might of the people guarding the fron-
tiers, they gave their own verdict that it was beyond Israel's power to conquer the land.

—NACHMANIDES.

[3]The Hebrew verb signifies more than 'spread'; it means 'they in-
vented a lie' concerning the Land. Seeing that the reassurance of Caleb
had made some impression on the bewildered people, they resorted to
lying, whereby they succeeded in bringing terror and despair into the
hearts of the whole community.

—NACHMANIDES.

[4]They then left Moses and Aaron and went round the tents to spread
their lies among the people.

—NACHMANIDES.

[5]The climate of the Land, they said, was so bad, and the produce of
its soil so coarse, that the country was a graveyard for ordinary people—
only giants with a very strong constitution could live there.

—SFORNO.

Only two among the twelve firmly disagreed with this report: Caleb of the tribe of Judah, and Joshuah of the tribe of Ephraim. Both these men declared their complete confidence in the Divine promises the Jews had received from the time of Abraham to inherit the land of Canaan. They felt that the attack should begin at once.[6] The other ten, however, persisted in their predictions of defeat.

The reaction of the people was complete panic, with a call to open revolt against God and Moses. They questioned God's motives in taking them out of Egypt: instead of making them a great nation, He would have them perish in the desert; their wives and children would now be a prey to their enemies; death in Egyptian slavery would have been better than falling into the hands of the Canaanites. So bitter were their protests that they prepared to appoint a leader to bring them back to Egypt. As Moses and the others vainly tried to calm their fears,[7] as well as renew their courage and faith, the vast majority of the people threatened to stone them.

It was at this moment that the Divine Presence appeared at the Tent of Meeting.[8]

And the Lord said unto Moses: 'How long will this people despise Me? And how long will they not believe in Me, for all the signs which I have wrought among them? I will smite them with the pestilence, and destroy them, and will make of thee a nation[9] greater and mightier than they.'

---

[6]True, they said, the natives of the Land are strong and their cities well fortified, but we are stronger than they.

—NACHMANIDES.

[7]They prostrated themselves before the whole assembly, imploring them to abandon their fatal plan of returning to Egypt.

—NACHMANIDES.

[8]In a pillar of cloud.

—RASHI.

[9]In order to fulfill the oath which God made with the Patriarchs that He would give the land to their descendants.

—RASHI.

Moses did not want this honor. He fervently prayed for the people and claimed that if they died in the desert, the nations of the world would interpret this as a sign that God was not capable of leading His People into the Promised Land. He pleaded with God to once more forgive the people. God granted his plea, but not without certain consequences.

And the Lord said: 'I have pardoned according to thy word.[10] *But in very deed, as I live—and all the earth shall be filled with the glory of the Lord*[11]*—surely all those men that have seen My glory, and My signs, which I wrought in Egypt and in the wilderness, yet have put Me to prove these ten times,*[12] *and have not hearkened to My voice; surely they shall not see the land which I swore unto their fathers, neither shall any of them that despised*[13] *Me see it. But My servant Caleb,*[14] *be-*

---

[10]I have answered your prayer not to destroy them outright. They will, however, perish in the wilderness in the course of forty years. Only their children will enter the Land.

—RASHBAM.

[11]It will be through their children inheriting Canaan that the glory of the Lord will be manifested.

—IBN EZRA.

[12]i.e. many times.

—RASHBAM.

Rashi, quoting the Talmud (Arakhin 15a) takes the number *ten* literally.

[13]This indicates their children under twenty years of age, who, though not included in the decree of retribution, will nevertheless perish in the wilderness if they, like their fathers, despise God. This actually happened in the conspiracy of Korah and because of other sins.

—SFORNO.

[14]No mention is made here of the part played by Joshuah in the expedition. The reason for this is as follows: As a reward for his trust in God, Caleb is promised that he would survive and enter the Land. Joshua's reward was even greater. He was to enter the Land as successor to Moses at the head of the people. This could not very well be revealed at a time when Moses was still at the height of his activities.

—NACHMANIDES.

*cause he had another spirit with him and hath followed Me
fully, him will I bring into the land whereinto he went; and his
seed shall possess it.'*

The ten spies who had caused such despair in the camp died of
a plague, and all those over the age of twenty were destined to die
in the wilderness. Only the young people, the new generation that
did not experience Egyptian slavery and were ready to heed the
word of God, would enter the land of Canaan under the leadership
of Joshua. The people, for their own protection, were now to turn
south, away from the threatening Canaanites and Amalekites, toward the Red Sea.

When Moses reported to the people what God had said, they
mourned and repented their actions. Impulsively, they determined to go into battle on their own initiative. Moses begged them
not to attempt this folly, warning them that neither he nor the Ark
would accompany them into battle.

*And Moses said: 'Wherefore now do ye transgress the com-
mandment of the Lord, seeing it shall not prosper?*[15] *Go not
up, for the Lord is not among you; that ye be not smitten down
before your enemies. For there the Amalekite and the Canaanite are before you, and ye shall fall by the sword; foras-
much as ye turned back from following the Lord, and the Lord
will not be with you.' But they presumed to go up to the top of
the mountain; nevertheless the ark of the covenant of the
Lord, and Moses, departed not out of the camp. Then the
Amalekite and the Canaanite, who dwelt in that hill-country,
came down and smote them and beat them down, even unto
Hormah.*

As if to underline the certainty that the next generation would
enter the land of Israel, the Torah here discusses the various sacrifices which would be offered by the Jews when they shall inhabit
Canaan.

Another law which took effect when the People entered the

---

[15]The violation of the law of God bears the seed of failure.

—IBN EZRA.

Land was that of *challah*. This commandment stipulated that the first part of a dough must be set aside for the priest prior to baking. In order for this law not to fall into disuse, the Rabbis ordained its observance even in lands outside of Israel. Since the priests do not officiate in the Holy Temple today, a small part of the dough is removed and burned.

At this point, the Torah relates the unfortunate execution of a man who publicly and willfully violated the Sabbath by gathering sticks on that day. This incident emphasizes the importance of the observance of the Sabbath.

Finally, the Torah presents the central commandment of the wearing of "fringes", known in Hebrew as *tsitsis*.

> *And the Lord spoke unto Moses, saying: 'Speak unto the children of Israel, and bid them that they make them throughout their generations fringes in the corners of their garments, and that they put with the fringe of each corner a thread of blue.* [16] *And it shall be unto you for a fringe, that ye may look upon it, and remember all the commandments of the Lord, and do them; and that ye go not about after your own heart and your own eyes, after which ye use to go astray; that ye may remember and do all my commandments, and be holy unto your God. I am the Lord your God, who has brought you out of the land of Egypt, to be your God:* [17] *I am the Lord your God.'*

When the exact source of the substance required for the blue thread became uncertain, only white fringes were used. Since men

---

[16] The blue dye was obtained from the blood of the *chalozon* (a kind of fish or snail).

—RASHI.

Blue, say the Rabbis, suggests the sea; the sea suggests the heavens; and the heavens suggest the Throne of Glory. Hence the fringes are a reminder of one's duties to God.

—IBN EZRA

[17] By redeeming the Jewish People from Egyptian slavery, God placed them under His special providential care. Their continued existence is thus guaranteed.

—SFORNO.

no longer wear four-cornered clothing, these fringes are placed on specially-made four-cornered garments.

Haftorah Shelach Lecha

JOSHUA II, 1–24

The Sidrah describes the saga of the twelve spies sent by Moses to investigate the land of Canaan prior to its capture by the Jewish People. Their report was filled with a lack of faith in God, and their scepticism destroyed the morale of the Nation.

Of the twelve, only Joshua and Caleb rendered a favorable report, filled with hope and faith.

The fears of the spies and the People resulted in long delay in the conquest of Canaan. It was not until the time that Joshua assumed the leadership of the People, that they were ready to enter the land.

The Haftorah tells how Joshua sent two spies into Canaan to search out the conditions of the country and the strength of its inhabitants.

This time, a hopeful opinion was rendered, culminating in the conquest of Canaan by the Jewish People.

> *Then the two men returned, and descended from the mountain, and passed over, and came to Joshua the son of Nun; and they told him all that had befallen them. And they said unto Joshua: 'Truly the Lord hath delivered into our hands all the land; and moreover all the inhabitants of the land do melt away before us.'*

קֹרַח

Korach

*R*EPEATEDLY, THE LEADERSHIP of Moses over the Jewish People in the wilderness was attacked and threatened. He was blamed by the people for every danger that confronted them and for every time they lacked food or water. Sometimes individuals opposed him; at other times the entire camp fought against his guidance, and once even his own brother and sister attempted to rebel against him.

Perhaps at no time was his authority endangered more than by Korah, one of the leading figures of the Hebrew camp.

Now Korah, the son of Izhar, the son of Kohath, the son of Levi,[1] with Dathan and Abiram, the sons of Eliab, and On, the son of Peleth, sons of Reuben, took men;[2] and they rose up in the face of Moses, with certain of the children of Israel, two hundred and fifty men; they were princes of

---

[1]The geneology of Korah stops short of Jacob, because on his death-bed he prayed that his name not be mentioned in connection with Korah's mutiny. His prayer is contained in the words: *Unto their assembly let my glory not be united* (Gen. xlix. 6).

—RASHI.

[2]The object *men* is not specified in the Hebrew text; it is an elliptical phrase often found in Scripture.

—IBN EZRA.

Korah and his associates succeeded in shaking confidence in Moses' leadership and stirring up a revolt, only after certain disastrous events had demoralized the people. These were the carastrophes which took place at Taberah (xi. 3) and Kibroth-hataavah (xi. 34), and the tragedy which befell the whole generation because of the treacherous sin of the spies.

—NACHMANIDES.

the congregation, the elect men of the assembly, men of renown; and they assembled themselves against Moses and against Aaron, and said unto them: 'Ye take too much upon you, seeing all the congregation are holy,[3] every one of them, and the Lord is among them; wherefore then lift ye up yourselves above the assembly of the Lord?'

It is generally agreed that Korah's attack upon Moses stemmed from purely selfish motives. He was angry that there were so many leaders from a single family. It especially angered him that this family was from Judah, his own tribe. The fact that only Aaron and his sons were permitted to offer the sacrifices in the Sanctuary further displeased him. He was unable to recognize the humility of Moses, nor to realize that Moses himself did not seek this leadership; it was imposed upon him by the command of God.

And when Moses heard it, he fell upon his face. And he spoke unto Korah and unto all his company, saying: 'In the morning the Lord will show who are His, and who is holy, and will cause him to come near unto Him: even him whom He may choose will He cause to come near unto Him . . .'

Moses told Korah and his group to appear the following morning, carrying fire censers with which to offer incense. Then, as they stood opposite the regularly appointed leaders and priests, God would decide whose authority was to prevail.

Moses concluded his instructions by rebuking Korah.[4]

---

[3]From the day God revealed Himself and gave the Torah to the people on Mount Sinai every Jew is holy.

—IBN EZRA.

[4]The Levites, being consecrated to the service of God, their participation in the revolt was far more serious than that of Israelites.

—SFORNO.

*And Moses said unto Korah: 'Hear now, ye sons of Levi:
is it but a small thing unto you, that the God of Israel hath
separated you from the congregation of Israel, to bring you
near to Himself, to do the service of the tabernacle of the
Lord, and to stand before the congregation to minister unto
them; and that He hath brought thee near, and all thy
brethren the sons of Levi with thee? and will ye seek the
priesthood also? Therefore thou and all thy company that
are gathered together against the Lord—; and as to Aaron,
what is he that ye murmur against him?*[5]

When Moses called for Dathan and Abiram,[6] two other
leaders of the revolt, to reason with them, they blatantly refused
to come.

—and they said 'We will not come up;[7] *is it a small thing
that thou hast brought us up out of a land flowing with
milk and honey, to kill us in the wilderness, but thou must
needs make thyself also a prince over us?*[8] *Moreover thou
hast not brought us into a land flowing with milk and
honey, nor given us inheritance of fields and vineyards;
wilt thou put out the eyes of these men?*[9] *We will not come
up.*

---

[5]What sin has he committed?

—IBN EZRA.

[6]From this the Rabbis deduced that it is proper to make every
effort to arbitrate a dispute.

—RASHI

[7]We shall not submit our case to you for your decision. Appearing
before a court of law is expressed in Hebrew by the term 'going up'.

—RASHBAM.

[8]Nachmanides renders: 'but thou hast also imposed a dictatorship
upon us'.

[9]Rashbam, Ibn Ezra and Sforno render: 'wilt thou blindfold these
people (so as not to see your fraud)?' We shall therefore not come up.

Moses was now very angry and asked God not to accept their incense offering, because he had never taken anything from any of the People nor done harm to a single one of them.

The next morning Korah and the two hundred and fifty princes appeared with their censers, together with Dathan and Abiram, as well as a large part of the camp which had been influenced by their accusations. When God's Presence was seen at the tent of Meeting, Moses received the commandment to separate himself and Aaron from this rebellious group, for it was to be destroyed. Both Moses and Aaron pleaded with God to direct His punishment only to those directly involved in this treachery. Then, following God's bidding, Moses and the elders told the people that had remained faithful to move away from the tents of Korah, Dathan, Abiram, as well as from all that group and its belongings.

Moses then announced to the camp that if those who attacked his and God's leadership would die a natural death,[10] it would mean that he was not sent by God. Otherwise, it would be a sign that Korah's group had committed a fatal sin which could have destroyed the camp, and, as a result, they would perish.

And it came to pass, as he made an end of speaking all these words, that the ground did cleave asunder that was under them.[11] And the earth opened her mouth, and swallowed them up, and their households, and all the men that apper-

---

[10]The punishment of the rebels was more severe than that of all previous offenders, because the conspiracy was a complete denial of all that God had done for Israel in Egypt and the wilderness.

—NACHMANIDES.

[11]The convulsion of the earth's surface was not a new thing. The novelty in the incident was that the earth opened, swallowed them up, and closed again. In natural earthquakes the ground remains open, the chasms being filled with water.

—NACHMANIDES.

tained unto Korah, and all their goods.[12] *So they, and all
that appertained to them, went down alive into the pit; and
the earth closed upon them, and they perished from among
the assembly. And all Israel that were round about them
fled at the cry of them; for they said: 'Lest the earth swallow
us up.' And fire came forth from the Lord, and devoured
the two hundred and fifty men that offered the incense.*

The brass censers which were employed by the two hundred and fifty men were to be melted down and converted into
a cover for the Ark, to serve as a reminder to the people of the
tragic consequences of rebellion against God.

The next day, many people again murmured against Moses
and Aaron, accusing them of being responsible for the death of
Korah and his camp.[13] When the people looked at the tent of
meeting, they saw that the cloud of God was over it. God asked
Moses and Aaron to move away from the congregation so that
He could destroy the new rebels. But Moses told Aaron to rush
into the congregation with his censer, to make atonement[14] for

---

[12]These, too, were destroyed lest righteous men derive some benefit from them and Korah and his associates gain merit for themselves
thereby.

—SFORNO.

[13]Their complaint was not about the fate of Dathan and Abiram,
the chief instigators of the rebellion, who had visibly died by the hand
of God. But they attributed the death of the two hundred and fifty men
to Moses and Aaron who had made them offer incense. Though the
people now believed that no one but Aaron and his descendants were
chosen for the priesthood, they still accused Moses of favoring his tribe
by appointing them to minister in the Tabernacle and so displacing the
firstborn of all the tribes.

—RASHBAM.

[14]To demonstate to the people that the incense which brings
death—if offered by unauthorized persons—brings life if it is offered
by lawful priests.

—RASHBAM.

this new act of hostility. The plague, which had already broken out among the people, was halted.

In order to clearly demonstrate that Aaron and his descendants were to serve as the priests, God told Moses to command the prince of each tribe to inscribe his name on a rod. These twelve sticks[15] were then placed before the Ark. One rod, with Aaron's name on it, representing the tribe of Levi, was among them. On the next day, the rod of Aaron sprouted with buds and almonds blossomed out of it. Moses showed this to the entire congregation and the authority of Aaron and his descendants was firmly established.

> *And the Lord said unto Moses: 'Put back the rod of Aaron before the testimony, to be kept there, for a token against the rebellious children; that there may be made an end of their murmurings against Me, that they die not.' Thus did Moses: as the Lord commanded him, so did he.*

The final section of the reading reviews the duties of the priests, and the responsibilities of the Levites in the Sanctuary. These tasks were solely theirs and the laity was not to approach anything pertaining to these matters.[16] In this way, they would not risk erring and bring about punishment by God.

Also listed are the taxes, tithes, and gifts which the priests and Levites are to receive from the people. Since the tribe of Levi obtained no land when Canaan was divided among the tribes, these gifts were their sole source of income. Thus they had no concerns with commerce and labor, but could totally devote themselves to the service of God and His Sanctuary.

---

[15]Aaron's rod was one of the twelve. Since Levi had to be included as one of the tribes, Joseph was counted only as one tribe and not separately as were Ephraim and Manasseh.

—NACHMANIDES.

[16]God told Moses to instruct Aaron that he should prevent the Israelites from approaching the Sanctuary.

—IBN EZRA.

Haftorah Korach

I SAMUEL XI, 14–XII, 22

Although Moses was the greatest prophet of the Jewish People, he never sought rank or rulership for himself. He conducted himself as a simple shepherd of his People and laborered only for their well-being.

The Sidrah recounts how Korach, with a large congregation, nevertheless, accused Moses of usurping power, and brazenly challenged his leadership.

The Haftorah tells of a similar event during which the Jewish People preferred a mortal king over the Divine rule of God. The prophet Samuel, like Moses, laborered selflessly for his people. He was very disappointed when they clamored for a monarch so they would be like all the nations around them.

He demanded to know if he had ever dealt dishonestly or selfishly and warns the People of the dire consequences they would face if they left the ways of God to ape those of the heathen nations.

But since the People had already decided to have a monarch rule over them, Saul was chosen as the first King of Israel.

Then said Samuel to the people: 'Come and let us go to Gilgal, and renew the kingdom there.' And all the people went to Gilgal; and there they made Saul king before the Lord in Gilgal; and there they sacrificed sacrifices of peace-offerings before the Lord; and there Saul and all the men of Israel rejoiced greatly.

חֻקַּת

Chukkat

CHAPTERS XIX–XXII, 1

*A*LTHOUGH IT IS not possible to have a precise understanding of the reasons for each of the six hundred and thirteen commandments of the Torah, most of them lend themselves to rational explanation. Some, however, seem to defy any logic or meaning. Tradition tells us that such laws serve as a test for the Jew to submit to the divine commandments even if his understanding cannnot grasp all the reasons. The Torah here describes such a commandment.

Contact with a dead person rendered the individual spiritually impure. Moses and Aaron now receive instructions as to how such a person could again become spiritually clean.

And the Lord spoke unto Moses and unto Aaron, saying: This is the statute of the law[1] which the Lord hath commanded, saying: Speak unto the children of Israel, that they bring thee a red heifer, faultless,[2] wherein is no blemish, and upon which never came yoke. And ye shall give her unto Eleazar the priest, and she shall be brought forth without the camp, and she shall be slain before his face.[3]

---

[1]Satan and the nations of the world ridiculed the paradoxical institution of the red heifer, according to which its ashes purified unclean and defiled the clean. Therefore the Torah employs the term *chukkah*—a statute whose reason is not disclosed—because it wishes to emphasize that this Divine law must be observed even though it is unfathomable.

—RASHI.

[2]Perfectly red; if there were two hairs of any other color, the heifer was disqualified for this purpose.

—RASHI.

[3]Eleazar supervised while a layman slaughtered it; (the slaughter-

Amid various rituals, the heifer was to be entirely burnt and its ashes, when mixed with running water, were to return all those who had contracted spiritual impurity to their former clean state.

Anyone who had touched a dead person, entered a structure which housed a corpse, or even came within close proximity of a grave, was considered unclean for a period of seven days. The waters were to be sprinkled on him on the third and seventh day of his impurity. Structures—and their contents—in which sources of uncleanliness rested were also to be sprinkled by these waters.

All water which was left uncovered overnight was no longer considered fit for use.

Besides the difficulty in explaining how this specially prepared water can bring about spiritual cleanliness, an even greater problem arises when we are told that whoever touches these waters in a state of purity became spiritually unclean. Thus: the priest performing the sacrifice, the one who burned the cow, the gatherer of the ashes and even those who sprinkled the waters, all became spiritually unclean until the following evening.

Tradition tells us that even King Solomon, in all his wisdom, could not understand the mystery of this ritual. Yet, as an act of faith, it was practiced during those periods in which sacrifices were offered.

The Torah now continues to relate the events of the fortieth year of the wanderings of the Jews in the desert on their way to the Promised Land. The camp[4] had reached Kadesh in the wilderness of Zin where Miriam, the sister of Moses, died and was buried.

At this sad time for Moses and Aaron, the people again

---

ing of a sacrifice was not regarded as a priest's function).

—RASHI.

[4]The addition of the phrase 'whole congregation' denotes the new generation which was to enter the Land; all those who were to perish in the wilderness on account of their sin had already died.

—IBN EZRA.

organized themselves in revolt because they had no water.[5]
They argued that it would have been better to die with the
former generation, or to have remained in Egypt where there
was food and water, even though they were slaves there. Moses
and Aaron turned away from the people to the Tent of Meeting,
where they bowed when God appeared to them.

> *And the Lord spoke unto Moses, saying: 'Take the rod, and
> assemble the congregation, thou, and Aaron thy brother,
> and speak ye unto the rock before their eyes, that it give
> forth its water; and thou shalt bring forth to them water
> out of the rock; so thou shalt give the congregation and
> their cattle drink.'*

But even Moses' patience had worn thin.

> *And Moses took the rod from before the Lord, as He
> commanded him. And Moses and Aaron gathered the as-
> sembly together before the rock, and he said unto them:
> 'Hear now, ye rebels; are we to bring you forth water[6] out
> of this rock?' And Moses lifted up his hand, and smote the
> rock with his rod twice; and water came forth abundantly,
> and the congregation drank, and their cattle. And the Lord
> said unto Moses and Aaron: 'Because ye believed not in*

---

[5]The death of Miriam is to be followed by the death of Aaron and
Moses who were not to enter the Promised Land. Hence the record of
the incident which was the cause of their exclusion now follows.

—IBN EZRA.

[6]'Or not' is to be supplemented. Moses put the question to the
rebellious people: Do you believe that God can bring forth water from
the rock, or do you think that it is beyond His power? The latter
appears to be your belief! The sin committed by Moses and Aaron
seems to be the expression used by the former, *are we to bring you forth
water?* which might have given the people the impression that it was
Moses and Aaron who by some device brought forth water from the
rock. He should have said, 'Is the Lord to bring you forth water?'

—NACHMANIDES.

*Me, to sanctify Me in the eyes of the children of Israel,
therefore ye shall not bring this assembly into the land
which I have given them.' These are the waters of Meribah
(Strife), where the children of Israel strove with the Lord,
and He was sanctified in them.*[7]

Because of the negative report of the spies who had previously been sent into Canaan, the people were now afraid to enter this country from the south. Moses sent messengers from Kadesh to the king of Edom, further to the east, seeking his permission to have the camp pass through his country on their way to the Promised Land. Not only did the king refuse this request, but he threatened war if the camp even moved in the direction of Edom. Moses turned the Jews away.[8]

Near the border of Edom, the camp now reached Mount Hor. The time had come for the death of Moses' brother, Aaron.

*And the Lord spoke unto Moses and Aaron in mount Hor,
by the border of the land of Edom, saying: 'Aaron shall be
gathered unto his people; for he shall not enter into the land
which I give unto the children of Israel, because ye rebelled
against My word at the waters of Meribah. Take Aaron*[9]
and Eleazar his son, and bring them up unto mount Hor.

---

[7]In the first incident of the rock (Exodus xvii. 1–7) where the people strove with Moses, only the elders were present when the water flowed from the rock; but on this occasion, which deprived Moses and Aaron of the right to enter the Land, the people *strove with the Lord* and the water gushed forth in the sight of all the people in whom God was to be sanctified.

—NACHMANIDES.

[8]The reason why the Jews did not use force against Edom is that they were forbidden by Divine command to attack them, as stated in Deutoronomy ii.4f.

—NACHMANIDES.

[9]This means, comfort him when he receives the news of his approaching death, by pointing out to him the great privilege of seeing his son succeed in the High Priesthood.

—RASHI.

And strip Aaron of his garments, and put them upon Eleazar his son; and Aaron shall be gathered unto his people, and shall die there'. And Moses did as the Lord commanded;[10] and they went up into mount Hor in the sight of all the congregation. And Moses stripped Aaron of his garments, and put them upon Eleazar his son; and Aaron died there in the top of the mount; and Moses and Eleazar came down from the mount. And when all the congregation saw that Aaron was dead, they wept for Aaron thirty days, even all the house of Israel.[11]

This Torah section concludes with the account of the battles which the Jews waged against the unfriendly and hostile nations whom they approached. One of these wars was against the king of Arad, of the land of Canaan. (This battle took place before the incident of the spies.)

When they left the site of Mount Hor, the people again murmured against God and Moses, as a result of which they were beset with a new plague.

And the people spoke against God, and against Moses: 'Whereof have ye brought us up out of Egypt to die in the wilderness? for there is no bread and there is no water; and our soul loatheth this light bread.' And the Lord sent fiery serpents among the people, and they bit the people; and much people of Israel died. And the people came to Moses, and said 'We have sinned, because we have spoken against the Lord and against thee; pray unto the Lord, that He take away the serpents from us.' And Moses prayed for the

---

[10]Although the Divine command to prepare Aaron for death was distressing to Moses, he carried it out without delay.

—RASHI.

[11]Both men and women, because Aaron had been the peacemaker in their quarrels.

—RASHI.

people.[12] *And the Lord said unto Moses: 'Make thee a fiery serpent, and set it upon a pole; and it shall come to pass, that every one that is bitten, when he seeth it, shall live.*[13] *And Moses made a serpent of brass,*[14] *and set it upon the pole; and it came to pass, that if a serpent had bitten any man, when he looked unto the serpent of brass, he lived.*

The Jews were victorious over two hostile kings: Sihon of the Amorites, and Og of Bashan. Having conquered their lands, they now lived in cities and prepared themselves to enter the Land which God had promised to Abraham, Isaac and Jacob.

Haftorah Chukkat

JUDGES XI, 1–33

Not only did the armies of Israel have to contend with hostile nations when they first entered Canaan, but they continued to be harassed and oppressed by them for many years after having entered the Promised Land.

---

[12]Moses complied with their request. The moral to be derived is that if an offender repents his sin and asks for forgiveness, it should be granted to him.

—RASHI.

[13]The Rabbis (*Rosh Hashanah* 29a) state that it was not the bronze serpent which cured them, but by looking up at it, they were reminded of the supremacy of God and submitted themselves to Him. The consequence was that the venom of the serpents did them no harm.

—RASHI.

[14]Because the sight of a serpent is harmful to persons who had been bitten, they were given the cure of looking at an artificial serpent, to make them realize that it is God Who kills, and it is God who preserves life.

—NACHMANIDES.

The Sidrah recounts the battle against the Amorites, one of the seven nations which originally inhabited Canaan.

In the Haftorah, we read of the efforts by Israel to extricate itself from the Ammonites, probable descendants of the northern part of the Amorite kingdom.

Jephta, a mighty warrior, had been driven away from his home by his brothers because he was the offspring of a questionable marriage. He became the leader of a group of bandits.

When the Ammonites began to battle against Israel, Jephta was approached by the leaders of his tribe, Gilead, with the request that he become their leader during the war.

At first, Jephta was reluctant to accept because he had been treated so badly by his family, He finally consented to be their chief if they would retain him as their leader after they had been victorious. They agreed, and Jephta prepared to battle against the Ammonites.

Prior to the conflict, Jephta made a terrible vow, for which future generations severely condemned him. He swore that if he were victorious, the first person coming out of his house to greet him upon his return from battle would be sacrificed as a burnt-offering. As it turned out, it was his own daughter who became the tragic victim of this vow.

Before going into battle, Jephta attempted to make peace with Ammon, but the king refused his offer. In the ensuing battle, the armies of Israel were victorious and the People again lived in safety.

בלק
Balak

CHAPTERS XXII, 2–XXV, 9

*T*HE CHILDREN OF Israel were now nearing the goal of their long wandering in the desert: the land of Canaan. Balak, one of the kings in the area, determined on a scheme to prevent the Jews from reaching their destination.

> *And Balak the son of Zippor saw all that Israel had done to the Amorites. And Moab was sore afraid of the people, because they were many; and Moab was overcome with dread because of the children of Israel. And Moab said unto the elders of Midian:*[1] *'Now will this multitude lick up all that is round about us, as the ox licketh up the grass of the field.'—And Balak the son of Zippor was king of Moab at that time.*[2]

It was nothing more than needless hatred which prompted Balak to pursue this course of action, since the Jews merely bordered on his land. They did not even request permission to pass through it or disturb the country in any way. Balak was afraid to openly attack the Jewish camp since he knew how badly the other armies who had attempted this were beaten.

Instead, he devised another scheme.

> *And he sent messengers unto Balaam the son of Beor, to Pethor, which is by the River, to the land of the children*

---

[1]Although Moab and Midian were enemies (cf. Gen. xxxvi. 35), they made peace to form a united front against Israel.

— RASHI.

[2]Although Moab's king at that time was Balak who was famous as a mighty warrior, he had yet no heart to fight the Jewish People.

— SFORNO.

of his people, to call him, saying: 'Behold, there is a people come out from Egypt; behold, they cover the the face of the earth, and they abide over against me. Come now therefore, I pray thee, curse me this people; for they are too mighty for me; peradventure I shall prevail, that we may smite them, and that I may drive them out of the land; for I know that he whom thou blessest is blessed, and he whom thou cursest is cursed.'

Through this curse, Balak hoped that his enemies would be weakened and then not be able to resist his intended onslaught. The chain of events which follows is very strange and the commentators on the Torah have many explanations for them.

The delegation of important dignitaries which the king had organized approached Balaam with many costly gifts.[3] The prophet told them to rest for the night in his home, during which time he would meditate about their request and communicate with God.

And God said unto Balaam: 'Thou shalt not go with them; thou shalt not curse the people; for they are blessed.'[4] And Balaam rose up in the morning, and said unto the princes of Balak: 'Get you into your land; for the Lord refuseth to give me leave to go with you.' And the princes of Moab rose up, and they went unto Balak, and said: 'Balaam refuseth to come with us.'

When Balak heard of the prophet's refusal, he sent a second delegation. This one was larger than the first and composed of

---

[3]Ibn Ezra renders: 'with all kinds of divination', that is: the messengers Balak sent to Balaam were sorcerers like him, and took their implements of magic with them.

[4]Israel is blessed by God, therefore Balaam's curse could have no effect.

—IBN EZRA.

even greater dignitaries who were authorized to offer Balaam greater rewards if he would consent to come with them and curse the Jews. Once more, the prophet informed them that without God's permission he could not go with them, regardless of the wealth and honor which he was offered. That night, God told him to accompany them, but only to say what God would directly command him.[5]

We now come to the difficult and strange passages in which the donkey upon which Balaam rode during the journey actually communicated with his master in an understandable manner. For reasons which are not exactly known, an angel of God stood in the donkey's way, ready to kill Balaam. The donkey, sensing the angel's presence, attempted to move away two times by stepping out of the path, thereby arousing the prophet's anger. Finally, when the animal no longer found a way to get by, it lay down and refused to go further. Balaam, now in a rage, struck the donkey, as he did the previous two times.

> And the Lord opened the mouth of the ass,[6] and she said unto Balaam: 'What have I done unto thee, that thou hast smitten me these three times?' And Balaam said unto the ass: 'Because thou hast mocked me; I would there were a sword in my hand, for now I had killed thee.' And the ass said unto Balaam: 'Am I not thine ass, upon which thou hast ridden all they life long[7] unto this day? was I ever wont to do so unto thee?' And he said: 'Nay'. Then the

---

[5]Although God told him at first not to go with them (verse 12), that instruction was given with the express purpose that he should not curse Israel. But now God permitted him to go with them for consultation only as long as he did not curse the people. Balaam, however, did not disclose this to Balak's emissaries.

—NACHMANIDES.

[6]The talking by the ass was real, brought about by the will of God.

—NACHMANIDES.

[7]That is: from the time you have been riding.

—IBN EZRA

Lord opened the eyes of Balaam,[8] and he saw the angel of the Lord standing in the way, with his sword drawn in his hand; and he bowed his head, and fell on his face. And the angel of the Lord said unto him: 'Wherefore hast thou smitten thine ass these three times? behold I am come forth for an adversary, because thy way is contrary unto me;[9] and the ass saw me, and turned aside before me these three times; unless she had turned aside from me, surely now I had even slain thee, and saved her alive.'

When Balaam realized that God was opposed to his mission, he offered to return to his home. The angel, however, told him to continue on his journey, reminding him only to say what God would permit him.

When Balaam reached the land of Moab, he was met by Balak, the king, and again was offered riches and honor. After the group offered sacrifices to their idols, Balaam was taken to a vantage point from where he could see the Jewish camp.[10] The prophet ordered seven altars[11] to be built upon which more sacrifices were offered. The time had now come for the curse and Balaam began to speak.

---

[8]That is was necessary to open his eyes to make him see the angel proves that Balaam was not a prophet but a magician. Only when he was on this mission did God appear to him as a prophet in honor of His people; but when Balaam returned to his native country, he again became a magician.

—NACHMANIDES.

[9]Inasmuch as Balaam was going to Balak with the intention of cursing Israel, though God only allowed him to act as a counsellor (see on verse 20).

—NACHMANIDES.

[10]Balak took Balaam to a high place from which he might see the Jews while uttering the curse, because the sense of seeing excersises great power on the soul of man.

—NACHMANIDES.

[11]The number *seven*, which plays a prominent part in Biblical institutions, is enveloped in deep mystery which only the few can understand.

—IBN EZRA.

And he took up his parable, and said:
From Aram Balak bringeth me,
The king of Moab from the mountains of the East:
'Come, curse me Jacob,
And come, execrate Israel.'
How shall I curse, whom God hath not cursed:[12]
And how shall I execrate, whom the Lord hath not
  execrated?

For from the top of the rocks I see him,
And from the hills I behold him:
Lo, it is a people that shall dwell alone,
And shall not be reckoned among the nations.[13]

Who hath counted the dust of Jacob,[14]
Or numbered the stock of Israel?
Let me die the death of the righteous,[15]
And let mine end be like his!

The king was very disturbed since Balaam not only refused to curse Israel but, in fact, actually had blessed them. He therefore took the prophet to another site and again had seven altars built upon which similar sacrifices were offered to the gods of Moab. Again, as before, the prophet blessed the camp by reciting another beautiful ode.

---

[12]Even when they deserved that God should so punish them.

—RASHI.

[13]The unique status of Israel as Balaam beheld it would be their characteristic feature for all time. They will always remain a separate entity, unlike any other nation and, as such, invincible and imperishable.

—NACHMANIDES.

[14]Although I see them from the top of the mountain as a separate mass of people, I cannot count them, for they are numberless like the dust of the earth.

—NACHMANIDES.

[15]That is: the Jews, who are assured of eternal life after death.

—NACHMANIDES.

Very agitated by this time, Balak requested that Balaam at least not bless Israel, if he could not curse them. Balaam answered, that he could only make those pronouncements which God permitted him.

Desperate now, the king took Balaam to a third and final place; a mountain-top overlooking the camp of Israel. Perhaps Balak had hopes that if the prophet saw the camp from a different direction, he might see something which would move him to pronounce a curse. When the prophet spoke this third time, however, he blessed Israel in an even more eloquent manner.

". . . . How goodly are they tents, O Jacob.
They dwellings, O Israel![16]

As valleys stretched out,
As gardens by the river-side;
As aloes planted of the Lord,
As cedars beside the waters;

Water shall flow from his branches,
And his seed shall be in many waters;
And his king shall be higher than Agag,
And his kingdom shall be exalted.

God who brought him forth out of Egypt
Is for him like the lofty horns of the wild-ox;
He shall eat up the nations that are his adversaries,
And shall break their bones in pieces,
And pierce them through with his arrows.

He couched, he lay down as a lion,
And as a lioness; who shall rouse him up?

---

[16]Balaam admired Israel's tents because they were so arranged as to safeguard privacy and modesty.

—RASHI.

Blessed be every one that blesseth thee,
And cursed be every one that curseth thee.

In great anger, the king told Balaam to flee to his home, since he had placed himself in great personal danger by blessing Israel again and again.

Soon after this event, a tragedy befell the Jews, caused by the Moabite women with whom they had begun to mingle. Many of the Jews started to worship the idols of Moab. A plague broke out and the guilty ones were executed.

As these events were taking place, a Jewish man walked into the camp of Israel with a Midianite woman. It was this type of behavior which was causing all the trouble. In a moment of fury, Aaron's grandson, Phinehas, rushed at these two people and thrust them through with a spear. The plague stopped.

Haftorah Balak

MICAH V, 6–VI, 8

Micah was a prophet who was raised in a simple village. Preaching at the same time as Isaiah (750–690 B.C.E.), he denounced the luxury and selfishness of the cities, and the hypocrisy of the religious leaders.

The Prophet reviews the faithfulness of God to His People. He reminds them of their miraculous departure from Egyptian bondage. Micah's reference to the failure of Balaam (as related in the Sidrah) to curse Israel is another example why Israel should show gratitude to their God.

The offering of empty sacrifices, the Prophet continues, is meaningless. The only relationship that Israel can forge with God must be based on mercy, humility and sincerity.

'. . . *Will the Lord be pleased with thousands of rams,*
With ten thousands of rivers of oil?

Shall I give my first-born for my transgression,
The fruit of my body for the sin of my soul?'

It hath been told thee, O man, what is good,
And what the Lord doth require of thee:
Only to do justly, and to love mercy, and to walk humbly
*   with thy God.*

פִּינְחָס

Pinchas

*T*HE PREVIOUS TORAH reading ended with a tragic and violent episode in which Phinehas, one of the grandsons of Aaron, killed a Jewish man and a Midianite woman as they publicly consorted in the Jewish camp. The Midianites, seeking a way to destroy Israel, were bent on leading them away from the life which God had commanded them to follow. Through idol-worship and immorality, the Midianites sought to do what they could not do in battle.

Phinehas was to be rewarded for his zealous action.

And the Lord spoke unto Moses, saying: "Phinehas, the son of Eleazar, the son of Aaron the priest, hath turned My wrath away from the children of Israel, in that he was very jealous for My sake[1] among them, so that I consumed not the children of Israel in My jealousy. Wherefore say: Behold, I give unto him My convenant of peace; and it shall be unto him, and to his seed after him, the convenant of an everlasting priesthood; because he was jealous for his God, and made atonement for the children of Israel.'

This position of the high priesthood continued in the family of Phinehas on an almost uninterrupted basis until the destruction of the Holy Temple.

---

[1]The description of God as *jealous,* which means He metes out retribution, is used in connection with the cardinal sin of idolatry (Exodus xx. 5). Phinehas, in punishing—at the risk of his own life—a prince in Israel whose offense was both idolatry and immorality, acted on behalf of God and averted a great disaster. Had it not been for Phinehas' prompt action, God would have destroyed the whole nation.

—IBN EZRA.

Because the Midianites had caused such havoc and tragedy in the Hebrew camp, the Jewish people determined, by divine decree, to harass and war against them.

The second census of the people was now about to take place. Again, the count was taken of all men over the age of twenty who were eligible for military service. The main purpose of this census was to prepare for the division of Canaan when the Jews would enter it. The division was to be decided by the casting of lots according to the names of the tribes[2] of their fathers.[3] The only tribe which was not to receive any land by proportionate distribution was Levi, whose function it was to be in the constant service of God.

It was generally assumed that only male sons could inherit land. At the time of the distribution, Moses was approached by the five daughters of a man from the tribe of Manasseh, who had died in the desert. These five daughters of Zelophehad claimed their right of inheritance since there were no sons in the family.

Moses placed the problem before God. The request of these daughters was deemed to be just, not only for themselves, but also for all similar cases in the future.

And Moses brought their case before the Lord. And the Lord spoke unto Moses, saying: 'The daughters of Zelophehad speak right: thou shalt surely give them a possession of an inheritance of their father to pass unto them. And thou shalt speak unto the children of Israel, saying:

---

[2]This refers to the individuals of the families which the Torah has just mentioned, whose number amounted to 601,730. No one who was under twenty years of age at the time of the last census was entitled to a share in the land.

—NACHMANIDES.

[3]Each family should receive an allotment proportionate to the number of its members. Although each tribe was allocated an equal share of land, that share was subdivided among its families, each family receiving a portion according to its numerical strength. For this reason the census in the plains of Moab took family groups into account.

—NACHMANIDES.

If a man die, and have no son, then ye shall cause his inheritance to pass unto his daughter. And if he have no daughter, then ye shall give his inheritance unto his brethren. And if he have no brethren, then ye shall give his inheritance unto his father's brethren. And if his father have no brethren, then ye shall give his inheritance unto his kinsman that is next to him of his family, and he shall possess it. And it shall be unto the children of Israel a statute of judgement,[4] as the Lord commanded Moses.'

Moses was now an old man approaching the end of his life, and it became necessary to choose his succesor. God commanded him to ascend Mount Abarim,[5] overlooking the Promised Land, so that he could see the country toward which he had been leading his people for such a great part of his life. Soon, God told Moses, he woud pass from this life, just as his brother Aaron died on Mount Hor, and that he could not, like the rest of his generation, enter the land of Canaan. Moses himself, thinking of the needs of the people, requested that a succesor be appointed to take his place after his death.

And Moses spoke unto the Lord, saying: 'Let the Lord, the God of the spirits[6] of all flesh, set a man over the congregation[7] who may go out before them, and who may come in

----

[4]The law of inheritance as here prescribed was not a temporary measure in respect to the Promised Land, but was to be observed for all time.

—NACHMANIDES.

[5]This mountain is identical with Mount Nebo (Deuteronomy xxxii. 1). It received the name *Abarim*, 'fords', because it was situated by the fords of the Jordan, opposite the land of Canaan.

—NACHMANIDES.

[6]God, Creator of all spirits, alone knows who is the most suitable to assume the leadership of Israel.

—IBN EZRA.

[7]Having been instructed to give the inheritance of Zelophehad to

before them, and who may lead them out, and who may bring them in; that the congregation of the Lord be not as sheep which have no sheperd.' And the Lord said unto Moses: 'Take thee Joshua the son of Nun, a man in whom is spirit, and lay thy hand upon him;[8] *and set him before Eleazar the priest, and before all the congregation; and give him a charge in their sight.*[9] *And thou shalt put of thy honor upon him, that all the congregation of the children of Israel may hearken. And he shall stand before Eleazar the priest, who shall inquire for him by the judgement of the Urim before the Lord; at his word shall they go out, and at his word shall they come in, both he, and all the children of Israel with him, even all the congregation.' And Moses did as the Lord commanded him; and he took Joshua, and set him before Eleazar the priest, and before all the congregation. And he laid his hands upon him,*[10] *and gave him a charge, as the Lord spoke by the hand of Moses.*

The balance of this Torah reading deals with a description of the various public sacrifices which were offered in the Sanctuary and later, in the Holy Temple in Jerusalem.

---

his daughters, Moses thought that his own sons, too, might inherit leadership. But God told him that none but Joshua would be his successor.

—RASHI.

[8]A symbolic action of transferring his office to Joshua and placing confidence in him.

—IBN EZRA.

[9]Appoint him as your successor publicly to inspire the people with loyalty towards their newly-elected leader.

—SFORNO.

[10]Moses had been commanded to lay his *hand* on Joshua (verse 18), but he went further and laid both his hands on him, thereby conferring a full measure of his own wisdom upon his successor.

—RASHI.

The first sacrifice described is the *tamid,* which is a regular daily offering. Each morning and evening, an unblemished lamb in its first year was offered. The sacrifice of this lamb was accompanied by a meal-offering of flour and oil, together with a drink-offering.[11]

On the seventh day of the week, the Sabbath, a special sacrifice was offered after the *tamid.* Whenever there was a special public sacrifice, such as on Sabbaths and holidays, the regular daily offering always preceded the others.

The beginning of each month is considered a minor festival and therefore a special sacrifice was offered.[12]

The springtime festival of Passover, commemorating the Exodus from Egypt, was celebrated by pilgrimages to Jerusalem where special holiday sacrifices were offered.

The Feast of Weeks is also known as the Festival of the First Fruits. This is the second of the pilgrim festivals, the sacrifices for which are here described.

The Torah next enumerates the offerings of Rosh Hashanah, the New Year. On that day the ram's horn, or *shofar,* [13] must be sounded. Yom Kippur, the Day of Atonement, takes place on the tenth day of the same month and is observed by fasting and other forms of abstinence.

The harvest festival of the Fall season is called the Feast of Tabernacles. Besides reviewing the sacrifices offered on each of

---

[11](Of strong drink). This exludes wine diluted with water.

—NACHMANIDES.

Rashi adopts the Rabbinic definition of newly pressed wine which is not as potent as aged wine.

[12]It was an ancient custom among the Jews to observe the new moon as a semi-festival, because the moon, being a dark substance and having to receive light from another planet, reflects the fate of Israel in this world. Hence the expression *your* in relation to the new moon and not to other festivals.

—SFORNO.

[13]This is a commandment that the ram's horn should especially be sounded on the first of the seventh month in addition to the usual sounding for the burnt-offering of every festival (cf.x.10).

—IBN EZRA.

these seven days, the Torah points out that the eighth day is one of "holy convocation".[14] This entire festival, known in Hebrew as *Succot* is the third of the three pilgrim festivals.

Since the destruction of the Holy Temple in Jerusalem in the year 70 C.E. (of the Common Era) all sacrifices have ceased.

Haftorah Pinchas

I KINGS XVIII, 46–XIX, 21

The fiery zeal of Phineas for God described in the Sidrah is matched by the prophet Elijah in the Haftorah.

In a great confrontation with the pagan priests of Baal (see page 117), Elijah had vindicated Israel's belief in their God.

Now Jezebel, the wicked Phoenician wife of King Ahab threatened to revenge herself by killing Elijah the very next day.

The Prophet, after leaving his disciple in Beersheba fled to the wilderness where an angel of God prepared food and drink for him.

Strengthened by this sustenance, Elijah wandered to Mount Horeb (Sinai) where he was assaulted by wind, earthquake and fire. Then God spoke to him. He was commanded to undertake a number of missions, the last of which was to appoint Elisha as his successor. Elijah did so by placing his mantle on Elisha's shoulders, thereby signifying that the mantle of prophecy was to pass from himself to his disciple.

---

[14]The eighth day was set apart for the exclusive rejoicing of God with Israel, while on the first seven days they offered sacrifices corresponding in number to the seventy nations.

—RASHI.

מטות

Mattot

And Moses spoke unto the heads of the tribes[1] of the children of Israel, saying: 'This is the thing which the Lord hath commanded. When a man voweth a vow unto the Lord,[2] or sweareth an oath to bind his soul with a bond, he shall not break his word; he shall do according to all that proceedeth out of his mouth. . . .

IF A PERSON uttered a voluntary oath, it was essential that he carefully carry out all the conditions of what he swore. He could, for example, promise to donate some of his belongings or perform certain acts to denote an added degree of religious fervor. On the other hand, he could pronounce a vow restraining himself from certain activities which would otherwise be permissable.

This injunction holds true only of a person who is fully responsible for his actions and has complete control over his property. However, should a girl[3] who lives in her father's

---

[1]Probably this legislation was not communicated to the people in general, because it contains the law that the father had the right to declare void certain vows of his daughter, and the husband those of his wife. This knowledge might have caused them to belittle the sanctity of the vows.

—NACHMANIDES.

[2]He specifies the name of God when uttering the vow.

—IBN EZRA.

[3]That is: in the first stage of womanhood, which is between twelve and twelve and a half years of age. Under twelve years she is regarded as a minor and her vow is null and void—except when she is eleven years and one day old and understands the significance of the vow. Above the age of twelve and a half years she is already in full woman-

house[4] and is under his jurisdiction utter an oath, the outcome would depend upon her father's reaction. If he openly agrees with his daughter's words, or merely remains silent, the vow would be binding upon her. If, however, the father protests and refuses to let her carry out her oath on the day that she made it, her vow is not binding. The Torah assures that God will forgive her for her statements since her father annuled her vows.

If a woman made a vow while she was single, and became married[5] while her oaths were still binding upon her, her husband would have the same choice as her father. If, on the day he heard about them, he protested and forbade her to continue to carry them out, she is automatically absolved of all her vows. Should her husband, however, agree to them, or say nothing, all her former vows would continue to be binding.

Any type of vow which was made by women who are either widowed or divorced are fully binding, just as if men had made them, since these women are of adult age and within their own jurisdiction.

The account of one of the most bloody battles fought by the army of the Israel is now related. In general, it is noted by historians how the Jews followed specified humane rules in the unfortunate periods of war and occupation. The battle against the Midianites was an exception in its cruelty and totality.

The Midianites,[6] partly through their prophet, Balaam, and

---

hood and her father no longer has the power of annulling her vows.

—RASHI.

[4]That means, under her father's control, even if she does not live in his house.

—RASHI.

[5]Talmudic teaching explains the words of a woman who is betrothed (betrothal in Talmudic times carried with it almost all the legal consequences of marriage). In that case the father and her betrothed must jointly annul her vow.

—NACHMANIDES.

[6]Although the Moabites were the instigators of the campaign against Israel, no war of retribution was decreed against them, because they had some excuse in that they saw themselves threatened by the

partly because of their women, caused many of the Jews to stray from the path of conduct taught by God and Moses. Many times, these events brought tragedy upon the camp of Israel. Now, the Jews determined, by God's decree, to bring the cause of these disasters to a firm conclusion.

One thousand men of each of the twelve tribes were recruited for the war. This army of twelve thousand soldiers won a complete and total victory over the Midianites, the majority of whom were slain. Only a limited group of the enemy was taken captive, together with a great deal of booty. Everything that was captured was divided between the Sanctuary, the Levites and the soldiers who fought the war.

The Torah relates that none of the Jewish troops were killed in the battle. Balaam,[7] the prophet who was requested to curse the camp of Israel, was one of those on the enemy side who was slain.

Before the Jewish People were ready to cross the Jordan River, prior to their conquest of the land of Canaan, Moses was approached by representatives of the tribes of Reuben and Gad. They requested that they be exempt from crossing the Jordan, since the land on the east bank was ideal for their cattle and they wanted to continue living in that region. They asked for permission to build their cities on the eastern bank of the Jordan River.

At first, Moses was very opposed to this plan.

And Moses said unto the children of Gad[8] and to the

---

approaching Jews. But the Midianites, who had no cause for entering into a quarrel with Israel, deserved punishment.

—RASHI.

[7]Balaam, whose home was in Mesopotamia, went to Midian to claim his reward for the 24,000 who fell in the plague brought about by his counsel (see on xxv. 1).

—RASHI.

[8]Whereas in the preceding verse the children of Reuben are named first in order of tribal seniority, in all the succeeding negotiations the children of Gad are mentioned first. The reason: the children

children of Reuben: 'Shall your brethren go to the war, and shall ye sit here? And wherefore will ye turn away the heart of the children of Israel⁹ from going over into the land which the Lord hath given them? . . .

Moses felt that it was selfish for these tribes to remain behind while the others had to wage war. Also, such an arrangement would be very bad for the morale of the rest of the nation. While the majority of the people would be engaged in battle, these two tribes would be busy building their cities.

The tribes who made this request offered a solution which was acceptable to all.

And they came near unto him, and said: 'We will build sheep folds here for our cattle, and cities for our little ones; but we ourselves will be ready armed to go before the children of Israel,¹⁰ until we have brought them unto their place; and our little ones shall dwell in the fortified cities because of the inhabitants of the land. We will not return unto our houses, until the children of Israel have inherited every man his inheritance. For we will not inherit with them on the other side of the Jordan, and forward, because

---

of Gad conceived the idea of settling on the east side of the Jordan; they were the spokesmen who presented the case to Moses; and because they were mighty warriors superior to the Reubenites, they were not afraid to settle away from the remainder of the people.

—NACHMANIDES.

⁹Moses suspected that the real motive behind their request was fear of taking part in the war against the inhabitants of Canaan. Therefore he warned them that by their action they might strike terror into the hearts of the people as did the spies; the same disaster would be repeated and the whole generation perish in the wilderness.

—RASHI.

¹⁰They offered themselves to form the vanguard in the campaign against Canaan, because the Gadites were mighty warriors.

—RASHI.

our inheritance is fallen to us on this side of the Jordan eastward.'

Moses was in agreement with the plan.

And Moses said unto them: 'If ye will do this thing: if ye will arm yourselves to go before the Lord to the war, and every armed man of you will pass over the Jordan before the Lord, until He hath driven out His enemies from before Him, and the land be subdued before the Lord, and ye return afterward; then ye shall be clear before the Lord, and before Israel, and this land shall be unto you for a possession before the Lord. . . .'

This arrangement was clearly transmitted by Moses to Eleazar and Joshua, as well as to the leaders of the camp. It stated that these tribes will receive the territory they desired only if they conform to the agreement. Moses then gave this land to the tribes of Gad, Reuben and half the tribe of Manasseh. [11]

Haftorah Mattot

I KINGS XVIII, 46–XIX, 21

Jeremiah is the prophet who foretold the destruction of the Southern Kingdom of Judah, and later witnessed its downfall in the year 586 B.C.E. As a result, this Haftorah was chosen as the first of the three "Haftorahs of Rebuke", which precede the fast-day of *Tisha B'Av* (the

---

[11]Originally only the children of Gad and Reuben asked for a possession on the east bank of the Jordan. But when it was found that the land was too extensive for the two tribes, part of it was offered to any other tribe. A portion of the tribe of Manasseh accepted the offer.
—NACHMANIDES.

9th day of *Av*), on which the destruction of both Holy Temples took place.

The Haftorah describes the first appearance of God to Jeremiah to appoint him Prophet over Israel. Through a number of symbols, God demonstrates to Jeremiah that He will fulfil all His promises to Israel. The Prophet is also informed that destruction will strike Jerusalem from its northern neighbors.

God charges Jeremiah to prophesy the downfall of the Jewish State to its inhabitants. Although he will be met with anger and hostility, Jeremiah must fearlessly spread the Word of God.

> *Thou therefore gird up thy loins, and arise, and speak unto them all that I command thee; be not dismayed at them, lest I dismay thee before them. For, behold, I have made thee this day a fortified city, and an iron pillar, and brazen walls, against the whole land, against the kings of Judah, against the princes thereof, against the priests thereof, and against the people of the land. And they shall fight against thee; but they shall not prevail against thee; for I am with thee, saith the Lord, to deliver thee.*

מסעי

Massey

CHAPTERS XXXIII–XXXVI

These are the stages[1] of the children of Israel, by which they went forth out of the land of Egypt by their hosts under the hand of Moses and Aaron. And Moses wrote their goings forth, stage by stage, by the commandment of the Lord. . . .

BY THE DETAILED description of the routes followed by the Jews in their forty year journey from Egypt to the Promised Land, future generations were informed of the details of this fateful period in the life of the Jewish People. Also reviewed are some of the highlights of the long trek through the wilderness. We again read how the former slaves left Egypt as a powerful nation; of the lack of water in the desert; of their encounters with unfriendly nations; and of the death of Aaron on Mount Hor.

The Jews were now encamped at the Jordan near the city

---

[1]A detailed geographical description of the places through which the Jewish People passed when crossing the wilderness was necessary for the sake of future generations. At the time, it was obvious that Israel's existence for forty years in a wilderness which was infested with wild beasts and lacked natural resources was a miracle of God. But in the course of time, people might be led to believe that the places in which Israel dwelt in the wilderness were either near to inhabited regions—such as are now inhabited by Bedouins—or that the places themselves contained food and water sufficient for the maintenance of Israel's population. It was necessary to name all these places for later generations to know they were not inhabited and did not contain natural resources.

—NACHMANIDES, QUOTING MAIMONIDES.

of Jericho. God's voice came to Moses commanding him to arrange for the total separation of the Canaanites from the Jews who were about to enter the land. Because of their pagan ways, it was assumed that the Canaanites would be a source of trouble and grief.

And the Lord spoke unto Moses in the plains of Moab by the Jordan at Jericho, saying: 'Speak unto the children of Israel, and say unto them: When ye pass over the Jordan into the land of Canaan, then ye shall drive out all the inhabitants of the land from before you, and destroy all their figured stones, and destroy all their molten images, and demolish all their high places. And ye shall drive out all the inhabitants of the land, and dwell therein; for unto you have I given the land to possess it. And ye shall inherit the land by lot according to your families—to the more ye shall give the more inheritance, and to the fewer thou shalt give the less inheritance; wheresoever the lot falleth to any man, that shall be his; according to the tribes of your fathers shall ye inherit'.

The Torah then outlines the exact boundaries which were to enclose the Land of Israel.[2] These were natural boundaries: desert, mountain and sea. Historically, the borders were often smaller, except during the reigns of King David and King Solomon. However, throughout history, the Jewish people have never relinquished their rights to the boundaries specified in the Torah.

Joshua, the disciple of Moses, and Eleazar, the son of Aaron, were appointed to supervise the division of the country. With them one prince of each tribe was to represent his respec-

---

[2]Since they were instructed to drive out all the inhabitants of the land (xxxiii. 52), it was necessary to give them a detailed account of its borders.

—IBN EZRA.

tive tribe to see that the land was properly divided. The tribes of Reuben and Gad which settled on the east bank of the Jordan did not send delegates since they were not involved in the distribution of the mainland.

Of the territory which each tribe was to receive, a number of cities had to be given by each one to the Levites,[3] who were to be in constant service to God. They were to be in charge of God's Sanctuary and to be the teachers of the people. As a result, they were to be spread out among all the tribes and had to live near them. They were also going to need fields around these cities for the cattle they would possess. Altogether, forty-eight cities were allotted to the tribe of Levi.

And the Lord spoke unto Moses in the plains of Moab by the Jordan at Jericho, saying: 'Command the children of Israel, that they give unto the Levites of the inheritance of their possession cities to dwell in; and open land round about the cities shall ye give unto the Levites. And the cities shall they have to dwell in; and their open land shall be for their cattle, and for their substance, and for all their beasts. And the open land about the cities, which ye shall give unto the Levites, shall be from the wall of the city and outward a thousand cubits[4] round about. And ye shall measure within the city for the east side two thousand cubits, and for the south side two thousand cubits, and for

---

[3]Although each tribe received an equal share of land, the families of each tribe were assigned portions according to their numerical strength. The number of the cities given to the Levites, however, was not in proportion to the size of the tribe, but related to the value of the particular city.

—NACHMANIDES.

[4]As is evident from the next verse, the Levite city was to be surrounded on each side by an area of two thousand cubits. The inner ring of a thousand cubits, spoken of in this verse, was to be an open space and the outer ring was for cultivation.

—RASHI.

*the west side two thousand cubits, and for the north side
two thousand cubits, the city being in the midst. This shall
be to them the open land about the cities. . . .'*

Six of these cities[5] were also designated to be cities of refuge. They were to serve as a haven for those who killed someone without deliberate intent.

*For the children of Israel, and for the stranger and for the
settler among them, shall these six cities be for refuge,[6] that
everyone that killeth any person through error may flee
thither. . . . then the congregation shall judge between the
smiter and the avenger of blood according to these ordinances; and the congregation shall deliver the manslayer
out of the hand of the avenger of blood, and the congregation shall restore him to his city of refuge, whither he was
fled; and he shall dwell therein until the death of the
high-priest,[7] who was annointed with the holy oil. But if*

---

[5]In addition to these six cities, the forty-two cities assigned to the Levites—thirty-six of which were in the land of Canaan and six beyond the Jordan—also served as places of refuge (cf. Makkoth 10a). That being so, the distribution of the cities of refuge was well balanced. Thirty-nine cities were given for the nine tribes and three-quarters of the tribe of Manasseh in Canaan, and nine for the two tribes and the one-quarter of Manasseh beyond the Jordan. This amounts to four cities to every tribe.

—NACHMANIDES.

[6]Although Moses during his lifetime set aside three cities on the east bank of the Jordan (Deuteronomy iv. 41), the appointment of all the six cities is recorded here because Moses' three cities did not function until the three on the western side of the Jordan were appointed by Joshua.

—RASHI, QUOTING MAKKOTH 9B.

[7]The exiled man gains his freedom through the death of the High Priest, because the latter should have prevented this calamity in Israel

the manslayer shall at any time go beyond the border of his city of refuge, whither he fleeth; and the avenger of blood find him without the border of his city of refuge, and the avenger of blood slay the manslayer; there shall be no blood-guiltiness for him; because he must remain in his city of refuge until the death of the high-priest; but after the death of the high-priest the manslayer may return into the land of his possession.

No fine or ransom could be paid for the life of the dead person.[8]

The fourth book of the Torah closes with some additional laws regarding inheritance. We learned from the case of the five daughters of Zelophehad (cf. *Pinchas* page 232) how, in the absence of sons, the right of inheritance reverted to daughters. These five women belonged to the tribe of Manasseh. A number of representatives of this tribe approached Moses and expressed the fear that if these women were to marry men of other tribes, the land which they had inherited would leave their domain. As a result, the equal distribution of land among the tribes would, after a period of time, be upset. It was then decided that the five daughters of Zelophehad would have to marry within their tribe of Manasseh, which they did. This ruling was extended to all women who inherited land, imposing upon them the duty to marry only within their own tribes.

---

by virtue of prayer. It is therefore only his death that expiates the sin of the homicide.

—RASHI, QUOTING MAKKOTH 11A.

[8]According to the twenty-fifth of the Thirty-two Hermeneutic Rules of Rabbi Eliezer, this sentence intimates that only murder cannot be expiated by ransom, but for physical injuries which are not fatal one has only to make monetary restitution to the injured party. Consequently the rule eye for eye, tooth for tooth (Exodus xxi. 24) really means that monetary compensation had to be paid for the loss of an eye, or any other limb.

—RASHBAM.

Haftorah Massey

JEREMIAH II, 4-28; III, 4; IV, 1-2

The theme of the previous Haftorah, by the same prophet, is continued in these chapters. In this second of the three "Haftorahs of Rebuke", Jeremiah chastises the People for turning their backs upon God.

By reviewing various periods in Jewish history, he demonstrates God's ever-present love and protection of His People. Why then, Jeremiah demands, do not the priests seek God? Why do not the teachers try to understand God? Why do the rulers betray their faith, thereby turning the entire People to the pagan worship of Baal?

The Prophet accuses the People of having committed two grave sins: they have forsaken their God who has been a Faithful Sheperd to them; and they have fashioned idols which they worship.

The People has also foolishly tried to form alliances with Egypt and Assyria, neither of whom will come to her aid in the day of retribution.

Only sincere repentance, the Prophet warns, can avert the imminent disaster.

If thou wilt return, O Israel,
Saith the Lord,
Yea, return unto Me;
And if thou wilt put away thy detestable things out of
My sight,
And wilt not waver;
And wilt swear: 'As the Lord liveth'
In truth, in justice, and in righteousness;
Then shall the nations bless themselves by Him,
And in Him shall they glory.

THE BOOK OF
DEUTERONOMY

ספר דברים

Deuteronomy (Second Law), the fifth and last book of the Torah is called Devarim *("These Are the Words") in Hebrew. Most of the chapters are composed of the closing addresses of Moses prior to his death. The great leader and prophet of the Jewish People, now an old man, reviews the travels in the wilderness; the wars and tribulations; and the commandments of God which the Jews had received during that period. Finally, after a beautiful song of praise to God and a blessing to each of the Tribes, Moses dies on Mount Nebo and the People of Israel prepare to enter Canaan under the leadership of Joshua.*

דברים

Devarim

CHAPTERS I–III, 22

$\mathcal{M}$OSES WAS NOW old: he had reached the age of one hundred and twenty years. As the end of his life came near, Moses gathered all the Jews[1] together in the wilderness on the east bank of the Jordan to review with them all that had transpired over the past forty years, as well as the divine commandments[2] they had received. He recalled their history and appraised their future. It was the eleventh month of the fortieth year since they had left Egypt. The army had fought a number of battles against hostile nations which they passed and the hour was almost at hand for them to enter the Promised Land under the leadership of Joshua.

---

[1]As the giving of the Torah on Mount Sinai was witnessed by the entire nation, so, on this occasion, when Moses expounded and completed the Torah, all Israel had to be present.

—NACHMANIDES.

[2]The reference is to all the ordinances contained in this Book beginning with the Decalogue. Some of these have been previously recorded in the other Books of the Torah and are now repeated for the benefit of the new generation which was to enter Canaan. Others are repeated with additional details and clarification. But there are some commandments which are reported here for the first time: laws dealing with divorce, levirate marriage, and other matters, although these too had been received by Moses either on Sinai or in the Tent of Meeting during the first year after the departure from Egypt. This explains the absence from the entire Book of the usual formula: 'And the Lord spoke unto Moses, saying, Speak unto the children of Israel,' or, 'Command the children of Israel.' As intimated in verse 5 and iv. 44, the main part of the Book begins with the Decalogue. What precedes is an introduction in which Moses admonishes the people and recalls God's mercy toward them.

—NACHMANIDES.

Moses begins his recollections by taking the minds of the people[3] back to Mount Sinai which he calls by its other name, Horeb.

The Lord our God spoke unto us in Horeb,[4] saying: 'Ye have dwelt long enough in this mountain; turn you, and take your journey, and go to the hill-country of the Amorites and unto all the places nigh thereunto, in the Arabah, in the hill-country, in the Lowland, and in the South, and by the sea-shore; the land of the Canaanites, and Lebanon, as far as the great river, the river Euphrates. Behold, I have set the land before you: go in and possess the land which the Lord swore unto your fathers, to Abraham, to Isaac, and to Jacob, to give unto them and to their seed after them.'

Because the people had multiplied greatly,[5] the burdens of teaching and judging the people became too heavy for Moses. As a result, he appointed elders and wise men of the tribes to share in these responsibilites. He warned the judges to be most cautious in their deliberations.

And I charged your judges at that time, saying: 'Hear the causes between your brethren, and judge righteously be-

---

[3]Moses' discourse was intended for the people who were about to enter the Holy Land. He therefore waited until the end of the journey by which time the older generation had died.

—SFORNO.

[4]Idential with Sinai.

—IBN EZRA.

Nachmanides is of the opinion that Horeb, where Israel encamped for some time, was the name of a place in the neighborhood of Mount Sinai.

[5]In Egypt, in fulfilment of Jacob's blessings.

—IBN EZRA.

tween a man and his brother, and the stranger that is with him. Ye shall not respect persons in judgement; ye shall hear the small and the great alike;[6] *ye shall not be afraid of the face of any man; for the judgement is God's;*[7] *and the cause that is too hard for you ye shall bring unto me, and I will hear it.' And I commanded you*[8] *at that time all the things which ye should do.*

After they had continued on their journey through the wilderness, they reached Kadesh-barnea. From this point, they were ordered to prepare for their entry into the Promised Land. But the people worried about their military strength. Disregarding God's promise, they feared they might not be able to overcome the Canaanites. Moses now reminds the people of their tragic rebellion.

And ye came near unto me every one of you,[9] *and said: 'Let us send men before us, that they may search the land for us, and bring us back word of the way by which we must go up, and the cities unto which we shall come.' And the*

---

[6]The judge should consider a lawsuit involving the smallest sum as seriously as one involving a great sum.

—RASHI.

[7]It is the will of God that justice be done on earth, and so He charged man with the task of executing His will. If man tolerates injustice, he is unfaithful to His Divine commission.

—NACHMANIDES.

[8]Though Moses appointed judges to assist him in settling civil differences, he did not delegate to them his function of propagating the word of God. He personally promulgated the teachings of the Torah to the people in accordance with Jethro's counsel (Exodus xviii. 20).

—NACHMANIDES.

[9]This implies a reproach. Moses complained that young and old, commoners and nobles, approached him in an unorderly crowd.

—RASHI.

thing pleased me well;[10] *and I took twelve men*[11] *of you, one man for every tribe; and they turned and went up into the mountains, and came unto the valley of Eshcol, and spied it out. And they took of the fruit of the land in their hands, and brought it down unto us, and brought us back word and said: 'Good is the land which the Lord our God giveth unto us.' Yet ye would not go up, but rebelled against the commandment of the Lord your God; and ye murmured in your tents, and said: 'Because the Lord hated us, He hath brought us forth out of the land of Egypt, to deliver us into the land of the Amorites, to destroy us. Whither are we going up? our brethren have made our heart to melt: The people is greater and taller than we; the cities are great and fortified up to heaven; and moreover we have seen the sons of the Anakim there.'*

In vain Moses tried to reassure the people, reminding them of all the miracles whereby God had supported and led the nation. Despite all encouragement, the people were in panic and too frightened to face the Canaanites. They murmured and complained against God and Moses. It was at this point that God determined not to let that generation enter the Promised Land, except for Caleb and Joshua,—the only two who brought back an encouraging report. Even Moses was included in this decree.[12] Only the children of the former Egyptian slaves who

---

[10]Only because you all demanded it.

—IBN EZRA.

[11]Though the twelve spies were heads of their tribes, Moses referred to them simply as *men* because they proved to be wicked men.

—NACHMANIDES.

[12]Not only were the Jews barred from entering the Holy Land because of their rebellion following the report of the spies, but Moses himself was also excluded on account of another sin committed by them at Meribah (Numbers xx. 12).

—NACHMANIDES.

grew up in the freedom of the desert would enter Canaan.

When the people learned of God's decision, they quickly repented and decided to attack the land without divine permission. Moses recalls how he warned them against taking such action without the direct consent of God. Nevertheless, the army marched against Canaan and were met by the Amorites. They suffered a heavy defeat and had to return to Kadesh where they remained for a long time.

Finally, the journey was resumed. These travels now saw the Jewish People pass a number of countries inhabited by people they were forbidden to harm or molest. One of these was situated at Mount Seir. Here lived the descendants of Jacob's brother, Esau, who were promised this region by God. The Jews paid them for food and water which they purchased[13] as they continued on their way.

The land of Moab also had to be left in peace, for God had promised this country to the descendants of Lot, the nephew of Abraham.

A number of kings now met the Jews in battle on their way to the Jordan. First, there was Sihon, King of Heshbon, who refused Moses' request to purchase food and water. He was so hostile that he also went to war against the Jews and was defeated by them in the ensuing battle. Another king, Og of Bashan, rushed out into battle against the Jews and was totally defeated.

As a result of these two victories, the Jews gained many cities and a great deal of land east of the Jordan. This territory was distributed to the tribes of Reuben and Gad, as well as to half the tribe of Manasseh. Although their women, children, and cattle remained on this land, all their armed soldiers had to pass over the Jordan with the rest of the camp, to return only when the entire Land of Israel was conquered.

---

[13]The Jews were required to buy food and drink from Esau, not because they were in need of them, but in order that the inhabitants might benefit from their presence and thus be assured of Israel's goodwill towards them.

—SFORNO.

Moses assured the future leader, Joshua, that if the people would have faith and follow the commandments of God, they would surely succeed in possessing the Promised Land, just as they had been victorious against the two hostile kings.

Haftorah Devarim

ISAIAH I, 1–27

Both this Sidrah and Haftorah always precede the Fast of *Tisha B'Av*, the day commemorating the destruction of both Holy Temples. It is the last of the three "Haftorahs or Rebuke".

Isaiah was a native of Jerusalem who was a prophet from 740 to 701 B.C.E. Despite the fact that this period preceded the Babylonian destruction of Jerusalem in 586 B.C.E., the Prophet foretold the coming disaster with complete clarity.

In a biting message, Isaiah delivers God's complaint against His People. Throughout history, God has watched over Israel as a father cares for his children, but the People has rebelled against Him. Israel stands condemned for its corruption, Godlessness and ingratitude.

Punishment has already begun with the destruction by the Assyrians of many Jewish cities. Were it not for God's mercy, the devastation would have equalled that of Sodom and Amorah.

The Prophet declares that God does not seek meaningless sacrifices. The Sabbaths, feasts and even prayers are an insult to God if they are practices in the midst of sin.

Isaiah warns that Israel must repent. The People must seek justice and relieve the oppressed.

The Prophet bemoans the terrible condition of Jerusalem which was once called the Faithful City and is now steeped in wickedness.

Yet if Israel will return to God, disaster can be averted.

And I will restore thy judges as at the first,
And thy counsellors as at the beginning;

Afterward thou shalt be called The city of righteousness,
The faithful city.

Zion shall be redeemed with justice,
And they that return of her with righteousness.

וָאֶתְחַנַּן

Va-Etchanan

Despite the fact that Moses had sheperded his people from Egyptian bondage to the very borders of the Promised Land, he was not destined to enter Canaan itself. Moses recalls his plea to God and its rejection.

And I besought the Lord at that time, saying: 'O Lord God,[1] thou hast begun to show Thy servant Thy greatness, and Thy strong hand; for what god is there in heaven or on earth, that can do according to Thy works, and according to Thy mighty acts? Let me go over, I pray Thee, and see the good land that is beyond the Jordan, that goodly hillcountry, and Lebanon.' But the Lord was wroth with me for your sakes, and hearkened not unto me; and the Lord said unto me: 'Let it suffice thee; speak no more unto Me of this matter. Get thee up into the top of Pisgah, and lift up thine eyes westward, and northward, and southward, and eastward, and behold with thine eyes; for thou shalt not go over this Jordan. But charge Joshua, and encourage him, and strengthen him,[2] for he shall go over before this people, and he shall cause them to inherit the land which thou shalt see.'

---

[1] The phrase denotes 'merciful God.' Even if justice demanded that he should be excluded from the Holy Land, Moses appealed to the merciful God to repeal the sentence.

—NACHMANIDES.

[2] By means of words, that is: he had the Divine assurance of success.

—RASHI.

Moses then continues with his last discourse to the throngs of people who were gathered to listen to the final words of their great leader.[3] He tells them that they are neither to add nor detract[4] from any part of the laws which they had received. He reminds them of all the miracles which they had been privileged to witness and of all the great victories they had won. By keeping God's commandments, the nation will be secure in its homeland and gain the respect of all peoples. The Jewish People will demonstrate their closeness to God and show their wisdom and understanding by accepting the way of life which God had taught them in the Torah. Not only was it important for the people of that generation to abide by the Torah, but it was essential that they teach this path of the Torah to their children and future generations.[5]

The great moment of destiny in the life of the Jewish people, when they stood at mount Sinai to receive the Decalogue is now reviewed by Moses.[6]

---

[3]Having concluded his words of reproach and pointed out that their fathers, as well as he, had forfeited their right of entering the Holy Land on account of their sins, Moses turned now to the people with the assurance that they were destined to take possession of the land, on condition that they remained faithful to God and His Torah.

—NACHMANIDES.

[4]Both addition to and subtraction from the word of God mar its Divine purpose.

—SFORNO.

[5]Having urged Israel to obey the statutes and ordinances which, he said, he was teaching them (verse 1), Moses now added that those precepts were not his own but God's, and that these Divine commandments should form the basis of their life in their national homeland.

—IBN EZRA.

[6]After exhorting the people to observe all God's commandments, Moses continued to impress upon them that they should never forget the awesome events at Mount Sinai, where amidst thunder and lightning they received those commandments. They should bear in mind the fact that God directly, and not through a mediator, revealed His

. . . And ye came near and stood under the mountain; and the mountain burned with fire unto the heart of heaven, with darkness, cloud and thick darkness. And the Lord spoke unto you out of the midst of the fire; ye heard the voice of words, but ye saw no form; only a voice. And He declared unto you His covenant, which He commanded you to perform, even the ten words; and He wrote them upon two tablets of stone. And the Lord commanded me at that time to teach you statutes and ordinances, that ye might do them in the land whither ye go over to possess it. . . . .'.

Once again, Moses warns the people never to make any form of idol, whether in the shape of a human figure, animal, bird, insect or fish. Nor may they worship the sun, moon, stars or any natural body. God alone was to be worshipped by the Jewish people.

These are the essential instructions which Moses reviewed with the Jewish people prior to their entry into the Promised Land. He again mentions sadly that he may not enter Canaan and warns the people against arousing God's anger by going contrary to His ways, thereby risking exile from their homeland.

Yet, Moses foresees that in the distant days ahead, Israel will make a "graven image" and tread those paths which God had taught are evil. When this tragic event takes place, the people will be scattered to the ends of the earth, after being driven out of their beloved Land. In the countries of their dispersion, they will serve foreign gods and only when they repent will God listen to their pleas and return them to their homeland.[7]

---

will to Israel, and no seer or dreamer can ever shake the authority of the Torah.

—IBN EZRA.

[7]A complete realization of God's law is not possible in the diaspora under foreign rule. Only as free men on their soil can Israel live a full religious life.

—IBN EZRA.

Moses then recalls how he appointed three cities on the eastern side of the Jordan to which those who killed someone accidentally could flee from family vengeance. These places were known as the Cities of Refuge.

Because of their extreme importance, Moses again recounts each section of the Decalogue which was previously spoken by God at Mount Sinai. With only slight variations, every commandment is repeated in detail.

I am the Lord thy God, who brought thee out of the land of Egypt, out of the house of bondage.

Thou shalt have no other gods before Me.[8] *Thou shalt not make unto thee a graven image, even any manner of likeness, of any thing that is in heaven above, or that is in the earth beneath, or that is in the water under the earth. Thou shalt not bow down unto them, nor serve them; for I the Lord thy God am a jealous God, visiting the iniquity of the fathers upon the children, and upon the third and upon the fourth generation of them that hate Me, and showing mercy unto the thousandth generation of them that love Me and keep My commandments.*

Thou shalt not take the name of the Lord thy God in vain; for the Lord will not hold him guiltless that taketh His name in vain.

Observe the sabbath day, to keep it holy, as the Lord thy God commanded thee. Six days shalt thou labor, and do all thy work; but the seventh day is a sabbath unto the Lord thy God, in it thou shalt not do any manner of work, thou, nor thy son, nor thy daughter, nor thy man-servant, nor

---

[8]It is not enough to believe in God; we must also believe that there is no other deity besides Him.

—RASHBAM.

thy maid-servant, nor thine ox, nor thine ass,[9] nor any of thy cattle, nor thy stranger that is within thy gates; that thy man-servant and thy maid-servant may rest as well as thou. And thou shalt remember that thou wast a servant in the land of Egypt, and the Lord thy God brought thee out thence by a mighty hand and by an outstretched arm; therefore the Lord thy God commanded thee to keep the sabbath day.

Honor thy father and thy mother, as the Lord thy God commanded thee; that thy days may be long, and that it may go well with thee,[10] upon the land which the Lord thy God giveth thee.

Thou shalt not murder.
Neither shalt thou commit adultery.
Neither shalt thou steal.
Neither shalt thou bear false witness against thy neighbor.

Neither shalt thou covet thy neighbor's wife; neither shalt thou desire thy neighbor's house, his field, or his man-servant, or his maid-servant, his ox, or his ass, or any thing that is thy neighbor's.

As is recorded in the book of Exodus, the people became so frightened at these sights and sounds when they heard God's

---

[9]These animals are not mentioned in the earlier version of the Decalogue (Exodus xx. 10). The addition intimates that even the vital work of tilling the soil, usually performed with these animals, must not be done on the Sabbath.

—NACHMANIDES.

[10]Some detect in this phrase an allusion to immortal life in the world to come.

—IBN EZRA.

voice, that they refused to listen further. Instead, sent Moses up to Mount Sinai to receive the rest of the Torah.

Moses took this point in his review of Israel's history to teach the very central belief of Jewish faith, affirming the absolute unity of God.

HEAR, O ISRAEL: THE LORD OUR GOD, THE LORD IS ONE.[11]
And thou shalt love the Lord[12] *thy God with all thy heart,*[13] *and with all thy soul,*[14] *and with all thy might.*[15] *And these words, which I command thee this day,*[16] *shall be upon thy heart; and thou shalt teach them diligently unto thy children, and shalt talk of them when thou sittest in thy house, and when thou walkest by the way, and when thou*

---

[11]The Lord, Who is now only *our God* and not of other peoples, will in time to come be acknowledged by all the world as the one and only God.

—RASHI.

[12]Obey His commands from love and not from fear.

—RASHI.

Rejoice to do what is pleasing in His sight, for there is no more glorious purpose in life.

—SFORNO.

[13]Heart denotes the mind.

—RASHI.

[14]Even at the sacrifice of your life.

—RASHBAM.

Soul denotes desire.

—IBN EZRA.

[15]With all your property.

—RASHI.

To the utmost of your power.

—IBN EZRA.

[16]The law of God should not be regarded as an antiquated ordinance, but as one which is newly promulgated and welcomed.

—RASHI.

liest down, and when thou risest up.[17] *And thou shalt bind
them for a sign upon thy hand,*[18] *and they shall be for
frontlets between thy eyes.*[19] *And thou shalt write them
upon the door-posts of thy house,*[20] *and upon thy gates.*[21]

Whenever Israel's children will ask about these laws and
beliefs,[22] they should be told of the exodus from Egypt and how
God brought them to the Promised Land. This great historical
event established the unique relationship between God and the
Jewish People.[23]

---

[17]That is: the time of evening and morning (when this section, the
Shema, is to be recited).

—RASHI.

[18]These are the phylacteries (*tefillin*) placed on the arm.

—RASHI.

[19]These are the phylacteries (*tefillin*) placed upon the head.

—RASHI.

[20]The singular form of the Hebrew word (apparently Rashi had a
text in which the *waw* was omitted) indicates that the *mezuzah* was to
be affixed to only one post.

—RASHI.

[21]The plural includes the gates of courts, provinces and cities.

—RASHI.

[22]Moses' warning to his contemporaries not to put the authenticity of the Torah to the test of miracles is now extended to all future
generations. The children should not wait for miracles as a proof of
the genuineness of the law of God. They should rather inquire of their
fathers who would pass on to them the historical facts which verify the
authority of the Torah and its commandments.

—NACHMANIDES

[23]To Israel God committed many more laws than to the other
nations, who are only required to observe the basic laws of humanity
known as 'the seven laws of the sons of Noah,' viz. not to worship idols,
not to blaspheme the name of God, to establish courts of justice, not
to kill, not to commit adultery, not to rob, and not to eat flesh cut from
a living animal.

—SFORNO.

The reading concludes with Moses explaining that God did not choose Israel because they were a large and powerful people.[24] On the contrary, they were few in numbers and the smallest of nations. God chose them because of his love for them, since they were willing to follow His commandments as taught in the Torah.[25] As long as they continued to do so, they would live happily and safely in the land which God swore to Abraham, Isaac and Jacob.

Haftorah Va-Etchanan

ISAIAH XL, 1–26

After the Fast of *Tisha B'Av*, the first of the seven "Haftorahs of Consolation" begin. Isaiah, the same prophet who denounced Israel and foretold the coming doom, now assures his People that God will bring them consolation.

The terrible troubles which befell Israel have more than erased her guilt. God's punishment—the result of love and not hatred of His People—has ended. He will now return Israel to its ancient Homeland.

The Jewish exiles in Babylon eagerly read these words. Forty-seven years after the downfall of Jerusalem, Babylon was about to succumb to the might of the now-powerful Persian Empire. Cyrus, king of Persia, proclaimed that the Judeans may return to their Homeland and rebuild the Holy Temple.

---

[24]Let Israel not think that they are more numerous than the people of Canaan and can therefore overcome them. The land will be theirs only because of God's love for them.

—RAShBAM.

[25]This corresponds to the phrase *choose you* in the preceding verse. Of all the peoples God found Israel worthy of becoming His chosen, and their qualification for this selection was their determined will to endure whatever trials would come upon them.

—NACHMANIDES.

Comfort ye, comfort ye My people,
Saith your God.
Bid Jerusalem take heart,
And proclaim unto her,
That her time of service is accomplished,
That her guilt is paid off;
That she has received of the Lord's hand
Double for all her sins.

עֵ֫קֶב

Ekev

CHAPTERS VII, 12–XI, 25

AS MOSES CONTINUES to speak to the entire camp of Israel, he outlines to them the rewards of faith in God and obedience to His commandments.

And it shall come to pass, because ye hearken to these ordinances, and keep, and do them, that the Lord thy God shall keep with thee the covenant[1] and the mercy which He swore unto thy fathers, and He will love thee, and bless thee, and multiply thee; He will also bless the fruit of thy body and the fruit of thy land, thy corn and thy wine and thine oil, the increase of thy kine and the young of thy flock, in the land which He swore unto thy fathers to give thee. Thou shalt be blessed above all peoples; there shall not be male or female barren among you, or among your cattle. And the Lord will take away from thee all sickness;[2] and He will put none of the evil diseases of Egypt,[3] which thou knowest, upon thee, but will lay them upon all them that hate thee. . . .

---

[1] If they proved faithful to God's law, He would fulfil His promise to the patriarchs in their own time (*with thee*) But if they rejected His commandments, the fulfilment of the promise would be deferred to a later generation.

—RASHBAM.

[2] Ordinary ailments from which people suffer.

—IBN EZRA.

[3] Supernatural diseases such as those with which He afflicted the Egyptians.

—IBN EZRA.

The people should not fear their enemies, for Israel shall dwell safely upon its land. Those who attack them shall be destroyed. Above all, the Jews must eliminate all forms of paganism and idol-worship, since these evil practices will surely bring God's punishment.

Moses continues to exhort the Jews to always remember[4] how they were tested for forty years as they wandered in the desert. During this period, they were under the constant protection of God. They had manna to eat, clothing to wear, and shelter for protection, throughout the many years of their journey. All these trials and tribulations, followed by the saving powers of God, were to prove to Israel that their ultimate faith and reliance must always rest with God.

And He afflicted thee, and suffered thee to hunger, and fed thee with manna, which thou knewest not, neither did thy fathers know;[5] that He might make thee know that man doth not live by bread only, but by every thing that proceedeth out of the mouth of the Lord doth man live.[6]

The people are also asked to realize that when God sends a rebuke, it is not the result of hatred against His people, but the type of correction and discipline which a father administers to a child whom he loves.[7]

---

[4]Their experience in the wilderness, where they received their daily bread in a supernatural way, proved that obedience to the law of God was the sure means of achieving security.

—NACHMANIDES.

[5]In providing them with manna, God showed greater kindness to them than to the patriarchs. Though they were Godfearing and righteous men, they did not receive their food from heaven.

—NACHMANIDES.

[6]Life does not depend entirely on physical food; it also needs the power which emanates from the regions above.

—IBN EZRA.

[7]A father does not punish his child to cause him to suffer, but to

The land into which they are passing, the Jews are told again, is a good and fertile country. It will sustain the population and permit its inhabitants to live in happiness and safety. Once the land has become prosperous, however, it will become very important for the nation not to forget their pact with God. Even in comfort and wealth[8] they must continue to walk in His paths by carrying out the commandments which were taught to them.

Moses now begins to recount some of the events which took place during the wanderings in the wilderness, especially the many revolts against God and Moses. Because they committed so many offenses, Moses calls them a "stiffnecked people".[9] They are entering Canaan, he tells them, not because of their righteousness, but because of the wickedness of the nations who are presently in that land and because of the oath which God swore to Abraham, Isaac and Jacob.

Moses reminds the people how they angered God at Mount Sinai when, after they heard the Ten Commandments, he went up to the top of the mountain for forty days and nights. He was to receive the two tablets on which these commandments were inscribed, as well as the rest of the Torah.

No sooner had these forty days passed, than the people made a golden calf which they began to worship. Moses recalls how he was sent down from the mountain by God. When he

---

direct him on the right path of life. This was the purpose of the hardships and trials which God imposed upon Israel during their wandering. The ultimate aim was their entry into the Promised Land with its rich resources.

—NACHMANIDES.

[8] In time of affluence they might forget their former state of slavery and the privations in the wilderness, and that God sustained them in those critical times.

—IBN EZRA.

[9] The description "stiffnecked people" is confirmed by the fact that throughout their wandering they repeatedly rebelled against God, although each rebellion was followed by the manifestation of God's greatness and judgement.

—SFORNO.

viewed this tragic sight, he smashed the tablets which were intended as the symbols of a covenant between God and the Jewish People. To avoid the total destruction of the nation through
God's punishment for this grave offense, Moses returned to the
top of Mount Sinai and prayed for divine pardon for the people
another forty days and nights. Not only did the pleas of Moses
result in God's forgiveness, but they also saved his brother
Aaron who played a leading role in this rebellion.[10]

Moses did not ascend the mountain the second time, until
he had completely destroyed the golden calf and ground it into
ashes which were strewn into a brook at the mountainside. God
told Moses to carve two new tablets[11] out of the stone and to
prepare a wooden ark. Throughout the forty days, Moses
pleaded with God to forgive the people.

*And I prayed unto the Lord, and said: 'O Lord God,
destroy not Thy people and Thine inheritance,[12] that Thou
hast redeemed through Thy greatness, that Thou hast
brought forth out of Egypt with a mighty hand. Remember
Thy servants, Abraham, Isaac, and Jacob; look not unto
the stubbornness of this people, nor to their wickedness, nor
to their sin; lest the land whence Thou broughtest us out
say: Because the Lord was not able to bring them into the
land which He promised unto them, and because He hated
them, He hath brought them out to slay them in the wilder-*

---

[10]Because he complied with the demand of the people to make
them the Calf.

—RASHI.

[11]While the first tablets were the work of God, the second were
made by Moses. In recalling this, Moses intended to inform the people
that although God forgave them the sin of the Golden Calf, the forgiveness was incomplete.

—SFORNO.

[12]Israel is God's *inheritance* because of His love for the patriarchs,
and His *people* because He had delivered them from Egypt.

—IBN EZRA.

ness. Yet they are Thy people and Thine inheritance, that Thou didst bring out by Thy great power and Thy outstretched arm.'

After the camp began to move again, Moses continues, the time of the death of Aaron, his brother, had come. He remembers how Eleazar became the new High Priest.

The tribe of Levi was then chosen by God to serve in the Sanctuary, instead of the first-born of all the tribes, since the tribe of Levi refused to participate in the worship of the Golden Calf.

Moses appeals to the people to follow in the ways of God and not to commit acts which will incur divine wrath.

And now, Israel, what doth the Lord thy God require of thee, but to fear the Lord thy God,[13] *to walk in all His ways, and to love Him, and to serve the Lord thy God with all thy heart and with all thy soul; to keep for thy good the commandments of the Lord, and His statutes, which I commanded thee this day? Behold, unto the Lord thy God belongeth the heaven of heavens,*[14] *the earth, with all that therein is. Only the Lord had a delight in thy fathers to love them, and He chose their seed after them, even you, above all peoples, as it is this day.*[15] *Circumcise therefore the*

---

[13]From this text the Rabbis derived the doctrine that everything is in the power of God except man's fear of God (which is left to his free will).

—RASHI.

[14]The Master of the Universe, who is glorified by the whole of creation, is not in need of Israel's obedience and worship. Only because of the merits of their forefathers God chose Israel of all the peoples as the custodian of His law for their own good.

—NACHMANIDES.

[15]This relationship between God and Israel will remain for all time.

—NACHMANIDES.

foreskin of your heart,[16] and be no more stiffnecked. For the Lord your God, He is God of gods, and Lord of lords, the great God, the mighty, and the awful, who regardeth not persons, nor taketh reward. He doth execute justice for the fatherless and widow, and loveth the stranger, in giving him food and raiment. Love ye therefore the stranger; for ye were strangers in the land of Egypt. Thou shalt fear the Lord thy God; Him shalt thou serve; and to Him shalt thou cleave, and by His name shalt thou swear. He is thy glory, and He is thy God, that hath done for thee these great and tremendous things, which thine eyes have seen. Thy fathers went down into Egypt with threescore and ten persons; and now the Lord thy God hath made thee as the stars of heaven for multitude.

If the Jewish People will always heed these words, the Land of Israel will be their homeland and haven. Moses explains this to the people.

For the land, whither thou goest in to possess it, is not as the land of Egypt,[17] from whence ye came out, where thou

---

[16]Remove the covering on your hearts which prevents My words from entering into them.

—RASHI.

Henceforth make your hearts receptive to the Divine truth, in contrast to your behavior in the past.

—IBN EZRA.

[17]It is far better; and even the district *from whence ye came out,* viz. Goshen, which was the best land of Egypt (Genesis xlvii. 11), is inferior to Canaan.

—RASHI.

Whereas the land of Egypt, with its rivers and streams for irrigation, yields its food for the good and bad alike, the Land of Israel, which relies for fertility upon rain, is only "flowing with milk and honey" when its inhabitants are faithful to the law of God. For His special attention is directed to that land, and He only gives it rain if His law is obeyed there.

—RASHBAM.

didst sow thy seed, and didst water it with thy foot, as a garden of herbs; but the land, whither ye go over to possess it, is a land of hills and valleys, and drinketh water as the rain of heaven cometh down; a land which the Lord thy God careth for;[18] *the eyes of the Lord thy God are always upon it,*[19] *from the beginning of the year even unto the end of the year.*

Haftorah Ekev

ISAIAH XLIX, 14–LI, 3

In the Sidrah, Moses continues to review the history of the Jewish People. He explains that "man does not live by bread alone", but must follow the dictates of God to live a full and satisfying life. Failure to do so would bring Divine retribution. Such punishment, however, is likened to that of a father who rebukes a wayward child.

Isaiah, in the second "Haftorah of Consolation" follows a similar theme. Israel may feel forsaken by God after the terrible destruction, but this is not so. Just as a mother can never forsake her own child, so will God never forsake His People.

> *Behold, the Lord God will help me,*
> *Who is he that shall condemn me?*
> *Behold, they all shall wax old as a garment,*
> *The moth shall eat them up.*

> *Who is among you that feareth the Lord,*
> *That obeyeth the voice of His servant?*

---

[18]But God cares for all lands (cf. Job xxxviii. 26)! He cares for them through His care for the Land of Israel.

—RASHI.

[19]Observing the deeds of its inhabitants, sending or withholding rain according as they are good or evil.

—SFORNO.

Though he walketh in darkness,
And hath no light,
Let him trust in the name of the Lord,
And stay upon his God.

ראה

Re-Eh

*A*s THE JEWS listen intently to Moses' discourse prior to his death, he places two alternatives before them.

> *Behold,[1] I place before you this day a blessing and curse:[2] the blessing, if ye shall hearken unto the commandments of the Lord your God, which I command you this day; and the curse, if ye shall not hearken unto the commandments of the Lord your God, but turn aside out of the way which I command you this day, to go after other gods,[3] which ye have not known. And it shall come to pass, when the Lord thy God shall bring thee into the land whither thou goest to possess it, that thou shalt place the blessing upon mount Gerizim, and the curse upon mount Ebal. . . . And ye shall observe to do all the statutes and the ordinances which I set before you this day.*

Above all, the Jewish People must destroy all traces of idol-worship in the land of Canaan. This pagan form of worship, with

---

[1]The Hebrew word is singular, addressed to each one of them.

—IBN EZRA.

[2]This refers to the blessings and curses which were to be pronounced on Mount Gerizim and Mount Ebal respectively on entering the Holy Land.

—RASHBAM.

[3]This text, which compares idol-worship to the denial of the whole Torah, served as a basis of the Rabbinical dictum that he who believes in the divinity of an idol is in the same position as if he entirely repudiated the Torah.

—RASHI.

its human sacrifice and other evils, had to be totally eradicated
from the Holy Land. All the offerings of the Jews were to be
sacrificed in no other place than God's Sanctuary which was
finally erected in Jerusalem and known as the Holy Temple.

Originally, only meat which was left over from sacrifices was
permitted to be eaten. After entry into the Holy Land, however,
those animals which the Torah specifically allowed (known as
kosher) could be consumed anywhere by anyone, as long as those
animals were properly slaughtered and all the blood was
removed.[4]

All food sacrifices and tithes from which the donor also ate,
were only to be eaten in God's Sanctuary.

Although the Jewish People were to tolerate and respect
other religions, they were to attack and destroy any form of
idol-worship. These pagan rites demanded human sacrifice and
brought many evils in their wake.

> *When the Lord thy God shall cut off the nations from before
> thee, whither thou goest in to dispossess them, and thou dis-
> possessest them, and dwellest in their land; take heed to thy-
> self that thou be not ensnared to follow them, after that they
> are destroyed from before thee; and that thou inquire not after
> their gods, saying: 'How used these nations to serve their
> gods? even so will I do likewise.' Thou shalt not do so unto
> the Lord thy God; for every abomination to the Lord, which
> He hateth, have they done unto their gods; for even[5] their
> sons and their daughters do they burn in the fire to their gods.*

---

[4]Eating blood has an evil effect on the mind of man who indulges
in it and even on his descendants after him. Hence the assurance that
abstention from blood would result in happiness also of one's offspring.

—IBN EZRA.

[5]The force of *even* is to include the practice of children sacrificing
their parents. Rabbi Akiba said, 'I once saw a heathen bind his father
who was then devoured by dogs'.

—RASHI.

(An allusion to a common practice in ancient times of putting old
people to death).

The ultimate central place of sacrifice and worship was in Jerusalem, where the Holy Temple was erected. Here the offerings and tithes were to be brought, accompanied by the prayers of the people. No sacrifices were permitted to be offered anywhere except where distinctly sanctioned by God. Such practices could have led to the very idol-worship which these limitations were intended to prevent. It is for this reason that the institution of sacrifices ceased with the destruction of the Holy Temple in the year 70 C.E.

Most of the sacrificial foods, including tithes of harvests, could only be eaten within the precincts of the Sanctuary, although some of the sacred foods were permitted to be consumed anywhere in Jerusalem. The Levites, whose only source of sustenance was the donations offered by the people, were never to be neglected or forgotten by them.[6]

Throughout history, religious leaders and false prophets have tried to mislead the Jewish people. Moses issues a stern warning against this danger.

If there arise in the midst of thee a prophet,[7] or a dreamer of dreams—and he give thee a sign or a wonder,[8] and the sign or the wonder come to pass, whereof he spoke unto thee-saying: 'Let us go after other gods, which thou hast not known, and let us serve them'; thou shalt not hearken

---

[6]Only in the Holy Land the Levite had a special claim for support, because he was landless. But in the diaspora the needy Levite was to be treated as any other poor man.

—RASHI.

[7]One who claims that God communicated a message to him while he was awake.

—NACHMANIDES.

[8]*Sign* denotes the prediction of a natural incident, while *wonder* implies the forecast of a supernatural event. By both methods the false prophet seeks to authenticate forms of idolatry .

—NACHMANIDES.

The former signifies a phenomenon in the heavens, the latter on earth.

—RASHI.

unto the words of that prophet, or unto that dreamer of dreams; for the Lord your God putteth you to proof, to know whether ye do love the Lord your God with all your heart and with all your soul. After the Lord your God shall ye walk, and Him shall ye fear, and His commandments shall ye keep,[9] and unto His voice shall ye hearken, and Him shall ye serve, and unto Him shall ye cleave. . . .

Whoever distorted God's teachings must be rejected, no matter who he is, and is liable to the death penalty. The same fate would apply to any city within Israel which fell prey to preachers of idol-worship or any other form of paganism.

The Jews are again cautioned against self-inflicted wounds[10] when mourning for the dead, a custom followed by the pagans.

Animals which chew their cud and have split hooves may be eaten. In the case of fish, they must have scales and fins to be permitted foods. The Torah lists those birds which are forbidden to be eaten. By careful examination, it has been established that these are birds of prey which do not have a food sack. Those which are not of a bird-of-prey species and have a food sack may be eaten. The Torah further states that all living things which died of themselves are forbidden for food.

By inference from several statements in the Torah relating to the prohibition of cooking a kid in its mother's milk, Jewish tradition forbids the mixing of meat and milk as part of the laws governing which foods may be eaten.

---

[9]This refers to the Torah of Moses.—RASHI; not new commandments devised by a prophet which are contradictory to the law of God.
—SFORNO.

[10]The heathen cut his flesh in bereavement as an expression of grief. This should not be practised among Jews who are the children of the true God. A father sometimes causes his children pain for their good; in the same way must the Jew accept the suffering which his heavenly Father inflicts upon him.
—IBN EZRA.

Farmers had to offer a portion of their crops and cattle, part of which became sacred food for the officials of the Sanctuary, and a portion of which they ate themselves. If the journey was too lengthy for them to bring the actual crops or cattle, their tithes could be converted into money. Once having arrived at the Holy Temple, they could purchase similar items.

Each seventh year was to be a "year of release".[11] Every debt entered into prior to that time was cancelled to prevent a poor class from developing in the land. The Torah warns against refusal to lend money to the needy before this year in the fear of not having it returned. The reward of helping one's neighbor is the blessing of God.

A Jewish slave was to work for six years and had to be released in the seventh. At that time, the master had to supply him with all the necessities to permit him to start a new life. The harsh experience of Egyptian slavery was to be a constant reminder to Jews to deal kindly with their fellow-men.

If a slave refused to go free when his time arrived, a special ceremony had to be performed at a door, wherein the slave's ear was pierced for rejecting freedom. Afterwards, the Torah permits him to serve his master forever. This is generally interpreted to mean until the following Jubilee year.

All first-born males of the flock had to be consecrated to God and offered as sacrifices, provided they had no blemishes.

The Torah reading concludes with a review of the three pilgrim festivals, describing the specific rituals and sacrifices of each of them. The three festivals thus described are Passover, the Feast of Weeks and the Feast of Tabernacles.

These festivals were a time of happy throngs coming to Jerusalem from all over Israel to rejoice in God's Holy Temple.

Three times in a year shall all thy males appear before the Lord thy God in the place which He shall choose: on the

---

[11]The term has two significances: the resting of the soil and the remission of debts.

—NACHMANIDES.

feast of unleavened bread, and on the feast of weeks and on the feast of tabernacles and they shall not appear before the Lord empty;[12] *every man shall give as he is able,*[13] *according to the blessing of the Lord which He hath given thee.*

Haftorah Re-Eh

ISAIAH LIV, 11–LV, 5

As the Sidrah continues to relate Moses' final message to his people, he places before them the free choice of Evil, resulting in death and destruction, or the way of Good, resulting in Life and Happiness.

The Prophet, in this "Third Haftorah of Consolation", assures the People that God will fulfil all His promises to restore Israel upon their soil if they will follow the paths of righteousness.

All of Israel's enemies, regardless of their superior numbers and greater strength, will fall away if Israel will heed the Word of God.

No weapon that is formed against thee shall prosper; And every tongue that shall rise against thee in judgement thou shalt condemn.

This is the heritage of the servants of the Lord, And their due reward from Me, saith the Lord.

---

[12]On appearing in the Sanctuary on the three pilgrim festivals, one had to bring a special burnt-offering and peace-offerings.

—RASHI.

[13]The number of the burnt-offerings and peace-offerings depends on the means of the donor and the size of his family.

—RASHI.

He must not be excessively liberal in this matter to the degree that he impoverishes himself.

—SFORNO.

Re-Eh

The Prophet pleads with the People not to rush after meaningless pursuits which will gain them nothing.

The teachings of God are for rich and poor alike.

If Israel will follow these Divine teachings, they shall live in happiness and security upon their own soil.

שׁפֹטים

Shofetim

CHAPTERS XVI, 18–XXI, 9

*A*N ORDERLY SOCIETY must have judges to decide and interpret the law, as well as officers to carry out the decisions of these judges. Moses now begins to outline the institutions which were to govern Jewish society.

> *Judges[1] and officers shalt thou make thee in all thy gates, which the Lord thy God giveth thee, tribe by tribe;[2] and they shall judge the people with righteous judgement. Thou shalt not wrest judgement; thou shalt not respect persons;[3] neither shalt thou take a gift ;[4] for a gift doth blind the eyes of the wise, and pervert the words of the righteous. Justice, justice shalt thou follow, that thou mayest live, and inherit the land which the Lord thy God giveth thee.*

Once more, the Torah repeats its solemn prohibition against any form of idol-worship. It is forbidden to plant a tree

---

[1]This subject follows immediately on the exhortation to appear at Jerusalem on the three festivals (at the end of the previous reading), to emphasize that, although every male went three times a year to the Holy City where he could consult the judicial authorities, it was still obligatory to have judges in every city.

—IBN EZRA.

[2]Rashi connects the phrase with "Shalt thou make thee"; judges were to be appointed for every tribe separately as well as for each town.

[3]The judge must treat both litigants alike during the proceedings. He should not, for example, let one stand and the other sit.

—RASHI.

[4]Even if the judge intends to act impartially and pronounce a just verdict.

—RASHI.

near God's altar in the manner of the pagans, nor to set up any types of altars not specified in the Torah. Only perfect animals, without any blemishes, were allowed to be sacrificed. Anyone who violated these outlined forms of worship would be liable to the penalty of death.

A High Court was to be established composed of priests and Levites who were to enact the necessary laws for the nation. This high tribunal which was to be located at the Sanctuary, was also to decide upon those cases which proved to be too difficult for the lower courts.[5] This Supreme Court was called the *Sanhedrin* and it carried out these functions during the existence of the Holy Temples and for some time afterwards. It was composed of seventy-one members. There were smaller courts of twenty-three judges in other communities. Courts which ruled only on monetary and civil matters were composed of three members.

The high office of King is discussed next. Moses predicted that the people would clamor for a monarch to rule them,[6] once they had settled in the land of Canaan. God, the people are told, would condone the appointment of a king, but only upon certain conditions. He would have to have the blessing of God and be a born Jew. He was not to amass many horses,[7] which were the instruments of war at that time. Nor was he to have an excess of wives,[8] who would turn his mind away from the responsibili-

---

[5]Although each city was to have it own court of law (xvi. 18) any difference of opinion on a matter of tradition must be referred to and decided by a majority of the highest court in Jerusalem.

—SFORNO.

[6]Here we have a prediction of what occurred later when the people asked of Samuel, "Now make us a king to judge us like all the nations" (1 Samuel viii. 5).

—NACHMANIDES.

[7]Unlike the rulers of other nations, Israel's king must not possess many horses from whatever land they come, that he should not put his trust in physical might but in God.

—NACHMANIDES.

[8]The maximum number allowed was eighteen.

—RASHI, QUOTING THE TALMUD.

ties of state.[9] Great riches were also to be avoided by the king. Each monarch had to write a copy of the entire Torah,[10] from which he was to read regularly. In this manner, he would always realize that he was bound by the Jewish law and was not permitted to create his own. He would not become arrogant and would not govern his people contrary to God's commandments.

Since the entire tribe of Levi, including the priests, did not receive a portion of the divided land, they were to live from the donations of part of the sacrifices and religious taxes.[11] Whenever a Levite came to the Sanctuary from another part of the country, he was to be permitted to participate in offering the sacrifices and take part in the services, thereby also receiving his due share.

After giving further warnings against all types of witchcraft and the like, Moses predicts that other prophets will arise to lead the people after his death. These prophets, in order to be heeded, must only speak in the name of God and everything they foretell in His name must come about. A true prophet must be followed, but the people must always beware of a false religious leader.

And the Lord said unto me: 'They have well said that which they have spoken. I will raise them up a prophet from among their brethren, like unto thee; and I will put My words in his mouth, and he shall speak unto them all

---

[9]Many wives would turn his heart to sensual passions.

—IBN EZRA.

[10]That is: two scrolls, one to deposit in his treasury and the other to be always with him.

—RASHI.

The sense is, a copy.

—RASHBAM.

[11]This includes those Levites who, because of physical disability, may not minister in the Temple.

—RASHI.

that I shall command him. And it shall come to pass, that whosoever will not hearken unto My words which he shall speak in My name, I will require it of him. But the prophet, that shall speak a word presumptuously in My name, which I have not commanded him to speak, or that shall speak in the name of other gods, that same prophet shall die.' And if thou say in thy heart: 'How shall we know the word which the Lord hath not spoken?' When a prophet speaketh in the name of the Lord, if the thing follow not,[12] *nor come to pass, that is the thing which the Lord hath not spoken; the prophet hath spoken it presumptuously, thou shalt not be afraid of him.*

Moses again reviews the designation of the three Cities of Refuge[13] to which someone who killed accidentally may flee. After all the land which was promised to the Jews had been settled, three more cities were to be chosen. If someone committed murder intentionally, he was liable to the full penalty of the court and could be removed from these cities. Otherwise, he remained there until the death of the High Priest and could not be attacked by any member of the slain person's family.

No landmark was to be moved unlawfully by a person in order to increase his property illegally.

Judgement could be brought against a person only by a minimum of two witnesses. If it was proven that a witness testified falsely against his neighbor, he could receive the same punishment that he intended to inflict on the other.[14]

---

[12]The authenticity of a prophet is established by his performing wondrous acts or by events which he had predicted.

—NACHMANIDES.

[13]The law concerning the Cities of Refuge is repeated here (cf. Numbers xxxv) for the sake of the addition that it only becomes operative after taking possession of the Land and dwelling in it.

—NACHMANIDES.

[14]The Rabbis took this verse to refer to witnesses who proved the

Some more instructions are now given regarding warfare. When the Jews had to go into battle, the leader of that time would first address the army. He would counsel the soldiers to have no fears, even if the enemy was more numerous, always trusting in the protection of God. Those who were nevertheless overly fearful were sent away. Also exempt from military service were the newly-married and the new owners of homes or vinyards.[15] During the battle, the destruction of all fruit-trees should be avoided.[16]

The Torah reading concludes with the case of a corpse found between two cities. If the murderer could not be found after due investigation, the elders of both cities had to measure the distance between the slain individual and the city borders. The elders of that city which was closest to the body had to offer a sacrifice, wash their hands, and affirm that they were innocent of this crime. Once the murderer was found he was, of course, brought to trial. In the meantime, the community had absolved itself of any guilt for the innocent blood which was shed.[17]

---

evidence of previous witnesses to be false by establishing an alibi. This is the only instance in which a witness can be declared to be false by evidence of others.

—NACHMANIDES.

Wherever Scripture uses the word "witness" it denotes two, unless one is specified.

—RASHI.

[15]The persons described would be in an unsettled state of mind and be the first to flee and cause others to retreat.

—IBN EZRA.

[16]Ibn Ezra renders: 'for man's life depends on the tree,' and the meaning of the verse is: do not cut down a fruit-tree which is necessary to man for food; you may eat of it but not use it as a weapon of offense against a besieged city.

[17]If the people adhere to the will of God, acts of bloodshed will not take place in their land.

—IBN EZRA.

Haftorah Shofetim

Isaiah LI, 12–LII, 12

As Moses commands the People to heed the commandment: "Justice, justice shalt thou follow" in the Sidrah, the Prophet Isaiah guides the Jewish People in a similar manner, in this fourth "Haftorah of Consolation".

Judah has paid dearly for its sins. No longer need they fear anyone. Their oppressors will fall before them as they triumphantly return to their Homeland.

Great joy shall again be felt in Judah and Jerusalem. The people who were conquered and exiled will be able to stand proudly and see the fulfilment of the promises of their God.

> *How beautiful upon the mountains*
> *Are the feet of the messenger of good tidings,*
> *That announceth peace, the harbinger of good tidings,*
> *That announceth salvation;*
> *That saith unto Zion:*
> *'Thy God reigneth!'*

> *Hark, thy watchmen! they lift up the voice,*
> *Together do they sing;*
> *For they shall see, eye to eye,*
> *The Lord returning to Zion.*

> *Break forth into joy, sing together,*
> *Ye waste places of Jerusalem;*
> *For the Lord hath comforted His people,*
> *He hath redeemed Jerusalem.*

Ki Tetze

CHAPTERS XXI, 10–XXV

*T*HROUGHOUT HISTORY, AND into the present times, armies have acted in extremely cruel ways, especially toward conquered peoples. The Torah realized that there would be times when Jewish armies would be engaged in warfare. In order to protect them from falling prey to the temptations of barbarism, very specific rules of conduct during battle and conquest are outlined.

If a victorious Jewish soldier sees a captured woman whom he wishes to marry,[1] he must first take her to his home. She is to remain there for a period of thirty days,[2] mourning her fate.[3] If after this span of time he still wished to marry her, he was able to do so. Otherwise, he had to free her entirely since he had humbled her.

The first-born son had the right of a double portion of the father's inheritance. Regardless of whom the father loved more, this law had to be adhered to.

If a man have two wives, the one beloved, and the other hated, and they have borne him children, both the beloved and the hated; and if the first-born son be hers that was

---

[1]Scripture makes a concession to human weakness.

—RASHI.

[2]Perhaps in that time he would lose his desire for her.

—IBN EZRA.

[3]As this was not the case of a voluntary proselyte but of compulsion to adopt the Jewish faith for the purpose of marrying a Jew, she was given a whole month to meditate on the new life she was entering and to find consolation therein for leaving her parents. This procedure was intended to break all connections with her past, and eventually to cause her to accept her new faith and new life.

—NACHMANIDES.

hated; then it shall be, in the day that he causeth his sons to inherit that which he hath, that he may not make the son of the beloved the first-born before the son of the hated, who is the first-born; but he shall acknowledge the first-born, the son of the hated, by giving him a double portion of all that he hath; for he is the first-fruits of his strength; the right of the first-born is his.

The case of a rebellious son is next discussed. If a child became completely undisciplined to the degree that he becomes a "glutton and drunkard"[4] and his parents could no longer control him, they were to bring him to the judges of the city who had the right to impose on him the severest penalty—even death. Jewish tradition records that this penalty was never meted out. Yet the law served as a warning to children to respect and heed the counsel of their parents.

In the rare cases that a Jewish court had to carry out a death penalty by hanging, the body was not allowed to be exposed overnight, but had to be buried on the same day of the execution.[5]

If a man came upon any lost property belonging to his neighbor, he could not simply leave it. He had to bring it to his home and take care of it until it was claimed.

In a similar spirit of friendship and kindness, a person who saw his neighbor's animal fallen on the ground could not pass by until he offered his assistance and helped them along the way again.[6]

The Torah continues to list a number of commandments.

---

[4]To satisfy his gross appetite he will resort to theft.

—SFORNO.

[5]Accoding to the Rabbis, this rule was extended also to the body of a person who died a natural death. A corpse should not be left overnight unburied.

—NACHMANIDES.

[6]The Hebrew word *immo*, meaning "with him", implies that one's duty is only to help him to lift up the fallen animal, but one is not obliged to do all the lifting while the owner of the animal remains idle.

—RASHI.

A woman shall not wear that which pertaineth unto a man, neither shall a man put on a woman's garment; for whosoever doeth these things is an abomination[7] unto the Lord thy God.

If a man wishes to remove baby birds or eggs from an nest, he may not do so in the presence of the mother bird, whom he must first drive away.[8]

When thou buildest a new house,[9] then thou shalt make a parapet for thy roof, that thou bring not blood upon thy house, if any man fall from thence.
Thou shalt not sow thy vineyard with two kinds of seed; lest the fulness of the seed which thou hast sown be forfeited together with the increase of the vineyard.

Thou shalt not plow with an ox and an ass together.[10]
Thou shalt not wear a mingled stuff, wool and linen together.
Thou shalt make thee twisted cords upon the four corners of thy covering, wherewith thou coverest thyself.

---

[7]The interchange of dress between the sexes tends to promiscuity.
—RASHBAM.

[8]The reason for this law, as well as for the commandment that an animal and its young should not be slaughtered on the same day (Leviticus xxii. 28), is that it is a cruel act. The principle here, is not to manifest God's pity for the animal, but to implant in man the virtue of mercy.

—NACHMANIDES.

[9]The sequence of the following sections intimates that one good deed leads to another. The fulfilment of the commandment in regard to the bird's nest will bring as its reward the possession of a new house, a vineyard (verse 9) and beautiful garments (verses 11f.), and so enable the possessor to fulfil the commandments these possessions entail.

—RASHI.

[10]The underlying principle of this law is prevention of cruelty, since the ass which is weaker than the ox would suffer in such a combination.

—IBN EZRA.

The commandments for which a reason is difficult to find are known as "statutes" (*chukim* in Hebrew), while those whose reasons seem clearer to us are called "laws" (*mishpatim* in Hebrew). Nevertheless all the laws of the Torah have been kept by the Jewish people as acts of faith in God and in His Torah.

A number of laws regarding the sanctity of marriage are next discussed. The honor of the woman, and the institution of marriage, are always to be protected.

Although the Jewish faith is open to all sincere converts, the Torah lists a number of classes of people who would not be eligible for admission into the faith.

The camp of the Jews had always to be pure and clean, both spiritually and physically. Those who were ritually impure had to remain outside of the camp until the evening when, after bathing, they were permitted to return.

If a slave fled from his master into the land of Israel, he was not allowed to be turned away, but had to be treated well and given the opportunity to rebuild his life as a free man.

In every way, morality was to prevail in the Holy Land.

Jewish people are forbidden to exact interest from each other and all vows for divine donations had to be carried out.[11]

That which is gone out of thy lips thou shalt observe and do; according as thou hast vowed freely unto the Lord thy God, even that which thou has promised with thy mouth.
When thou comest into thy neighbor's vineyard, then thou mayest eat grapes until thou have enough at thine own pleasure; but thou shalt not put any in thy vessel.
When thou comest into thy neighbor's standing corn, then thou mayest pluck ears with thy hand; but thou shalt not move a sickle unto thy neighbor's standing corn.

Although these last two verses seem to indicate that anyone may satisfy his appetite in his neighbor's field, the Rabbis have restricted this privilege to laborers actually working in the fields.

---

[11]The fulfilment may not be deferred beyond the three following pilgrim festivals.

—RASHI.

If a man divorced his wife and she married another man, the first husband may not remarry her, even though she became divorced or widowed from her second husband.

A groom should spend as much time as possible with his bride[12] during their first year of marriage and excessive responsibilities should not be heaped on him.

A person may not take a millstone or any necessary tool for a pledge, since he would then be depriving his neighbor of the basic needs of his livelihood.

Kidnapping for the purpose of selling the victim into slavery is a capital crime punishable by death.

Sickness, such as leprosy,[13] had to be treated with great care and the instructions of the priests and Levites had to be scrupulously obeyed, thereby avoiding further contamination in the camp.

> *When thou dost lend thy neighbor any manner of loan, thou shalt not go into his house to fetch his pledge. Thou shalt stand without, and the man to whom thou dost lend shall bring forth the pledge without unto thee. And if he be a poor man, thou shalt not sleep with his pledge;[14] thou shalt surely restore to him the pledge when the sun goeth down,[15] that he may sleep in his garment, and bless thee; and it shall be righteousness unto thee before the Lord thy God.*

---

[12]One that is new to him, even though she was a widow; but the law does not apply to a man who remarries his divorced wife.

—RASHI.

[13]Every leper, even the king, must be isolated, as was done to Miriam the prophetess by Divine command (Numbers xii. 14).

—RASHBAM.

[14]Keep not the pledge overnight.

—RASHI.

[15]The text refers to a garment for use during the night. If the pledge be a garment worn during the day, it must be returned in the morning.

—RASHI.

Thou shalt not oppress a hired servant that is poor and needy, whether he be of thy brethren, or of thy strangers that are in thy land within thy gates. In the same day thou shalt give him his hire, neither shall the sun go down upon it;[16] *for he is poor, and setteth his heart upon it;*[17] *lest he cry aganst thee unto the Lord, and it be sin in thee.*

The fathers shall not be put to death for the children, neither shall the children be put to death for the fathers; every man shall be put to death for his own sin.

Thou shalt not pervert the justice due to the stranger, or to the fatherless;[18] *nor take the widow's raiment to pledge. But thou shalt remember that thou wast a bondman in Egypt, and the Lord thy God redeemed thee thence;*[19] *therefore I command thee to do this thing.*

If a farmer forgot to pick some of his crops, he could not later retrieve them, but had to leave them for the poor.[20] The

---

[16]The day laborer whose work is finished at evening should be paid before sunset.

—NACHMANIDES.

[17]He relies on his daily earnings for his sustenance.

—IBN EZRA.

[18]Because it is easier to act unjustly towards these defenceless persons the Torah repeats the prohibition (cf. xvi. 19).

—RASHI.

A warning to the judge not to embarrass people of humble standing in any way lest it lead to perversion of justice.

—SFORNO.

[19]Recalling their sojourn as strangers in Egypt will help them to appreciate the warning against the ill-treatment of strangers.

—IBN EZRA.

[20]Even though the forgotten sheaf is an unintentional charitable act, the owner will receive God's blessing; how much more so, if one

same rule applies to anything which was left on an olive-tree after it was beaten or shaken by the farmers,[21] as well as all grapes which were left over in the vineyard.

The application of lashes—one of the forms of punishment prescribed in the Torah—had to be administered in a controlled and non-excessive manner.

Thou shalt not muzzle the ox when he treadeth out the corn.[22]

If a man was married and died before a child was born it was the duty of the late husband's brother to marry the widow, in order to carry on the family name.[23] If he refused, he had to formally release her before she could remarry.

The only case of mutilation as punishment recorded in the Torah is mentioned at this point regarding a woman who immodestly attacks a man wrestling with her husband. The stated punishment of "cutting of her hand" was understood to mean monetary compensation.

---

helps the needy intentionally.

—RASHI.

[21]According to the Rabbis, the intention is "thou shalt not entirely remove the fruit." Consequently, this serves them as a source for the law that as one had to leave a corner of grain in the field for the poor, so had one to leave a quantity of fruit on trees.

—RASHI.

[22]The law applies to any animal that is engaged in work in connection with food. The ox is only specified because that animal is normally employed for this kind of work.

—RASHI.

[23]This does not mean that the first child should be given the same name as the dead man (as Ibn Ezra explains), but by her marrying the deceased husband's brother the name of the dead man will be continued in their children.

—NACHMANIDES.

By this marriage, he receives the deceased brother's share of their father's estate.

—RASHI.

Thou shalt not have in thy bag diverse weights, a great and a small. Thou shalt not have in thy house diverse measures, a great and a small. A perfect and just weight shalt thou have; a perfect and just measure shalt thou have; that thy days may be long upon the land which the Lord thy God giveth thee. For all that do such things, even all that do unrighteously, are an abomination unto the Lord thy God.

The Torah reading concludes with an admonition to the Jewish People always to remember how the tribe of Amalek treacherously attacked them when they left Egypt.[24] They were in all times to blot out the memory of the evil of Amalek.

Haftorah Ki Tetze

ISAIAH LIV, 1–10

The Sidrah outlines the rules of conduct to guide the Jewish People in battle. Even in such periods, they must be governed by kindness and compassion.

The Prophet, in this fifth "Haftorah of Consolation" assures the People that God will, in turn, show great kindness to Israel.

In a stirring description of Israel's return to their Homeland, Isaiah describes how the cities shall once more be populated by the Jewish People.

God's punishment was only a passing moment in the eternal relationship of love for Israel. Just as God's anger relented after Noah's Flood, so will His mercy endure for Israel.

---

[24]The history of Amalek's unprovoked attack should be passed on from one generation to another.

—NACHMANIDES.

For the mountains may depart,
And the hills be removed;
But My kindness shall not depart from thee;

Neither shall My covenant of peace be removed,
Saith the Lord that hath compassion on thee.

כי תבא

Ki Tavo

CHAPTERS XXVI–XXIX, 8

*T*HE LAND OF Canaan, which the Jews were about to enter under
the leadership of Joshua, was primarily an agricultural country.
Its main crops were wheat, barley, grapes, figs, pomegrantes,
olives and date-honey. Moses now tells the people that they
must always remember that the yield of the earth brought about
through rain, sunshine and proper climate, is a direct result of
the blessings of God. To keep this fact clearly before the nation
at all times, we read about the ceremony in which the farmers
brought offerings of the first-fruits of the Land.

> *And it shall be, when thou art come in[1] unto the land*
> *which the Lord thy God giveth thee for an inheritance,*
> *and dost possess it, and dwell therein; that thou shalt*
> *take of the first of all the fruit[2] of the ground, which*
> *thou shalt bring in from thy land that the Lord thy*
> *God giveth thee; and thou shalt put it in a basket, and*
> *shalt go unto the place which the Lord thy God shall*

---

[1]As the concluding words of the previous chapter dealt with the
commandment to blot out the memory of Amalek, which was to be
obeyed when the Jews were securely settled in Canaan (see on xxv. 10),
this section introduces a series of enactments which had to be carried
out when the land was in their possession, such as: bringing the first-
fruits to the Temple; giving tithes; writing the Law upon the stones;
building an altar; and pronouncing the blessing and curse upon Gerizim and Ebal.

—IBN EZRA.

[2]The expression "of the first", and not "the first", suggests that
not all fruits were subject to this law. By means of an analogy it is
deduced that the law applied only to the seven species which were the
special produce of the Land of Israel (viii. 8).

—RASHI.

choose[3] *to cause His name to dwell there. And thou shalt come unto the priest that shall be in those days,*[4] *and say unto him: 'I profess this day unto the Lord thy God, that I am come unto the land which the Lord swore unto our fathers to give us.' And the priest shall take the basket out of thy hand, and set it down before the altar of the Lord thy God . . .*

After the priest[5] had received the basket of first-fruits, the donor repeated an expression of gratitude to God, in which he proclaimed that the Jewish People stemmed back to a wandering Armenean,[6] who came to Egypt as a small group.[7] There they

---

[3]After the building of the Temple, the first-fruits had to be brought only there; until then they were brought to the temporary Sanctuarys in Shiloh, Nob and Gibeon.

—NACHMANIDES.

[4]One was not allowed to choose one's own priest and give him the first-fruits; they had to be presented to the priests who were on duty in the Temple.

—NACHMANIDES.

[5]By bringing his first-fruits to the House of God, the Jew expressed his thanks to Him for fulfilling His oath to his ancestors to give their descendants a land of their own.

—IBN EZRA.

[6]The traditional rendering is: "An Armenean (Laban) planned to destroy my father (Jacob)".

—RASHI.

On grammatical grounds this translation is impossible. The meaning is: while living in Aram, Jacob was destitute, and also in Egypt he was a stranger. Consequently Israel's land was not an inheritance from their ancestor but a gift of God.

—SFORNO.

Rashbam explains the reference to Abraham who was a wanderer from his native country.

[7]With seventy souls.

—RASHI.

multiplied and became a great nation. During their stay, the Egyptians enslaved them and severely persecuted the Jews. God responded to their prayers for deliverance and redeemed them out of their slavery with great miracles. From there, the Jews travelled to the land of Canaan, described in the Torah as a land "flowing with milk and honey". In gratitude, the donor concluded, he is bringing these first-fruits as an offering to be eaten by the priests, the Levites and the strangers, all of whom had no share in the Land.

Besides the first-fruits, there were a number of other religious taxes or tithes which the Jewish landowners were responsible for. The regular annual tithe was ten percent of the value of his harvest, which he had to give to the landless Levites. These taxes were the main source of sustenance for the members of this tribe, whose sole task was to serve in God's Sanctuary and to teach the Torah and the Jewish religion to the people.

Another ten percent was put aside by the farmer for the times that he and his family made their pilgrimages to Jerusalem on the festivals of Passover (*Pesach*), the Feast of Weeks (*Shavuot*), and the Feast of Tabernacles (*Succot*). These were the festivals when he offered sacrifices in the Holy Temple in a spirit of joy and thanksgiving.

Finally, during each third year of the cycle, the balance of this second tithe had to be distributed among the poor, widows and orphans. None of the money could be saved for the new three year cycle. Thus, this second tax also became known as the "poor tithe".

After giving these instructions, Moses commanded the people to inscribe all the words of the Torah on twelve stones on Mount Ebal, where an altar was to be erected upon which sacrifices would be offered.

And Moses and the elders of Israel[8] *commanded*

---

[8]After concluding the Torah, Moses summoned the elders—who had great influence with the people—so that they should join him in his exhortations.

—NACHMANIDES.

the people, saying: Keep all the commandment which I command you[9] this day. And it shall be on the day when ye shall pass over the Jordan unto the land which the Lord thy God giveth thee, that thou shalt set thee up great stones,[10] and plaster them with plaster.[11] And thou shalt write upon them all the words of this law, when thou art passed over; that thou mayest go in unto the land[12] which the Lord thy God giveth thee, a land flowing with milk and honey, as the Lord, the God of thy fathers, hath promised thee. And it shall be when ye are passed over the Jordan, that ye shall set up these stones, which I command you this day, in mount Ebal, and thou shalt plaster them with plaster. And there shalt thou build an altar unto the Lord thy God, an altar of stones; thou shalt lift up no iron tool upon them. Thou shalt build the altar of the Lord thy God of unhewn stones; and thou shalt offer burnt-offerings thereon unto the Lord thy God. And thou shalt sacrifice peace-offerings, and shalt eat there; and thou shalt rejoice before the

---

[9]Though Moses and the elders addressed the people, the singular form is used because the main speaker was Moses and the elders merely supported him.

—NACHMANIDES.

[10]According to the Rabbis, three sets of stones were to be erected: one set in the Jordan (Joshua iv. 9); another at Gilgal (Joshua iv. 20); and a third on mount Ebal (verse 4).

—RASHI.

[11]That they may endure.

—IBN EZRA.

[12]The inscription of the Torah on the stones by the banks of the Jordan was to serve as a reminder to the People that they were to observe those laws in their daily life, and thereby be worthy of entering and possessing the land.

—NACHMANIDES.

Lord thy God.[13] *And thou shalt write upon the stones all the words of this law very plainly.'*[14]

Upon their entry into Canaan, the children of Israel were to participate in a ceremony of great dramatic and spiritual import. Wending their way into the Land, they would pass between two mountains: one named Gerizim and the other Ebal. The Twelve Tribes were to be divided between these two mountains. Simeon, Levi, Judah, Issachar, Joseph and Benjamin were to stand on mount Gerizim to symbolize the blessing. Reuben, Gad, Asher, Zebulun, Dan and Naphtali were to take their positions on Mount Ebal to represent the curse.

The Levites, standing between these two mountains, were then to pronounce the various commandments. When they declared those who would observe them as blessed, they turned to Mount Gerizim and all the people said "amen" ("so may it be"). Then, turning to Mount Ebal, they declared those who violated the commandment as cursed, and all the people on this mountain responded "amen".

These are the commandments which the Levites pronounced;

Cursed be the man that maketh a graven or molten image, an abomination unto the Lord, the work of the hands of the craftsman, and setteth it up in secret.[15] *And all the*

---

[13]The renewed covenant between God and Israel on Mount Gerizim and Mount Ebal was to be an occasion for rejoicing.

—SFORNO.

[14]In legible script.

—IBN EZRA.

In the seventy languages of the peoples of the world.

—RASHI.

[15]The eleven (twelve according to Rashbam) sins enumerated for the curse are such as could be committed in secret; otherwise they would be punishable by a court of law.

—IBN EZRA.

people shall answer and say: Amen.
Cursed be he that dishonoreth his father or his mother. And
all the people shall say: Amen.
Cursed be he that removeth his neighbor's landmark. And
all the people shall say: Amen.
Cursed be he that maketh the blind to go astray in the
way. [16]
And all the people shall say: Amen.
Cursed be he that perveteth the justice due to the strangers,
fatherless, and widow. [17] *And all the people shall say: Amen.*
Cursed be he that lieth with his father's wife; because he
hath uncovered his father's skirt. And all the people shall
say: Amen.
Cursed be he that lieth with any manner of beast. And all
the people shall say: Amen.
Cursed be he that lieth with his sister, the daughter of his
father, or the daughter of his mother. And all the people
shall say: Amen.
Cursed be he that lieth with his mother-in-law. And all the
people shall say: Amen.
Cursed be he that smiteth his neighbor in secret. And all
the people shall say: Amen.
Cursed be he that taketh a bribe to slay an innocent person.
And all the people shall say: Amen.
Cursed be he that confirmeth not the words of this law to
do them. [18] *And all the people shall say: Amen.*

---

[16]Misleading the inexperienced by giving them wrong advice (see on Leviticus xix. 14).

—RASHI.

[17]With these defenseless persons the act of injustice is likely to remain unexposed and is therefore included with the curses. Other victims of injustice would make the crime public.

—IBN EZRA.

[18]This refers to a person who denies the Divine origin of any commandment of the Torah and considers its fulfilment valueless.

—NACHMANIDES.

Finally, the Torah repeats the great rewards of peace and security for the nation of Israel if they will follow the ways of God's Torah. On the other hand, a detailed description of "the curse" is given—should the people fall into rebellion. The terrible sufferings of war, famine and exile which will overcome the Jews are enumerated with all their horrible consequences.

Moses does not close on this sad note. He asks the people to remember how God protected them throughout their history and led them safely through the wilderness to the Promised Land.[19] Therefore, they should always take great heed to follow these divine commandments for their future welfare and prosperity.

Haftorah Ki Tavo

ISAIAH LX

In the sixth "Haftorah of Consolation", the Prophet describes the triumphant return of the exiles to their Promised Land and Jerusalem. As the Sidrah details the commandments regarding the Land of Israel, so does Isaiah explain how the waste cities shall be rebuilt. The very nations which participated in their destruction will now humbly assist in their reconstruction.

The exiled sons and daughters of Israel shall find their way back from every part of the earth. Once again upon their native soil, they will enjoy in full measure the blessings of God.

From the addition of "to do them" it follows that the imprecations were pronounced upon those who violated the negative commands and failed to observe in secret the positive commands.

—IBN EZRA.

[19]If they did not respond to God's mercies in the past, surely it is time that they should acknowledge His providential care for them now after forty years' stay in an inhospitable desert, and after acquiring the territories of Sihon and Og.

—SFORNO.

Violence shall no more be heard in thy land,
Desolation nor destruction within thy borders;
But thou shalt call thy walls Salvation,
And thy gates Praise.

The sun shall be no more thy light by day,
Neither for brightness shall the moon give light unto thee;
But the Lord shall be unto thee an everlasting light,
And thy God thy glory.

Thy sun shall no more go down,
Neither shall thy moon withdraw itself;
For the Lord shall be thine everlasting light,
And the days of thy mourning shall be ended.

Thy people also shall be all righteous,
They shall inherit the land forever;
The branch of My planting, the work of My hands,
Wherein I glory.

The smallest shall become a thousand,
And the least a mighty nation;
I the Lord will hasten it in its time.

נצבים

Nitzavim

*P*RIOR TO THE death of Moses, all the Jews had assembled to hear the final words of their great leader and to enter into a covenant with God before their entry into the Promised Land.

As Moses looks at the multitude before him, he singles out the various groups, and describes the purpose of the assembly.

Ye are standing this day all of you[1] before the Lord your God: your heads, your tribes, your elders, and your officers, even all the men of Israel, your little ones, your wives, and thy stranger that is in the midst of thy camp, from the hewer of thy wood unto the drawer of thy water; that thou shouldest enter into the covenant of the Lord thy God—and into His oath—which the Lord thy God maketh with thee this day; that He may establish thee this day unto Himself for a people,[2] and that He may be unto thee a God, as He spoke unto thee, and as He swore unto thy fathers, to Abraham, to Isaac, and to Jacob. . . .

---

[1]On the day before his death, Moses assembled all Israel to initiate them into the covenant with God.

—RASHI.

The whole nation was still standing before Moses who had previously summoned them to assemble.

—RASHBAM.

[2]The purpose of the second covenant was to impress upon the People the eternal bond which exists between God and themselves. Since God had sworn never to exchange Israel for any other nation, their fidelity to Him had to be reaffirmed under solemn oath.

—RASHI.

This entire congregation had to realize that they were individually and collectively responsible to live the life which they had been taught by God in order to be considered His people. The Torah, which was to be the blueprint of this life, was the inheritance of the whole nation and was not to be relegated to a select clergy caste.

Moses also indicated that this covenant was not only being established with the people at that time, but also with all those yet unborn generations who would arise in the future. The people of Israel must always consider themselves a unity of the past, present and future.

> *Neither with you only do I make this covenant and this oath; but with him that standeth here with us this day before the Lord our God, and also with him that is not here with us this day—. . . .*[3]

The nation is reminded how God redeemed them out of the bondage of Egypt[4] and guided them through the wilderness for forty years, in order to bring them to the Promised Land. They will continue to merit this protection in the future only by adhering to the commandments of the covenant. If they lapse into paganism and turn from God's ways, the children of Israel would risk the destruction of their land, followed by exile to foreign countries. Should such a catastrophe occur, the nations of the world[5] will be amazed at how the Land of Israel, which

---

[3]That is: future generations.

—NACHMANIDES.

Therefore you have the duty to inform your children that the possession of the land is contingent upon obedience to the covenant.

—SFORNO.

[4]Some are still here who saw the abominations in Egypt.

—IBN EZRA.

[5]Among whom Israel will be forced to live in exile.

—SFORNO.

was once so beautiful and fertile, could fall into such disuse and barrenness.

Such a catastrophe, however, would not endure forever.[6] The exile of the Jewish people, even if it should last a long time, would certainly come to an end. Sooner or later, the people would come to their senses[7] and return to the ways of God. Then God will seek out the Jewish People from among all the nations among whom they were scattered in their exile, and return them to the Promised Land. No matter to which distant land the exiles may have been scattered, they will be brought back to their ancient homeland. Once returned, they will again multiply and live in prosperity and security, even more so than before. At such a time, it will be the enemies of Israel who will face destruction, should they oppose the return of the children of Israel to their Land.

Moses assures the congregation before him that the way of life which God is asking them to follow is neither hard to understand not difficult to observe.

For this commandment which I command thee this day, it is not too hard for thee, neither is it far off. It is not in heaven,[8] that thou shouldest say: 'Who shall go up for us

---

[6]The whole of this section refers to the distant future. None of its predictions has so far been fulfilled.

—NACHMANIDES.

[7]After the people have taken the initiative in returning to God, they will receive His support in attaining the highest spiritual achievement; the purification of the heart.

—IBN EZRA.

The eyes of the people will be opened, and they will turn from the errors which corrupted their heart.

—SFORNO.

This is a prediction of the Messianic era when man's dual character —good and evil—will end and goodness will be his only natural instinct.

—NACHMANIDES

[8]For the purpose of repentance, Israel has no need of a message brought by a prophet.

—SFORNO.

*to heaven, and bring it unto us, and make us to hear it,
that we may do it?' Neither is it beyond the sea,*[9] *that thou
shouldest say: 'Who shall go over the sea for us, and bring
it unto us, and make us to hear it, that we may do it?' But
the word is very nigh unto thee, in thy mouth, and in thy
heart,*[10] *that thou mayest do it.*

Since nothing impossible is being asked of them, nor of the
generations which are to follow, they are making a clear and
intelligent choice by entering into God's covenant. If they heed
these teachings, a happy and secure life awaits them in their
land. Should they rebel, death and evil lurk in the future.

*See, I have set before thee this day life and good, and death
and evil,*[11] *in that I command thee this day to love the
Lord thy God, to walk in His ways, and to keep His
commandments and His statutes and His ordinances; then
thou shalt live and multiply, and the Lord thy God shall
bless thee in the land whither thou goest in to possess it. But
if thy heart turn away, and thou wilt not hear, but shalt*

---

[9]You have no need of wise men who reside in distant lands to
explain this to you.

—SFORNO.

[10]These are the two aspects of repentance: sincere regret from the
heart, and verbal confession.

—NACHMANIDES.

[11]One is dependent upon the other: if you do good, you will have
life, otherwise you will have death.

—RASHI.

Long life and happiness, or premature death and disaster.

—IBN EZRA

The Jews, endowed with free will, have the choice in their own
hands.

—NACHMANIDES.

*be drawn away, and worship other gods, and serve them;
I declare unto you this day, that ye shall surely perish; ye
shall not prolong your days upon the land, whither thou
passest over the Jordan to go in to possess it.*

As Moses exhorts the nation to choose life and blessing, he
makes it clear that humans will always have free choice in decid-
ing what type of life to lead. Because of this, their reward for
choosing the life of the Torah will be great. Moses calls eternal
witnesses, heaven and earth, to testify to the truth of the words
he speaks.

*I call heaven and earth to witness against you this day,
that I have set before thee life and death, the blessing and
the curse; therefore choose life, that thou mayest live, thou
and thy seed;*[12] *to love*[13] *the Lord thy God, to hearken to
His voice, and to cleave unto Him; for that is thy life, and
the length of thy days; that thou mayest dwell in the land
which the Lord swore unto thy fathers, to Abraham, to
Isaac, and to Jacob, to give them.*

---

[12]In conclusion Moses calls heaven and earth to witness his declaration in which he impressed upon the people that the fate of life and
death rested with them, and he counselled them to choose life.

—NACHMANIDES.

God did not exhort them to choose life like one who serves for a
reward; He meant that they should choose what really is life.

—SFORNO.

[13]To be connected with the preceding verse: the life you are urged
to choose should be inspired by love of God.

—IBN EZRA.

Haftorah Nitzavim

ISAIAH LXI, 10–LXIII,9

The seventh and last of the "Haftorahs of Consolation" is always read on the Sabbath before *Rosh Hashanah*, the Jewish New Year. It depicts the spiritual joy which is felt during that season by the Jewish People, ever faithful to God.

The Return to Zion continues to be the main theme of the Prophet's discourse. Israel's period in exile was like a seed in the earth: though covered in darkness, they will burst forth into glorious sunshine.

Isaiah vows to ceaselessly plead with God for Zion's sake.

For Zion's sake will I not hold My peace,
And for Jerusalem's sake I will not rest,
Until her triumph go forth as brightness,
And her salvation as a torch that burneth.

The Prophet concludes by assuring the People that God feels their misery and the pangs of exile. He depicts God as a warrior who Himself is engaged in battle, winning the victory from the hostile nations and assuring the Return to Zion.

וילך

Va-Yelech

*T*HE LIFE OF MOSES was nearing its end. He had reached old age and the time had come to give a final message to his beloved people, as well as to transfer his leadership to Joshua.

And Moses went[1] and spoke these words unto all Israel. And he said unto them: 'I am a hundred and twenty years old this day;[2] I can no more go out and come in;[3] and the Lord hath said unto me: Thou shalt not go over this Jordan. The Lord thy God, He will go over before thee; He will destroy these nations from before thee, and thou shalt dispossess them; and Joshua, he shall go over before thee, as the Lord hath spoken.'

Moses assures the nation that they need have no fears because of his impending death. God would continue to guide them. Also, Joshua would be invested with the spirit of God and

---

[1]After concluding his exhortations to the whole assembly which then dispersed, Moses went from tribe to tribe to announce his approaching end, to comfort the people and encourage them to put their faith in his successor.

—IBN EZRA.

[2]Today I complete the number of my years. On this day (the seventh of Adar) I was born and on this day I am to die.

—RASHI.

I have reached a good age, so do not grieve over my death.

—SFORNO.

[3]Not because of declining strength (cf. xxxiv. 7), but for the reason that the leadership is being transferred to Joshua.

—RASHI.

successfully bring the Jews into the Promised Land. The nations of Canaan who will wage war against the Jews will not succeed. Above all, Moses reminds the people, they must at all times be strong and infused with complete faith in God.

> *Be strong and of good courage, fear not, nor be affrighted at them; for the Lord thy God, He it is that doth go with thee; He will not fail thee, nor forsake thee.*

Moses now summons Joshua to appear before the entire congregation. In solemn phrases, he charges his disciple to show the same strength which is demanded of the nation. His great task will be to lead the children of Israel into the land which God had sworn to their fathers. Just as he had assured the People, so Moses affirms to Joshua that God will surely guide his way in leading the People to their destination. As the new leader of the nation he, above all others, must be strong and fearless.

> *And Moses called unto Joshua, and said unto him in the sight of all Israel: 'Be strong and of good courage; for thou shalt go with this people into the land which the Lord hath sworn unto their fathers to give them; and thou shalt cause them to inherit it. And the Lord, He it is that doth go before thee; He will be with thee, He will not fail thee, neither forsake thee; fear not, neither be dismayed.*

The next task of Moses was to write down the words of the Torah which he had learned from God when he was on Mount Sinai for forty days and nights. This text was handed to the priests and elders for future safekeeping to always keep the Word of God known and alive among the Jewish people.

To be certain that all Israel will constantly be informed of the word of God, Moses commands the public reading of a portion of this book[4] every seven years,[5] on the festival of *Succot* (Tabernacles).

And Moses commanded them, saying: 'At the end of every seven years, in the set time of the year of release, in the feast of tabernacles, when all Israel is come to appear before the Lord thy God in the place which He shall choose, thou shalt read this law before all Israel in their hearing. Assemble the people, the men and the women and the little ones,[6] and thy stranger[7] that is within thy gates, that they may hear, and that they may learn, and fear the Lord your God, and observe to do all the words of this law; and that their children,[8] who have not known, may hear, and learn to fear the Lord your God, as long as ye live in the land whither ye go over the Jordan to possess it.

This command of Moses was carried out for many years. We know from Jewish historical sources that the Torah was thus publicly read on *Succot* by the High Priest and, at other times, by the king of the Jewish nation.

---

[4]According to the Rabbis, the Book of Deuteronomy *only* was read in public by the king on this occasion.

—RASHI.

[5]i.e. the beginning of the first year of a new cycle of seven years.

—IBN EZRA.

[6]The men to learn, the women to listen, and the children for the parents to gain merit by bringing them.

—RASHI.

[7]That he might perhaps embrace the faith of Israel.

—IBN EZRA.

[8]This refers to "the little ones" in the preceding verse. The children nearing the age when they would be subject to the Torah were to listen. They would be prompted to ask questions which their fathers would answer, and so learn to fear God when grown up.

—NACHMANIDES.

As Jewish history continued, the Torah was read publicly in such a manner that no three days passed without its being read at religious services. Thus, it is publicly read on Mondays and Thursdays, as well as on Sabbaths, holidays and fastdays. The Jews of ancient Israel divided the Torah into one hundred and fifty-six sections, so that the reading of the Scroll was completed every three years. In Babylonia, the Jewish community arranged the readings so as to complete the cycle every year. Our present custom follows that of Babylonian Jewry. By adhering to this practice, the entire Jewish people will constantly hear and study the revealed word of God and thereby follow His commandments.

After Moses had committed the text of the Torah to writing, the voice of God came to him, reminding him that the time of his death was at hand. Moses was commanded to bring Joshua to the Tent of Meeting, where the new leader was to receive instruction by God.

> *And the Lord said unto Moses: 'Behold, thy days approach that thou must die; call Joshua, and present yourselves in the tent of meeting, that I may give him a charge.' And Moses and Joshua went and presented themselves in the tent of meeting. . . . And he gave Joshua the son of Nun a charge,[9] and said: 'Be strong and of good courage; for thou shalt bring the children of Israel into the land which I swore unto them; and I will be with thee.'*

At the Tent of Meeting, God also told them that after Moses will "sleep with his fathers", the people will enter the Promised Land. After a period of prosperity and security, they will turn away from God and thereby evoke His wrath. Soon thereafter they will be scattered among the nations.

Instead of realizing the cause for all their troubles, they will

---

[9]The subject in this verse is God.

—SFORNO.

314

question whether God is still concerned with His people. In order to avoid the perpetuation of such an error among the people, Moses is commanded to prepare a song before his death, which will outline the course history will take for the Jewish people. In possession of this song, future generations will not lose faith, but will always realize that as soon as they repent of the evil ways into which they have fallen, God will again be their Guide and surely return them to the Land which He swore unto their fathers.

Finally, after having written the words of the Torah and the song, Moses commands the Levites, whose task it was to carry the Ark containing the two tablets of the Ten Commandments, to place the Scroll by the side of the Ark[10] as a constant witness of the Word of God.

Haftorah Va-Yelech

HOSEA XIX, 2-10; MICAH VII, 18-20; JOEL II, 15-27

HOSEA

This Haftorah is read during the Ten Days of Penitence—between *Rosh Hashanah* and *Yom Kippur*. Hosea calls upon the Jewish People to return to God. They have only "stumbled" in their sin, for no Jew would consciously oppose God. The Prophet appeals to the People to stop relying on alliances with other nations and to return to God with love, wisdom and sincerity.

---

[10]Some Rabbis maintained that a board projected from the ark on which the Book rested; others that it lay within the ark beside the Tablets of the Commandments.

—RASHI.

315

MICAH

The words of Micah echo the theme of Divine Pardon—the theme of the Ten Days of Penitence.

Who is a God like unto Thee, that pardoneth the iniquity,
And passeth by the transgression of the remants of His heritage?
He retaineth not His anger for ever,
Because He delighteth in mercy.

He will again have compassion upon us;
He will subdue our iniquities;
And Thou wilt cast all their sins into the depth of the sea.

Thou wilt show faithfulness to Jacob, mercy to Abraham,
As Thou hast sworn unto our fathers from the days of old.

JOEL

Since this Haftorah is read on the Sabbath before the Fast of *Yom Kippur*, it describes a fast of repentance which the Prophet announces. Everyone is called upon to participate and rededicate himself to return to God in sincere repentance.

If the People will truly turn away from their evil ways, Joel assures them of God's salvation.

And ye shall eat in plenty and be satisfied,
And shall praise the name of the Lord your God,
That hath dealt wonderously with you;
And My people shall never be ashamed.

And ye shall know that I am in the midst of Israel,
And that I am the Lord your God, and there is none else;
And My people shall never be. ashamed.

הַאֲזִינוּ

Ha-A-Zinu

Chapter XXXII

IN THE BOOK of Exodus, we read the beautiful song which Moses offered to God after he crossed the Red Sea with the children of Israel. It was at that time that he began his mission of leading the Jews through the long and difficult years of the wilderness on their journey to the Promised Land.

Moses now composes another song to God. This one is to conclude not only his leadership, but his life. He had reached the age of one hundred and twenty years and had assembled all the People before him. When the entire nation had gathered, Joshua was appointed as Moses' successor. Moses then wrote down the words of the Torah and recited this farewell ode to his beloved People.

To give lasting strength and meaning to the words he is about to utter, Moses calls heaven and earth to witness the truth of his statements.

> *Give ear, ye heavens, and I will speak;*
> *And let the earth[1] hear the words of my mouth.*
> *My doctrine shall drop as the rain,*
> *My speech shall distil as the dew;[2]. . .*

---

[1]Moses called heaven and earth to witness his last exhortation because they are eternal.

—RASHI.

[2]The Torah is life to Israel as rain is to the world; but whereas rain is troublesome to wayfarers and others, Moses adds "as the dew" which is acceptable to all.

—RASHI.

Just as rain and dew do not fail in their effect of fertilizing the soil, so, prays Moses, may his words find receptive minds among Israel.

—IBN EZRA.

Moses begins by affirming that all the ways of God, as well as His laws are perfect and just. At all times, God was and will be faithful to His people.

> *The Rock,[3] His work is perfect;*
> *For all His ways are justice;[4]*
> *A God of faithfulness[5] and without iniquity,[6]*
> *Just and right is He.[7]*

There is no sin or wrong in God. He knows of no corruption. The evils and upheavals which face His people during various phases of history are caused by Israel's faithlesness and rebellion.

Moses become very stern with the congregation before him. He calls them a crooked and perverse generation. So often have they revolted and gone astray. They made the Golden Calf soon after hearing the very words of God at Mount Sinai. Whenever there was a lack of food or water, they challenged the leadership of Moses, as well as his divine mission. Throughout the forty years in the desert, there was strife and contention.

---

[3]God is as unalterable as a rock in His relations with man.

—IBN EZRA.

[4]Whether tending to happiness or misfortune.

—IBN EZRA.

[5]He is faithful to give their reward to the righteous in the hereafter if they do not receive it in this world.

—RASHI.

He will faithfully fulfil His promise to the Patriarchs concerning the descendants.

—SFORNO.

[6]Even the wicked receive God's reward for any good acts performed by them.

—RASHI.

[7]Just in His merciful acts, and right in meting out punishment.

—NACHMANIDES.

Is corruption His? No; His children's is the blemish;
A generation crooked and perverse.
Do ye thus requite the Lord,
O foolish people and unwise?[8]
Is He not thy father that hath gotten thee?
Hath He not made thee and established thee?

Moses takes the people back to their ancient history. He invites the younger ones to ask their fathers and learn about the early days of Israel. God found them during their Egyptian slavery. Amid many miracles, He redeemed them and brought them to freedom. Then, He watched closely over them during the many years of their wandering in the desert.

However, after God saw to it that the Jews had all their needs satisfied, they grew fat and rebelled. They searched for strange and false gods to worship.

But Jeshurun[9] *waxed fat, and kicked—*
Thou dist wax fat, thou didst grow thick, thou didst become
gross—
And he forsook God who made him,
And contemned the Rock of his salvation.
They roused Him to jealousy with strange gods,
With abominations did they provoke Him
They sacrificed unto demons, no-gods,
Gods that they knew not,
New gods that came up of late,
Which your fathers dreaded not.

---

[8]The word *nabal* (fool) denotes a person who repays his benefactor with evil. In breaking God's law, Israel acted ungratefully, forgetting all the wonderful deeds God had performed for them. They also proved to be "unwise," because they did not realize that it was not God but they who would suffer in consequence of their sin.

—NACHMANIDES.

[9]A designation for Israel, from the root *yashar*, "to be upright".

—IBN EZRA.

It was then that the vengeance of God was aroused and He considered bringing about their destruction. The downfall of the nation would come about at the hands of unfriendly peoples and exposure to the dangers of the wilderness.

Israel was finally saved, not because of its repentance and righteousness, but because of God's respect for His own Name. Because other nations would mockingly claim that the destruction of Israel was the result of their own strength[10] and that God was helpless to prevent the disaster, God decreed that they should be spared.[11]

If only the nations realized, Moses continues, from where Israel's strength comes.

> *If they were wise, they would understand this,*
> *They would discern their latter end.*[12]
> *How should one chase a thousand,*[13]
> *And two put ten thousand to flight,*
> *Except their Rock had given them over,*[14]
> *And the Lord had delivered them up?*

---

[10]Israel's enemies fail to realize that his suffering is the work of God as a punishment for sin.

—NACHMANIDES.

[11]The survival of dispersed Israel will not be due to their merit, but will be an act of God in the interests of mankind. For Israel is the eternal custodian of the Sovereignty of God and the Torah.

—NACHMANIDES.

[12]The cause of Israel's calamity.

—RASHI.

If Israel's enemies were wise to understand that sin was the cause of the suffering, they whose transgressions were of a more serious nature would know that their own end would be even worse.

—IBN EZRA.

[13]One of the enemy chase a thousand Jews.

—RASHI.

[14]The extraordinary character of Israel's defeat should serve the enemy as proof that the defeat was from God.

—NACHMANIDES.

Israel's enemies will enjoy great triumphs, but their day of retribution will come. Israel's terrible plight at the hands of its oppressors will finally move God to come to its aid. Conversely, the false gods of Israel's enemies will not come to their aid.

Then, all the nations will sing aloud[15] the praises of God, together with Israel, when divine justice will have been meted out and the Promised Land will again be redeemed.

> *See now that I, even I, am He,*[16]
> *And there is no god with Me;*
> *I kill, and I make alive;*
> *I have wounded, and I heal;*
> *And there is none that can deliver out of My hand.*

On that very day of Moses' song, God commanded him to go up on Mount Nebo, to die as he looks upon the Promised Land.

> *And the Lord spoke unto Moses that selfsame day,*
> *saying: 'Get thee up into this mountain of Abarim,*
> *unto mount Nebo, which is in the land of Moab, that*
> *is over against Jericho; and behold the land of Ca-*
> *naan,*[17] *which I give unto the children of Israel for*
> *a possession; and die in the mount whither thou goest*
> *up, and be gathered unto thy people; as Aaron thy*

---

[15]When Israel's blood will be avenged, the nations will change their attitude toward the people of God, hate giving place to praise.
—IBN EZRA.

[16]Israel should deduce from the suffering sent upon him, and from which none could save him—as also from the help that would eventually come—that none can thwart God's plans.—Rashi. To the heathen challenge: Where were Israel's gods?—God's answer is that there is only one Divine Power Who is neither helped nor opposed by any other.
—NACHMANIDES.

[17]To give it your blessing.
—SFORNO.

brother died in mount Hor, and was gathered unto his people. Because ye trespassed against Me in the midst of the children of Israel at the waters of Meribath-kadesh, in the wilderness of Zin; because ye sanctified Me not in the midst of the children of Israel. For thou shalt see the land afar off;[18] but thou shalt not go thither into the land which I give the children of Israel.

Haftorah Ha-A-Zinu

II Samuel XXII

In the Sidrah, Moses delivers his farewell message to the Jewish People. As his leadership began with a song of thanksgiving to God after the Crossing of the Red Sea, so his life now ends on a note of gratitude.

The Haftorah offers a similar song of thanksgiving by King David after he was saved from the attacks of King Saul who sought to kill him.

David, as Moses before him, declares that whenever he was in distress, his prayers and pleas were directed to God. He affirms that God is interested in the individual destiny of each creature.

David declares that by living the life desired by God, man can hope for Divine Salvation.

> *For thou art my lamp, O Lord;*
> *And the Lord doth lighten my darkness.*
>
> *For by Thee I run upon a troop;*
> *By my God do I scale a wall.*

---

[18] I grant you this privilege because I know how dear the Land is to you.

—RASHI.

As for God, His way is perfect;
The word of the Lord is tried;
He is a shield unto all them that take refuge in Him.

Therefore I will give thanks unto Thee, O Lord,
among the nations,
And will sing praises unto Thy name.

A tower of salvation is He to His king;
And showeth mercy to His annointed,
To David and to his seed, for evermore.

וְזֹאת הַבְּרָכָה

Vezot Ha-Berachah

CHAPTERS XXXIII–XXXIV

𝒯HE FINAL ACT of Moses was to bless his beloved people. As he approached Mount Nebo, the site of his imminent death, Moses bestowed an individual blessing upon each of the tribes.

And this is the blessing,[1] wherewith Moses the man of God[2] blessed the children of Israel before his death. And he said:

The Lord came from Sinai,
And rose from Seir unto them;
He shined forth from Paran,[3]
And he came from the myriads holy.

---

[1] Like the patriarch Jacob who blessed his children on his death-bed, so Moses blessed Israel before his death.

—IBN EZRA.

[2] Added to indicate that Moses, in these blessings, was inspired by God.

—IBN EZRA.

[3] The presence of God among Israel was particularly manifest at three stages. At Sinai God first revealed Himself to Israel and communicated His Law to Moses on the Mount and afterwards in the Tabernacle. After leaving Sinai, the Jews halted in the wilderness of Paran. There the cloud of the *Shechinah* (Divine Presence) descended (Numbers x. 12), but disappeared after the episode of the spies. Not until they reached Seir, the territory of Esau, was God's communication with Moses resumed.

—NACHMANIDES.

At His right hand[4] was a fiery law[5] unto them.

Yea, He loveth the peoples,
All His holy ones—they are in Thy hand;[6]
And they sit down at Thy feet,
Receiving of Thy words.

Moses commanded us a law,[7]
An inheritance of the congregation of Jacob.[8]

And there was a king in Jeshurun,[9]

---

[4]Though myriads of angels were present, the Torah was communicated to Israel directly by God.

—NACHMANIDES.

[5]A law given from the midst of fire and lightning, or a law that combines mercy with justice.

—NACHMANIDES.

[6]The abode of the tribe of Levi, chosen for holy service, was about the ark, and they enjoyed special protection from the Guardian of Israel.

—IBN EZRA.

[7]The Torah will be accepted by every succeeding generation and remain the everlasting possession of Israel.

—NACHMANIDES.

[8]The word "congregation", instead of "house" or "seed", intimates that numerous gentiles would join the fold of Israel, and they would share in the heritage of the Torah.

—NACHMANIDES.

[9]This verse is to be connected with the preceding. As with the Torah, so will the Sovereignty of God be accepted by all future generations, following the acknowledgement of His supremacy by the entire nation at Sinai. Moses here concludes his introductions in which he pointed to three outstanding merits of Israel which made them worthy of his blessing: God made His abode among them; they accepted His Torah; they acknowledged His sovereignty.

—NACHMANIDES.

> *When the heads of the people were gathered,*
> *All the tribes of Israel together.*

The first blessing, extended to Reuben, included the prayer that the tribe shall live and not disappear through a decrease in its numbers. (The Reubenites were to live away from the main body of the nation and could become a prey to external attacks.)

The tribe of Simeon did not receive a separate blessing, probably because their nineteen cities were in Judah's territory and the blessing extended to Judah thereby included them.

Moses prays to God to accept the pleas of Judah, since this tribe was to be in the forefront of the attack against Canaan and to be surrounded, for a time, by the hostile Canaanites.

The tribe of Levi received the blessing of being the custodian of the faith. This tribe refused to associate itself with the sin of the Golden Calf, and warred against its own relatives for the honor of God, Their task was to bring the offerings, as well as to be the religious teachers among the people. Moses prays for their prosperity and protection.

> *Bless, Lord, his substance,*
> *And accept the work of his hands;*
>
> *Smite through the loins of them them that rise up*
> *   against him,*
> *And of them that hate him, that they rise not again.*

Benjamin, who was the beloved son of Jacob, is assured that God's love will also abide with that tribe. The Holy Temple was to be situated in Benjamin's territory.

As Jacob blessed his son Joseph with the "dew of heaven", so Moses now blesses this tribe with the bounties of nature and military strength. He extends this blessing to the two tribes emanating from Joseph—Ephraim and Manasseh.

Zebulun was the sea-faring tribe, living on the shores of

Lake Tiberias (the Sea of *Kinneret*) and the Mediterranean Sea. Both the blessings of Jacob and Moses bid the tribe well in their maritime enterprises.

The tribe of Issachar dwelt quietly in their tents, engaged in working the land and study. Moses blessed them with success in these pursuits.

Gad was to fight with the other tribes to conquer the land of Canaan, although they would return to the eastern banks of the Jordan after the war. Moses blesses the tribe for its courage and prays that they may have abundant territory.

Dan, the tribe from which Samson was to emerge, was known as an adventurous group and is so described in the blessing of Moses.

Naphtali is blessed for the beautiful and fertile land it was to inherit around the Sea of Kinneret.

Finally, the tribe of Asher was blessed, even more than the other tribes, with prosperity and security. The other tribes would rejoice in his good fortune.

Moses concludes his blessings to the tribes with a praise of God, who extends His protection over all Israel.

> *There is none like unto God, O Jeshurun,*[10]
> *Who rideth upon the heaven as thy help,*
> *And in His excellency on the skies. . . .*

> *And Israel dwelleth in safety,*
> *The fountain of Jacob alone,*
> *In a land of corn and wine;*
> *Yea, his heavens drop down dew.*

> *Happy art thou, O Israel, who is like unto thee?*

---

[10]In conclusion, Moses passed from individual blessings to a benediction upon the entire nation.

—IBN EZRA.

A people saved by the Lord,[11]
The shield of thy help,
And that is the sword of thy excellency![12]
And thine enemies shall dwindle away before thee;
And thou shalt tread upon their high places.[13]

Having completed his blessing of the tribes, Moses approaches Mount Nebo and climbs to its peak.[14] From this vantage point, he sees large areas of his beloved and beautiful Land of Israel[15] with its palm-trees, seas, hills and valleys. God again assures Moses that this is the land which He swore to Abraham, Isaac and Jacob, as well as to their descendants.

So Moses the servant of the Lord died[16] *there in the land of Moab, according to the word of the Lord.*[17]

---

[11]Israel's salvation will not be secured by might of arms but by Divine aid.

—SFORNO.

[12]God is the sword which will enable Israel to prevail over their enemies.

—SFORNO.

[13]Even their kings will humble themselves.

—SFORNO.

[14]The last chapter of the Torah was, in my opinion, written by Joshua.

—IBN EZRA.

[15]God permitted Moses to see the land in order that he may bless it.

—NACHMANIDES.

[16]Even at the time of his death Moses fulfilled the commands of God.

—IBN EZRA.

[17]The Rabbis explained this as meaning by "Divine kiss" (a painless death).

—RASHI.

And he was buried[18] in the valley of the land of Moab over against Beth-peor; and no man knoweth of his sepulchre unto this day.[19] And Moses was a hundred and twenty years old when he died; his eye was not dim, nor his natural force abated. And the children of Israel wept for Moses in the plains of Moab thirty days; so the days of weeping in the mourning for Moses were ended.[20] And Joshua the son of Nun was full of the spirit of wisdom; for Moses had laid his hands upon him; and the children of Israel hearkened unto him, and did as the Lord commanded Moses. And there hath not risen a prophet since in Israel like unto Moses, whom the Lord knew face to face;[21] in all the signs and the wonders,[22] which the Lord sent him to do in the land of Egypt, to Pharaoh, and to all his servants, and to all his land; and in all the

---

[18]Literally: 'he buried him'. Some Rabbis interpreted that God buried him; others that Moses buried himself.

—RASHI.

[19]Joshua added these words at the end of his life.

—IBN EZRA.

[20]This sentence is to be connected with the next verse. When the period of mourning for Moses was over, the people turned to Joshua and submitted to his leadership.

—IBN EZRA.

[21]Moses spoke with God at any time he wished.

—RASHI.

[22]To be connected with the preceding verse. The superior standard of Moses' prophetic spirit was evidenced in all the great acts which he performed both among the Egyptians and Israel. "Signs" are events predicted before they occur; "wonders" are supernatural acts, such as turning the rod into a serpent.

—NACHMANIDES.

mighty hand,[23] *and in all the great terror, which Moses wrought in the sight of all Israel.*

Haftorah Vezot Ha-Berachah

JOSHUA I

Jewish history is a Golden Thread of survival and continuity of the People. As Moses, the greatest of Jewish Prophets, goes to his rest (as described in the Sidrah), the mantle of leadership is bestowed upon Joshua. It is for this reason that the Book of Joshua, the first book of the Prophets, provides the Haftorah at the close of the annual cycle of Torah reading.

The Haftorah tells how God commanded Joshua to cross the Jordan and enter Canaan immediately after the death of Moses. Joshua is told: "Be strong and of good courage." He is never to deviate from the Word of God as transmitted to Moses.

When Joshua commanded the People to prepare themselves to cross the Jordan within three days, they accepted his leadership and were ready to carry on.

And they answered Joshua, saying: 'All that thou hast commanded us we will do, and whithersoever thou sendest us we will go. According as we hearkened unto Moses in all things, so will we hearken unto thee; only the Lord thy God be with thee, as He was with Moses. Whosoever he be that shall rebel against thy commandment, and that shall not hearken unto thy words in all that thou commandest him, he shall be put to death; only be strong and of good courage.

---

[23]A reference to the splitting of the waters of the Red Sea.

—IBN EZRA.

List of Commentators

RASHI—

Rabbi Solomon ben Isaac was born in France in 1040 and died in Worms in 1105. Most of his life was spent in the Rhineland. He is famous for his clear and concise explanations of the Torah and Talmud. His commentaries exhibit a wise knowledge of Rabbinic literature. Rashi's explanations are generally homiletical with occasional Midrashic interpretations.

IBN EZRA—

Abraham Ibn Ezra was born in Spain in 1092, where he mastered both the Hebrew and Arabic languages. He spent about half his life travelling the world, spreading the Arabic culture of Spain. His commentaries are largely of a literary style, stressing grammar and diction. He is very terse and concerned with the exact meaning of the text.

RASHBAM—

Rabbi Shemuel ben Meir (1085–1174) was the grandson of Rashi, who was also his teacher. Often taking exception to his famous grandfather, he primarily laid emphasis on the plain meaning of the verse (*peshat*).

NACHMANIDES— Rabbi Moshe ben Nachman was born in Spain in 1194, where he lived most of his life. Besides attaining fame as a Talmudist, he was also deeply interested in the Cabalah (Jewish mysticism). In 1263, he defended the Jewish religion in a disputation against the convert, Pablo Christiani, as a result of which he was forced to leave Spain. He went to the Holy Land, his love for which is often expressed in his commentaries, where he died c. 1270. His commentary on the Torah embodies legal discourses which demonstrate the connection between the Torah and rabbinic law (*Halachah*), the moral values of the narratives, mystical allusions and literal interpretations which often take issue with Rashi's views.

SFORNO— Obadiah ben Jacob Sforno was born in Italy C. 1475 and died at Bologna in 1550. Besides his proficiency in theological studies, he was deeply conversant with mathematics, philosophy and medicine. He rejects mystical and forced interpretations, always seeking to discover the plain and basic meaning of the text. He takes every opportunity to demonstrate the ethical teachings which are implicit in the text.